2005–2006

Unbelievably Good Deals and Great Adventures

That You Absolutely Can't Get Unless You're Over 50

Joan Rattner Heilman

McGraw·Hill

New York   Chicago   San Francisco   Lisbon   London   Madrid   Mexico City
Milan   New Delhi   San Juan   Seoul   Singapore   Sydney   Toronto

Library of Congress Cataloging-in-Publication Data

Heilman, Joan Rattner.
Unbelievably good deals and great adventures that you absolutely can't get unless you're over 50 / by Joan Rattner Heilman.—2005-2006 [ed.].
    p.   cm.
Includes index.
ISBN 0-07-143829-7
1. Travel.   2. Discounts for older people.   I. Title.

G151.H44   2005
910'.2'02—dc22   2004023131

3 4 5 6 7 8 9 0   DOC/DOC   3 2 1 0 9 8 7 6 5

ISBN 0-07-143829-7

McGraw-Hill books are available at special quantity discounts to use as premiums and sales promotions, or for use in corporate training programs. For more information, please write to the Director of Special Sales, Professional Publishing, McGraw-Hill, Two Penn Plaza, New York, NY 10121-2298. Or contact your local bookstore.

This book is printed on acid-free paper.

Contents

1

Introduction to Good Deals and Great Adventures

This book is a guide to the perks, privileges, discounts, and special adventures that are now yours simply because you've been around for at least 50 years.

On your 50th birthday (or on your 60th, 62nd, or 65th), you qualify for hundreds of special opportunities and money-saving offers that make younger people wish they were older—all for a couple of good reasons. First, as a person in your prime, you deserve them.

Second, as part of the fastest-growing demographic group in the United States, you represent an enormous market of potential consumers, a fact that has become quite apparent to the business community. More than a quarter of the U.S. population today is over 50. By 2020, that proportion is expected to increase to a third as the baby boomers turn 50 at a rate of about four million a year. About 35

1

million Americans—almost 13 percent of the total population—are now over 65, and it is estimated that by 2030
that number will exceed 70 million, nearly a quarter of the
U.S. population. Besides, life expectancy is higher today
than ever before (today, more than four million Americans
are 85 and older), and most of us can expect to live a long,
healthy, and active life.

Those of us over 50 control most of the nation's wealth,
including half of the discretionary income (the money that's
left over after essentials have been taken care of) and almost
80 percent of its financial assets. Very often, the children
have gone, the mortgage has been paid off, the house is fully
furnished, the goal of leaving a large inheritance is not a
major concern, and the freedom years have arrived at last.

As a group, we're markedly different from previous older
generations who pinched pennies and saved them all. We,
too, know the value of a dollar, but we feel freer to spend our
money because we're better off than our predecessors, a significant number of us having accumulated enough resources
to be reasonably secure. We also are far better educated than
those before us, and we have developed many more interests and activities. Besides, we have more time to enjoy ourselves. Although many people continue to work after age
65, the average age of retirement has dropped to 61.

Most important, we as a group are remarkably fit,
healthy, and energetic. We're living longer and feeling better. In fact, a survey has shown that most of us feel at least
15 years younger than our chronological age and rate our
health as good or excellent.

The business community is actively courting the mature
population because now many of us have the time to spend

our money doing all the things we've always put off before. With the recognition of our numbers and financial power, our flexible schedules, and our vast buying power, we are finally being taken very seriously. To get our attention, we are increasingly presented with some real breaks and good deals, all detailed on these pages. We are also invited on trips and adventures specifically tailored to suit our interests, needs, and abilities.

In this book, you will learn how to get what's coming to you—the discounts and privileges that are among the advantages of getting older. Here are some that you absolutely couldn't get if you were younger:

- Discounts at hotels and motels; at car-rental agencies; and on buses, trains, and boats
- Price breaks on airfares
- An education at colleges and universities that offer you bargain rates
- Travel adventures all over the world designed specifically for older travelers
- Clubs, trips, and services for mature singles
- Skiing for half price—or nothing
- Tennis tournaments, golf vacations, walking trips, bike tours, and senior softball leagues designed for you
- And much more!

Because every community in this country and abroad has its own special perks to offer you, make a practice of *asking* if there are breaks to which you are entitled, from movies to museums, concerts to historic sites, hotels to ski resorts and theme parks, restaurants to riverboats. Don't expect clerks, ticket agents, tour operators, restaurant hosts, or even travel agents to volunteer them to you. First of all, they may not think of it. Second, they may not realize you have reached the appropriate birthday. And third, they may not want to call attention to your age, just in case that's not something you would appreciate. You never know whether you're being offered the best possible deal unless you ask. Many bargains and privileges are available only to people who speak up.

Remember to request your privileges *before* you pay or when you order or make reservations, and always carry proof of age, an over-50 club membership card, or—better yet—both. Sometimes the advantages come with membership in a senior club, but usually they are available to anyone over a specified age.

To make sure you're getting a legitimate discount when you're using your special privileges, call the hotel, airline, car-rental company, or tour operator and ask what the regular or normal prices are. Find out if there's a special sale or promotion going on. Ask about other discounts—corporate, weekend, government, or auto-club membership breaks, for example. Most important, always ask for *the lowest available rate* at the time you plan to travel and compare that with the discounted senior rate. Then decide whether you are getting a good deal. Sometimes you'll find that even better specials are available.

With the help of this guidebook, completely revised and updated at least once a year, you will have a wonderful time and save money too.

2

Travel: Making Your Age Pay Off

People over 50 are the most ardent travelers of all. We travel more often, farther, more extravagantly, and for longer periods of time than anybody else. Since the travel industry discovered these facts, it's been going after our business.

It has fallen in love with our age group because we have more discretionary income than people of other ages and more time to spend it. Besides, we are remarkably flexible. Many of us no longer have children in school, so we're free to travel off-peak or whenever we feel the need for a change of scenery. In fact, we much prefer spring and fall to summer. Some of us have retired, and others have such good jobs that we can make our own schedules. We can take advantage of midweek or weekend slack times when the industry is eager to fill space.

But, best of all, we are energetic, and we're not sitting in rocking chairs on the porch. People over 55 account for one-third of all overnight domestic travel at least 50 miles from home, overseas packaged tours, and hotel/motel nights, as well as 70 percent of bus trips and cruises.

Contrary to what a younger person might think, people in the mature generation aren't content with watching the action. Instead, we like to get right into the middle of it. There's not a place we won't go or an activity we won't try. Though many of us prefer escorted tours, almost half of us choose to travel independently.

Not only that, but we're shrewd—we look for the best deals to the best places. We are experienced comparison shoppers and want the most for our money.

For all of these reasons, we are now offered astonishing numbers of travel-related discounts, reduced rates, special tour packages, and other perks. Many agencies and tour operators have designed all or at least part of their trips to appeal to a mature clientele. Others include seasoned travelers along with everyone else but offer us special privileges.

So many good deals and great adventures are available to you when you are on the move that we'll start off with travel.

But, first, keep in mind:

- Rates, trips, and privileges tend to change at a moment's notice, so check out each of them before you make your plans. Airlines are particularly capricious, and it's hard to tell what they offer from one week to the next. The good deals in this guidebook are those that are available as we go to press.

■ Many airlines, cruise lines, tour operators, and travel agencies have gone out of business recently, and others are struggling to stay afloat. Protect yourself by charging your travel expenses to a major credit card and purchasing comprehensive travel insurance that covers carrier default and trip cancellation as well as other potential problems.

■ Always ask for your discount or special privilege when you make your reservations or at the time of purchase, order, or check-in. If you wait until you're checking out or settling your bill, it may be too late.

■ Remember that your privileges may apply only between certain hours, on certain days of the week, or during specific seasons of the year. Research this before making reservations, and always remind the clerk of the discount when you check in or pay your fare. Be flexible when you can, and travel during the hours, days, or seasons when you can get the best deals.

■ When traveling, it's particularly important to carry identification with proof of age or membership in a senior club. In most cases, a driver's license or passport does the job. In some cases, the organization's membership card, a birth certificate, a resident alien card, or any other official document showing your date of birth will suffice. If you're old enough for a Medicare card or Senior ID card, use that.

■ Look before you book. Don't always spring for the senior discount without checking out other rates. Often special promotional rates or discounts that are available to anybody of any age turn out to be better deals. The car-rental companies and airlines, for example, are famous for this. Ask your travel agent or the ticket seller to figure out the *lowest possible available rate* for you at the time you want to travel.

■ Some senior privileges are available whether you make reservations by telephone or online, but frequently they are not to be found on the websites. If you want them, you or your travel agent must call. On the other hand, you may find that Web fares or prices are the lowest, beating the price you would get on the telephone. The only solution is to try it both ways before you make your reservation.

■ Pay for all travel with a major credit card if possible. If there are problems or disputes, you will have less difficulty resolving them.

■ The age of a "senior" varies from 50 upward. Some special privileges are yours at age 50, usually but not always tied to membership in a senior organization. Others come along later at varying birthdays, so watch for the cutoff points. Also, in most cases, if the person purchasing the ticket or trip is the right age, the rest of the party, a traveling companion, or the people sharing the room are entitled to the same reduced rates.

3

Airfares: Improving with Age

One thing that improves with your age is airfare. That's still true today although the largest U.S. airlines, in dire financial straits, have abandoned the money-saving senior coupons we all loved and the standard 10 percent discount on just about all fares for senior travelers.

But all is not lost. Some domestic airlines, particularly the smaller ones, are bucking the trend and continue to cater to older travelers. So do many foreign carriers. And even the major players haven't abandoned us completely. Most of them schedule "senior fares" to travelers 65 and older on some domestic routes for some departures that can take about 10 percent off the cost of a 14-day advance-purchase ticket. The senior fares, unlike the earlier programs, are usually loaded with restrictions and are often hard to find—most of them are not available online, and reservations clerks can't be relied on to volunteer information about them when you call—but they can help cut costs when you can't hunt down a better fare. The major benefit of the senior fares is that the maximum stay is now up to 180 days rather than the 30 days on almost all other cheap tickets, making life easier for snow-birds and others who migrate with the seasons.

But, first, look before you book:

- Make sure you are getting the *lowest available fare* to your destination at the time you want to fly. Ask about senior discounts and senior fares, but be prepared to jump ship if you can get a better deal with a seasonal sale or a supersaver fare. Remember that senior discounts are usually subtracted from the "published fares," usually the highest fares, so they might not be the best deals out there.
- Even when you speak to an airline's reservations agent, you might not get the correct information about senior fares or discounts. If you doubt the validity of the information given to you, insist on speaking to a supervisor and check it out on the website. Reservation agents have been known to be wrong.
- Always check airline websites and travel sites and call the airline's reservations number, or talk to a travel agent before purchasing airline tickets. Often, the lowest fares are available only online. On the other hand, senior discounts and senior fares are rarely mentioned on airline websites. To get Southwest's special fares for travelers 65-plus, for example, you must make your reservations by phone.
- Keep in mind that the restrictions you must fly by may not be worth the savings. Always examine the fees and

conditions and decide whether you can live with them. There may be blackout periods around major holidays when you can't use your privileges, departures only on certain days or at certain hours, restrictions on the season of the year, or stiff penalties for flight changes. It's not always easy to sort out the offers.

■ Be prepared to present valid proof of age at the check-in counter. It's possible that your special fare will not be honored if you don't have that proof with you, and you will have to pay the difference.

■ Almost all airlines that continue to offer senior discounts extend the courtesy to a younger companion when you fly together.

■ Book your travel as early as possible for the best fares and the most available seats. Discounted seats are limited and may not be reserved at all on some flights.

■ Be flexible. To get seats and the best fares, plan to fly at off-peak times when the rest of the population isn't rushing off to faraway places. For example, noontime or late-night flights can be much cheaper than early-morning or dinnertime flights. Consider leaving on a different day—fares are often lower midweek or on Saturday. Avoid Monday mornings and Friday afternoons. And fly off-season, when children aren't on vacation and there are no major holidays, to get better prices.

■ For cheaper airfares, check out the many rapidly proliferating low-cost airlines, such as Southwest, ATA, and JetBlue. They all have limited routes and may not fly out of a city or airport that's convenient for you—and they may not feed you more than a minor snack—but they usually offer other important advantages besides cheap tickets. For example, on some of these niche airlines, you may fly only one way, paying just half the round-trip fare, book your trips at the very last minute without penalty, and have no worries about Saturday-night or minimum stays. Some offer special senior fares that can't be beat.

■ Membership in a private airline VIP club means you can spend your waiting time at the airport in comfort, complete with snacks and free drinks, copy machines, private telephones, luggage storage areas, and sometimes even showers. At this writing, you can buy a lifetime club membership at age 62 or 65 from two airlines— Continental and Northwest—for about half what other adults pay. The break applies to single memberships as well as those that include your spouse. Not only that, but you may also bring guests to the lounges and sometimes use the clubs even when you are not ticketed for a flight that day.

■ Some European airlines give senior discounts on fares for domestic flights within their borders or to other cities in Europe. To get the breaks, it is usually necessary to book these flights at the same time and in conjunction with your international ticket.

Be advised that airfares and airline policies can change overnight—and often do—so always call the airline for an update.

U.S. AIRLINES
AMERICA WEST AIRLINES

America West is the only domestic carrier at this writing that retains its senior coupons and a 5 percent discount on almost all of its fares. The discount is available to you at 62 or more and to a younger companion who travels with you on the same flight. The Senior Saver Pack, also for passengers 62-plus, gives you four one-way coupons good for coach travel on any of the airline's flights within the U.S. and from the U.S. to Canada and Mexico. The coupons must be exchanged for tickets within a year. Two coupons are required for flights to Alaska, and international travel must be round-trip.

On this airline, which flies to 93 U.S. cities, you may use the coupons for one or two grandchildren between the ages of 2 and 12 when they travel with you. Also included in the packet are coupons for bonus miles and discounts on land packages and car rentals. You may fly any day, anytime, if seats are available. Reservations must be made at least 14 days in advance, although you may use your tickets to fly standby on valid travel days. You're entitled to frequent-flyer points for your miles, and unused coupons are refundable.

For information: 800-235-9292; www.americawest.com.

AMERICAN AIRLINES (AA)

On some routes at some times, AA offers special senior fares to passengers 65 or over. These give you a 10 percent discount on a 14-day advance-purchase nonrefundable booking with a Saturday-night stay. They must be booked using the reservations number and are not available online, although sometimes you can find an even better deal on the airline's website. Senior fares are also usually available on American Eagle flights, including the Business Express shuttle that links New York, Boston, and Washington, D.C.

For information: 800-433-7300; www.aa.com.

ATA AIRLINES

A low-fare nationwide airline based in the Midwest, ATA (American Trans Air) has periodic senior fares for travelers age 62 and older. Although they may save you money, they are not always the lowest fares available, so the airline recommends that you check the website before booking your flight and select the senior designation as your passenger type to be sure you are getting the lowest fare possible for a particular route. On ATA, you may purchase one-way tickets and you don't have to stay over a Saturday night.
For information: 800-435-9282; www.ata.com.

CONTINENTAL AIRLINES

Although it has forsaken its senior coupons, senior club, and the automatic 10 percent senior discount, Continental now offers special senior fares on certain routes for travelers 65 and over. Ask about them when you make reservations by telephone, or select the "seniors" category when you book online. You will be quoted the senior fare if one is available for your flight. As always, make sure it's the lowest fare you can get.

If you want to spend your airport waiting time in comfort, check out Continental's Presidents Club, its collection of airport lounges. A lifetime membership in the club is half the regular fee for those who are 62-plus.
For information: 800-525-0280; www.continental.com. For the Continental Presidents Club: 800-322-2640.

DELTA AIRLINES

Delta once offered wonderful privileges to senior travelers but no more. Its special discounts, senior coupons, and

senior clubs are gone. You may, however, find that Delta sometimes offers some nice low promotional fares available to everybody.
For information: 800-221-1212; www.delta.com.

DELTA SHUTTLE

Delta offers reduced senior fares for its East Coast shuttle service between New York and Boston or Washington, D.C. It's a good deal for travelers age 62 or older and requires no advance purchase. However, you must fly between 10:30 A.M. to 2:30 P.M. and 7:30 P.M. to 9:30 A.M. on weekdays. On Saturdays and Sundays, you may fly anytime.
For information: 800-221-1212; www.delta.com.

HAWAIIAN AIR

Passengers over the age of 60 and their younger companions are offered special flat-rate senior fares that are about 10 percent lower than the published fares on all flights from West Coast cities to Hawaii. These fares are the best you can get except for the occasional promotional seat sale and must be booked by telephone.
For information: 800-367-5320; www.hawaiianair.com.

HORIZON AIR

A regional airline, Horizon Air serves 46 western destinations from Alberta to Arizona. It occasionally offers senior fares on some routes for passengers 65-plus, so ask if they are available when you make a booking.
For information: 800-547-9308; www.horizonair.com.

MIDWEST AIRLINES

Midwest Airlines, the Milwaukee-based carrier that flies to many cities throughout the U.S., offers senior fares to anyone over the age of 55 on 14-day advance-purchase flights when seats are available. The special fares allow a maximum stay of 180 days, useful for seasonal snowbird migration or long-term travel. These fares are not available online and must be booked by telephone.

For information: 800-452-2022; www.midwestairlines.com.

NORTHWEST AIRLINES

At age 65, you become eligible for Northwest Airlines' Senior Fare for flights within the U.S. or to Canada, Mexico, or the Caribbean. This fare is priced at about 10 percent less than the standard leisure fares and allows a stay of up to 180 days, a bonus for snowbirds and others who like to go somewhere and stay put for a while.

A lifetime membership in Northwest's World Club costs people who are 65 or over only half of what it costs their younger friends and relatives. Join as an individual or with a spouse and spend your waiting time in comfort.

For information: 800-225-2525; www.nwa.com. For Northwest Airlines World Club: 800-692-3788.

SOUTHWEST AIRLINES

A low-cost carrier known for its bargain fares, Southwest Airlines flies coast to coast to about 60 cities. Its senior fares, discounted 20 to 70 percent off the full fare and capped at $129 one way, are available on every flight every day of the week to people 65 or older. Because the number of senior seats is limited, you should reserve yours as early as possible.

Your senior tickets are fully refundable, exchangeable, and changeable. In other words, you can change your flights or cancel at any time without penalty. No advance booking is required which means you won't be paying exorbitant last-minute rates, there's no minimum or maximum stay or Saturday-night requirements, and you may purchase a one-way or round-trip ticket so you can return whenever you like. All seats are coach. Sometimes the fares for all ages are even cheaper, although they have more restrictions, so check them out too.

The bad news is that few long-haul flights are nonstop, no meals are served, the senior fares are not available to younger travel companions, and they must be booked by phone as they are not available on the website.

For information: 800-435-9792; www.southwest.com.

UNITED AIRLINES

The only special deal offered to seniors by United Airlines these days is the Silver Wings Plus program. Join the club at age 55 or more and you will be offered zone-based fares that are sometimes—but not always—better than other available rates. A two-year membership costs $75, a lifetime membership is $225. In addition, you must buy a book of four certificates for $25 for four round-trip flights, then reserve your flights using the certificates. The same fare applies to one travel companion. The club also offers vacation packages, cruises, and hotel and rental-car deals.

For information: 800-241-6522; www.united.com. For United Silver Wings Plus: 800-720-1765; www.silverwings plus.com.

US AIRWAYS

At this writing, AARP members receive special fares on US Airways that are often a good deal for travelers age 50 and over. The fares are zone-based and can be used for travel in the U.S. and to Canada, the Caribbean, and sometimes to Europe. To purchase AARP Savers tickets for yourself and a travel companion, you must book by telephone at least 14 days in advance. They are not available online or through travel agents. A Saturday-night stay is required and there are some blackout dates, but there is no minimum stay. *For information:* 800-428-4322; www.usairways.com. Call 866-886-2277 for AARP Savers fares.

US AIRWAYS SHUTTLE

Here's a good deal that's still around. Fly on the US Airways Shuttle that operates between New York, Boston, and Washington, D.C., with no advance purchase and save yourself some money on last-minute flights with the Senior Fare for which you qualify at age 62. You must, however, go off-peak, and that means you must fly between 10 A.M. and 2 P.M. or between 7 P.M. and midnight, Monday through Friday (anytime on Saturday and Sunday). *For information:* 800-428-4322; www.usairways.com.

GOOD DEALS IN CANADA
AIR CANADA

If you are over 60, you and a travel mate are eligible for a 10 percent reduction on published fares, including sale fares, for flights within Canada and from Canada to destinations in Europe and Asia. The discount also applies to trips from the U.S. to the U.K. but not to flights between the U.S. and Canada, although Air Canada is the largest carrier between

the two countries and operates about 500 nonstop flights daily between 59 U.S. and 8 Canadian cities.
For information: 888-247-2262; www.aircanada.ca.

GOOD DEALS ON FOREIGN AIRLINES

Always inquire about special senior discounts when you book your flights. Many foreign airlines offer a 10 percent discount to passengers at age 60 or 62 on transatlantic flights originating in the U.S., although a younger companion may not always be entitled to the same deal. Many foreign carriers will also give you a break on domestic flights within a nation's borders or to other nearby countries. Remember that seasonal promotional fares that are available to travelers of all ages may be lower than the senior fare, so be sure to do your homework before committing yourself.

AEROMEXICO

Mexico's largest airline, Aeromexico flies to 84 destinations in the U.S., six countries in Europe and South America, and 43 cities in Mexico. It gives passengers 62-plus and a younger traveling companion a 10 percent discount off most fares on its international routes. On many flights within Mexico, you and a younger companion can get the same deal if you're age 60.
For information: 800-237-6639; www.aeromexico.com.

AIR JAMAICA

Fly to Jamaica or about 15 other Caribbean destinations from the U.S. on Air Jamaica and take advantage of a 10 percent discount for passengers 60 and over and a companion at least 18 years old. The discount applies to most published fares. *For information:* 800-523-5585; www.airjamaica.com.

AUSTRIAN AIRLINES

The Austrian Airlines Group serves 123 destinations in 64 countries on five continents. On its frequent two-class, non-stop service across the Atlantic to Vienna and beyond from its gateway cities (New York, Montreal, Toronto, and Washington, D.C.), it offers a 10 percent discount to passengers 62 and over—and a travel companion of any age—on all but promotional sale fares.
For information: 800-843-0002 in the U.S.; 888-817-4444 in Canada; www.austrianair.com.

BWIA WEST INDIES AIRWAYS

If you are at least 60 years old, a 10 percent discount is yours on most fares from the U.S. and Canada. The same discount applies to a younger companion.
For information: 800-538-2942; www.bwee.com.

CATHAY PACIFIC AIRWAYS

This airline's senior-friendly "Worry Free" fares are a good deal if you have a U.S. passport and have turned 55. You and a travel companion of any age can get about 10 percent off the published fares from Los Angeles, New York, or San Francisco to Hong Kong and nine other Southeast Asian destinations. You pay no fee to change your flights and get a full refund if you must cancel your trip anytime up until departure. Tickets must be purchased online, and reservations can be made only four days in advance.
For information: 800-233-2742; www.cathayusa.com.

CAYMAN AIRWAYS

This small airline that flies from Miami, Tampa, Fort Lauderdale, Chicago, or Houston to the Cayman Islands will take 10 percent off some fares for you and a younger travel mate if you are 62.

For information: 800-422-9626; www.caymanairways.com.

EL AL ISRAEL AIRLINES

El Al, Israel's national airline, flies four times more weekly nonstop flights to Israel from the U.S. than any other airline. It offers passengers over 60 and their spouses over 55 special senior fares that are 10 percent less than most other fares between the two countries.

For information: 800-223-6700; www.elal.com.

FINNAIR

On flights between Finnair's U.S. and Canadian gateway cities and Helsinki, you and a companion of any age get a discount of 10 percent on most transatlantic fares if you are 62 or older. You'll get an even better discount—a whopping 70 percent or thereabouts—off the cost of flights within Finland, but you must be 65 for this privilege and pay for your tickets within 72 hours of booking your flight.

For information: 800-950-5000; www.finnair.com.

IBERIA AIRLINES OF SPAIN

If you are 62 years old, Iberia gives you and a companion 10 percent off most published nonsale fares for round-trip transatlantic flights originating in North America and for flights within Europe if your travel originates here.

For information: 800-772-4642; www.iberia.com.

LUFTHANSA GERMAN AIRLINES

Once you've turned 60, Lufthansa offers you and a travel mate over 18 a discount of 10 percent off most fares across the Atlantic to Germany or its other European destinations. The same discount applies to domestic travel as well if it is booked at the same time as your international flights.
For information: 800-645-3880; www.lufthansa-usa.com.

MARTINAIR HOLLAND

On Martinair's flights from Florida to Amsterdam, travelers 60-plus and their younger travel companions (at least 16 years old) are entitled to a 10 percent discount on most fares. Travelers 55 and older get the same 10 percent discount when they fly from Florida to Costa Rica, but younger companions do not. And flying from the Canadian cities of Vancouver, Toronto, Calgary, or Edmonton to Amsterdam, 60-plus passengers get the discount, but travel mates don't get the same deal.
For information: 800-MARTINAIR (800-627-8462); www .martinairusa.com.

MEXICANA AIRLINES

On international flights between the U.S. or Canada and Mexico, Mexicana takes 10 percent off most published fares for passengers who are at least 62 and their travel companions. It does the same for domestic flights within Mexico that are reserved in the U.S. at the same time.
For information: 800-531-7921; www.mexicana.com.

SCANDINAVIAN AIRLINES SYSTEM (SAS)

On flights across the Atlantic from gateway cities in the U.S. or Canada to Scandinavian countries or other international destinations, SAS passengers age 62 and older (but no companions) get a 10 percent discount on most fares.

On domestic flights in Sweden, SAS offers special senior fares too, depending on the route, for those 65 or older.

But before flying with a senior fare, tempting as it might be, look into the cost of going with an air pass such as the Star Alliance Air Pass. It can make your travel, transatlantic and domestic, even cheaper.

For information: 800-221-2350; www.scandinavian.net.

SWISS INTERNATIONAL AIRLINES

This airline occasionally offers a 10 percent discount on published fares to passengers who are 62 or older and a travel companion of any age. The discount is applied to non-sale fares on transatlantic flights from the U.S. to its many European destinations.

For information: 877-FLY-SWISS (877-359-7947); www.swiss.com.

TAP AIR PORTUGAL (TAP)

TAP, Portugal's national airline that serves 30 cities worldwide, gives travelers over the age of 62 a 10 percent discount on most nonpromotional transatlantic fares originating in the U.S. The same discount applies for one traveling companion of any age.

For information: 800-221-7370; www.tapusa.us.

VIRGIN ATLANTIC AIRWAYS

Turn 60 and Virgin Atlantic gives you a 10 percent discount on all published nonsale fares for flights between the U.S. and London. In addition, members of AARP and one travel mate each are offered discounts ranging from 11 to 17 percent on some advance-purchase premium economy fares to London.

For information: 800-862-8621; www.virginatlantic.com.

4

Hotels and Motels: Get Your Over-50 Markdowns

Now that you're over 50, you'll never have to pay full price for a hotel room again. Across the U.S. and Canada and often in the rest of the world, virtually all lodging chains and most individual establishments go out of their way to give you a break on room rates. You don't even have to wait until you're eligible for Social Security to cash in on your maturity because most hotels, inns, and motels offer discounts to you at age 50, usually requiring only proof of age or membership in a senior organization.

What all this means is that you should *never* make a lodging reservation without making sure you are getting a special rate—a senior discount of at least 10 to 15 percent or an even better deal.

With all of the competition within the lodging industry today, the senior discount isn't always the cheapest route to a hotel room. You may find the best rates through a travel agency, a hotel broker, a half-price program, chain websites, an online discounter, or a hotel chain's own club or simply by asking the reservations clerk what's available. Perhaps there's a promotional off-peak sale going on that beats your age-related discount. The message is, don't get too enthusiastic about your senior privileges until you've investigated all the possibilities and found the *lowest available rate*.

But, first, keep in mind:

If you want to use the privileges coming to you because of your age, you must do some advance research and planning with your travel agent or on your own.

In this rapidly changing world, rates and policies can be altered in a flash, so an update is always advisable.

■ Always ask whether there is a senior discount, whether or not one is posted on the website or mentioned in the hotel's literature. You'll find that just about every hotel has one.

■ The basic senior discounts of 10 to 15 percent are about as good as you'll get at budget hotel chains, so take the deal and run. At more expensive hotels, however, it pays to save the paltry 10 or 15 percent senior discount for the times when you can't get anything better some other way through special promotions. You can often get a much better deal if you pursue all other options.

Some of the biggest senior discounts are available only with major restrictions such as a 21-day, nonrefundable advance purchase, so make sure you're willing to live with those restrictions before committing yourself.

Information about discounts is seldom volunteered. In most cases, you must arrange for them when you make your reservations and confirm them when you check in. Do not wait until you're settling your bill because then it might be too late. Some hotels and motels require that you make advance reservations to get their discounts. "Advance" may mean a considerable period of time such as three weeks, but it may also mean only a week, a day, or even a few hours. Check it out before making your plans.

■ Although many senior discounts are available every day of the year, some are subject to "space availability." This means it may be hard to get them when you want to travel because only a limited number of rooms may be reserved for special rates. If these are already booked or are expected to be booked, you won't get your discount. And some hotels have "blackout" dates during special events or holiday periods when the discount is not available. So always book early, ask for your discount privileges, and try to be flexible on your dates in order to take advantage of them. Your best bets for space are usually weekends in large cities, weekdays at resorts, and nonholiday seasons.

■ Many hotels, particularly in big cities and warm climates, cut their prices drastically in the summer. Others that cater mostly to businesspeople during the week try to encourage weekend traffic by offering bargain rates if you stay over a Saturday night. Resorts are often eager to fill their rooms on weekdays.

■ When you travel in other countries, remember that your senior discount is valid at participating foreign locations of many major American hotel chains, such as Choice Hotels International, Hilton Hotels, Holiday Inn, Marriott, Radisson, and Sheraton.

■ If you are traveling with children or grandchildren, remember that at many hotels, children under a specified age, usually 16 or 18, may stay in your room for free. And at some big chains, they may eat free, too.

■ In some cases, not every hotel or inn in a chain will offer the senior discount. Those that do are called "participating" hotels or motels. Make sure the one you are planning to visit is participating in the senior plan.

■ In addition to the chains, many independent hotels and inns are eager for your business and offer special reduced rates. Always *ask* before making a reservation. Your travel agent should be able to help you with this.

■ Some hotel restaurants will give you a discount, too, whether or not you are a registered guest.

■ By the way, your discount usually applies only to the regular rates and, in most cases, will not be given on top of other special discounts. One discount is usually all you get.

■ Keep in mind that "extras" included at no additional charge are worth money. Some hotel chains include a full hot breakfast rather than the usual unimaginative continental variety. Others provide no-cost high-speed Internet access, local calls, or evening "happy hours." Free parking is another option that can save you plenty. Find out about these possibilities by going online or calling the hotels directly.

AMERIHOST INN

These new-construction economy hotels across the country, all with indoor swimming pools, give a discount of 15 percent off the regular room rates to members of AARP and 10 percent at participating locations to all other guests age 50 or over. Continental breakfast is included.

For information: 800-434-5800; www.amerihost.com.

AMERISUITES

All of these all-suite hotels with swimming pools and fitness centers in 32 states give members of AARP a discount of 15 percent on the regular room rates every day of the year. Buffet breakfast is included.

For information: 800-833-1516; www.amerisuites.com.

ASTON HAWAII

At properties that range from economy hotels to luxury condominium resorts located on four of Hawaii's major islands, Aston Hawaii takes 25 percent off the regular room rates when one guest in the room is at least 50. An additional privilege is a seventh night free at many participating properties.

For information: 800-922-7866, in Hawaii, 800-321-2558; www.astonhotels.com.

BAYMONT INNS & SUITES

Baymont Inns & Suites operates more than 180 affordable properties in 33 states, most of them located near shopping areas, major highways, restaurants, and entertainment. Guests who are over 55 get a 10 percent discount, and AARP members get the same privilege at age 50. A free breakfast buffet and, in many locations, free high-speed Internet connections are included.

For information: 877-BAYMONT (877-229-6668); www .baymontinns.com.

BEST INNS & SUITES

At these economy inns, the Best Traveler Silver Edition program gives guests over the age of 50 a discount of 10 percent off the regular rates, plus a tenth night free. Continental breakfast comes with it. Join the free program by calling the reservations number.

For information: 800-237-8466; www.bestinn.com.

BEST WESTERN INTERNATIONAL

You'll get a simple 10 percent off the regular room rates any day of the year at all 2,300 Best Westerns in the U.S. and Canada and at most of the 1,700 elsewhere in the world, if you belong to AARP or CARP. Because the hotels in this group are individually owned, they are all different and may even offer you other privileges such as late checkout, upgrades, and breakfast.

For information: 800-WESTERN (800-937-8376); www .bestwestern.com.

BUDGET HOST INNS

A network of about 160 mostly family-owned economy inns in the U.S. and Canada, almost all Budget Host Inns offer senior discounts—usually 10 percent off the regular rates— that vary by location. Call the toll-free reservations number and you will be transferred directly to the front desk of the inn you want, where you can ask about the accommodations, facilities, rates, discounts, and directions to the property.

For information: 800-283-4678; www.budgethost.com.

CANDLEWOOD SUITES

Candlewood Suites, a group of about 100 affordable all-suite hotels, takes 10 percent off the regular room rates for members of AARP at all of its locations.

AMERICAN EXPRESS SENIOR CARD

The major benefit of the American Express Senior Member Card, designed specifically for people 62 or over, is a reduction in the annual fee—$35 for a standard card or $55 for a Gold Senior Member Card and $20 or $25 for each additional cardholder on the same account—along with the usual charge privileges and customer services. Other benefits are a quarterly newsletter; savings on travel, shopping, and dining; and a 24-hour global hotline for emergency assistance on legal, medical, or financial problems.
For information: 800-THE-CARD (800-843-2273); www.americanexpress.com/senior.

For information: 888-226-3539; www.candlewoodsuites.com.

CASTLE RESORTS & HOTELS

Castle's 18 hotels and resort condominiums in Hawaii, Saipan, and New Zealand offer guests 50 and over a discount of up to 25 percent off the regular rates every day of the year, as well as special rates on rental cars.
For information: 800-367-5004; www.castleresorts.com.

CHOICE HOTELS INTERNATIONAL

Among the better deals at major hotels are those offered by Choice Hotels, an international group of about 4,500 locations in 48 countries with brand names that include Main-Stay Suites, Sleep Inn, Comfort Suites, Comfort Inn, Quality, Clarion, Econo Lodge, and Rodeway Inn. All of them take catering to older travelers very seriously, and most give you a choice of three options.

If you're 60 or older, the Sixty-Plus Rate gives a reduction of 20 to 30 percent when you make reservations in advance at any U.S. participating hotel. Call the toll-free number and be sure to request the special rate.

If you're not yet 60 or the Sixty-Plus Rate is not available at the hotel you want, ask for the Fifty-Plus Rate. It takes 10 percent off and is available every day of the week at all Choice hotels with or without advance reservations.

The AARP Rate is even better, giving members of this estimable organization a discount of 15 percent at age 50 at participating hotels around the world. Book by telephone or online, but be sure to quote the special discount code ID #00333300.

On top of the senior rates, you are also eligible for the special promotions offered every spring and fall that give you a chance to save even more.

Most Choice hotels include complimentary continental breakfast, and two brands—Econo Lodge and Rodeway Inns—have designed special senior rooms.

For information: 800-4-CHOICE (800-424-6423); www .choicehotels.com.

CLARION HOTEL & CLARION SUITES

See Choice Hotels International. These upscale, full-service hotels and resorts—190 of them in 15 countries—have special accommodations for both business travelers and families. All have swimming pools, exercise rooms, business centers, and restaurants.

For information: 800-4-CHOICE (800-424-6423); www .choicehotels.com.

COMFORT INN

See Choice Hotels International. You'll find Comforts, about 3,000 of them, around the world, all of them offering reasonable rates and comfortable lodgings. Most provide complimentary continental breakfast, swimming pools, or exercise facilities.
For information: 800-4-CHOICE (800-434-6423); www.choicehotels.com.

COMFORT SUITES

These all-suite hotels feature oversized rooms with partially divided sleeping and seating areas, a living/workspace, microwaves, and refrigerators. All have swimming pools or exercise rooms and serve continental breakfast every morning.
For information: 800-4-CHOICE (800-434-6423); www.choicehotels.com.

CONRAD HOTELS

See Hilton Hotels. Many Conrad Hotels in the U.S., Europe, Australia, Hong Kong, Egypt, Singapore, Turkey, Uruguay, and the Caribbean participate in Hilton's Senior HHonors Worldwide program for over-60s. Members are entitled to up to 50 percent off the regular room rates and 20 percent off the bill for dinner for two.
For information: 800-HILTONS (800-445-8667); www.hilton.com.

COUNTRY HEARTH INN

Most of these economy motels in the South and Midwest take 10 percent off the room rates for visitors over 50.
For information: 800-848-5767; www.countryhearth.com.

COUNTRY INNS & SUITES BY CARLSON

At its more than 320 locations worldwide, Country Inns offers its own Senior Power rate of 10 percent off the published rate for guests over 50. If you prefer, you can ask for the AARP member rate that saves you the same 10 percent. These affordable hotels with traditional architecture and a bed-and-breakfast ambience include a complimentary breakfast.

For information: 800-456-4000; www.countryinns.com.

COURTYARD BY MARRIOTT

If you're 62 or older, you'll get 15 percent off the regular room rates every day of the year at participating locations of these moderately priced hotels, most of which feature swimming pools, exercise facilities, and free Internet access. Advance reservations are recommended.

For information: 800-321-2211; www.courtyard.com.

CROWNE PLAZA HOTELS & RESORTS

Any day of the year, Crowne Plaza offers members of AARP a 10 percent discount off the regular room rates at about 100 participating locations in North America. As upscale accommodations in 49 countries around the world, these hotels and resorts are designed to cater especially to business travelers, providing business centers, fitness rooms, restaurants, concierge services, and meeting rooms.

For information: 800-227-6963; www.crowneplaza.com.

DAYS INNS WORLDWIDE

One of the first national brands of economy lodgings in the country, Days Inns—all 1,900 of them around the world—

have discontinued their September Days Club and replaced it with a discount of 15 percent off the regular rates for members of AARP with an advance reservation. Anybody else over the age of 50 gets 10 percent off at participating properties.

For information: 800-DAYS-INN (800-329-7466); www .daysinn.com.

DELTA HOTELS

Delta Hotels, Canada's largest first-class hotel company, with more than 40 properties across the country, is a subsidiary of Fairmont Hotels and Resorts. Most of its locations offer members of AARP and CARP a discount of 10 to 15 percent off the best available room rates.

For information: 800-268-1133; www.deltahotels.com.

DOUBLETREE HOTELS

At many Doubletrees, you are offered a senior discount if you are 60 or more. Because each location has its own policy, ask the hotel you are considering whether there is a senior discount and how much it can save you. When there is one, it is yours anytime, any day, no advance reservations required, if rooms are available. Not only that, but you'll get a reduction on food and nonalcoholic beverages at some Doubletree restaurants if you are guests of the hotel.

For information: 800-222-8733; www.doubletreehotels .com.

DOWNTOWNER INNS

See Red Carpet Inn. 800-251-1962; www.bookroomsnow .com.

DRURY INNS

Concentrated in the Midwest and the South, these inexpensive hotels offer about 10 percent off the regular rates. You must be at least 50 to qualify and have proof of age handy. A free breakfast is included.
For information: 800-DRURYINN (800-378-7946); www .druryinn.com.

ECONO LODGE

See Choice Hotels International. In addition to three varieties of senior discounts, these affordable hotels feature special accommodations for older travelers. Its "senior rooms" feature bright lighting, large-button telephones, easy-to-read alarm clocks, and grab bars in the bathroom.
For information: 800-4-CHOICE (800-424-6423); www .choicehotels.com.

EMBASSY SUITES HOTELS

At participating Embassy Suites Hotels, guests who are over the age of 50 will receive a 10 percent discount off the regular rates on their two-room suites. Embassy offers amenities such as a free cooked-to-order breakfast each morning, and guests can enjoy a Manager's Reception with hors d'oeuvres and beverages every evening.
For information: 800-EMBASSY (800-362-2779); www .embassy-suites.com.

EXEL INNS OF AMERICA

A small group of budget motels in the Midwest, most Exel Inns offer a 10 percent discount to guests who are 55 and over.
For information: 800-356-8013; www.exelinns.com.

FAIRFIELD INN BY MARRIOTT

At this midprice group of hotels, you are eligible for a 15 percent discount on the regular room rates for up to two rooms for an unlimited number of nights when rooms are available, but only if you are 62 or older. A continental breakfast and free Internet access are included.
For information: 800-228-2800; www.fairfieldinn.com.

FAIRMONT HOTELS & RESORTS

These grand hotels and resorts—which include the elegant Canadian Pacific Hotels—are located in Canada, the U.S., Bermuda, Mexico, Dubai, and Barbados and give 50-plus travelers special breaks. Members of AARP receive a 10 to 25 percent discount off the regular room rates, and CARP members get a 20 percent discount off the bed-and-breakfast rates—subject, of course, to space availability.

Many of these luxury hotels also design off-peak, three-night, almost all-inclusive packages for older travelers.
For information: 800-441-1414; www.fairmont.com.

FOUR POINTS HOTELS BY SHERATON

Four Points Hotels, located in 15 countries, are full-service hotels with affordable prices. Like other members of the Starwood group of lodgings, they give a good deal to AARP members—up to 50 percent off the published room rates with a 21-day, nonrefundable advance purchase that includes a Thursday, Friday, or Saturday arrival. Without the advance booking, you can save up to 25 percent any day of the week. You may also sign up for complimentary membership in the Starwood Preferred Guest Program at the Preferred Plus Tier, earning points for frequent stays, upgrades on rooms at check-in, instant rewards, and late checkout, based on availability.

For information: 800-368-7764 or 877-778-2277; www
.fourpoints.com or www.starwood.com/aarp.

HAMPTON INN/HAMPTON INN & SUITES

These moderately priced hotels and suites, part of the Hilton
family, have more than a thousand locations in the U.S.,
Canada, and Latin America. When you make a reservation,
ask for the AARP discount that varies from inn to inn. A
breakfast buffet is included, and many of the hotels have
swimming pools and exercise facilities.
For information: 800-HAMPTON (800-426-7866); www
.hampton-inn.com.

HAWAIIAN HOTELS & RESORTS

There's good news for travelers over the age of 50 at two
full-service oceanfront resorts in Hawaii. At both the Royal
Lahaina Beach Resort on Maui and the Royal Kona Resort on
the Big Island, the deal is a 50 percent discount on rooms.
Ask for the 50-plus specials when you make reservations.
For information: 800-22-ALOHA (800-222-5642); www
.hawaiihotels.com.

HAWTHORN SUITES HOTELS

Although there is no official senior discount at these upscale
hotels designed for extended stays, many properties do offer
a 10 percent savings to older travelers. So ask when you are
making a reservation. Each suite includes kitchen facilities
and offers a hot buffet breakfast daily.
For information: 800-527-1133; www.hawthorn.com.

HILTON GARDEN INN

These intimate and affordable hotels are located in many cities and major suburban areas and close to many airports. All feature convenience marts, restaurants, swimming pools, fitness centers, and free parking. And they all offer the Hilton Senior HHonors Club members (see Hilton Hotels) discounted hotel rates guaranteed to be lower than any others available, a second room for family or friends at the same cost, and 20 percent off the bill for a meal for one or two at participating hotel restaurants. You may join the club at age 60.

Guests without a membership get a 10 to 15 percent discount at age 50 just by asking for it.

For information: 877-STAY-HGI (877-782-9444); www .hiltongardeninn.com. For Hilton Senior HHonors Worldwide: 800-492-3232; www.hiltonhhonors.com.

HILTON HOTELS

If you're over 60 and do a lot of traveling, an outstanding deal is waiting for you at Hilton Hotels as well as Conrads and Hilton Garden Inns. If you join Senior HHonors, Hilton's travel club, you'll get discounted rates at more than 450 participating hotels in 60 countries guaranteed to be lower than any other publicly available rate and often up to half off the regular rates. The cost of membership for you and a companion is $55 in the U.S. ($75 elsewhere) for the first year, then $40 (or $60) annually.

Other privileges come with membership in the club too. One major attraction is that you can reserve not only your own room at a discount but a second one at the same rate for family and friends of any age. Another perk allows you to eat in participating Hilton, Conrad, or Hilton Garden Inn restaurants and get 20 percent taken off the bill for dinner for one or two people, whether you are a guest of the hotel or merely dropping in. At most locations, the deal applies only to dinners; at hotels that do not serve dinner, it applies only to breakfast. For a list of restaurants participating in the plan, visit the club's website.

As a member of the senior club, you're automatically enrolled in Hilton HHonors, a frequent-stay program, and earn points and miles when you stay in Hiltons, Conrads, Hilton Garden Inns, and the other brands that belong to this group of hotels: Doubletree, Embassy Suites Hotels, Hampton Inn, Homewood Suites, and Scandic Hotels.

If you don't join the club but are over the age of 50, you'll get a discount of 10 to 15 percent off the regular rates at participating hotels just by asking for it.

For information: 800-HILTONS (800-445-8667) or 800-492-3232; www.hilton.com. For Hilton Senior HHonors Worldwide: 800-548-8690.

HISTORIC HOTELS OF AMERICA

All of these landmark hotels are independently owned and differ on their savings for seniors, but most give visitors over the age of 50 a 10 percent discount and some offer even more.

Historic Hotels of America is a program of the National Trust for Historic Preservation that has identified 203 hotels that have maintained their historic integrity, architecture, and ambience. They must be at least 50 years old, listed in or eligible for the National Register of Historic Places, or recognized locally as having historic significance.

For information: Call each hotel directly. Or contact National Trust Historic Hotels of America, 1785 Massachusetts Ave. NW, Washington, DC 20036; 800-678-8946 or www.historichotels.org.

HOLIDAY INN

At Holiday Inns around the world, members of AARP get 10 percent off nondiscounted room rates every day of the year. The privilege is subject, of course, to space availability. Kids under 12 stay and eat free at all locations in the U.S. and Canada. Amenities include swimming pools, restaurants, 24-hour business services, meeting facilities, and fitness rooms.

For information: 800-HOLIDAY (800-465-4329); www .holiday-inn.com.

HOLIDAY INN EXPRESS

With about 1,200 locations worldwide and more opening every week, Holiday Inn Express provides clean, modern, uncomplicated accommodations at affordable rates. What's equally important to us, however, is the 10 percent discount on nondiscounted room rates for guests who are members of AARP and therefore over the age of 50.

For information: 800-HOLIDAY (800-465-4329); www .hiexpress.com.

HOMEWOOD SUITES BY HILTON

At participating Homewood Suites by Hilton throughout the U.S., guests age 50 or over get up to 10 percent off the regular room rates. Accommodations are one- or two-bedroom suites with fully equipped kitchens. Among the amenities

are a free breakfast every day and an evening Manager's Reception with hors d'oeuvres and beverages Monday through Thursday.
For information: 800-CALL HOME (800-225-5466); www .homewood-suites.com.

HOWARD JOHNSON INTERNATIONAL

A famous American landmark, Howard Johnson opened its first hotel in 1954 and is now found throughout the U.S. and many other countries. To AARP members who make an advance reservation, its several brands—Howard Johnson Hotels, Howard Johnson Inns, Howard Johnson Express Inns, and Plaza Hotels—give a discount of 20 percent off the published room rates. To all others over the age of 50, they offer a 10 percent discount at participating properties.
For information: 800-I-GO-HOJO (800-446-4656); www .howardjohnson.com.

HYATT HOTELS & RESORTS

A collection of upscale lodgings all over the world, most Hyatt Hotels offer guests who are 62-plus special senior rates that vary from property to property but can give you a discount of up to 50 percent off the regular rates. Advance reservations are required, and the senior rates are subject to availability.
For information: 800-233-1234; www.hyatt.com.

INTERCONTINENTAL HOTELS & RESORTS

InterContinental Hotels, with about 140 properties in 65 countries, offer services and amenities specifically designed for the international business traveler in key destinations

around the globe. With upscale restaurants, concierge services, complimentary breakfast and evening cocktails, meeting rooms, business service centers, fitness centers, and other amenities, participating properties in this group of hotels give a 10 percent discount to members of AARP on the nondiscounted room rates when space is available.
For information: 800-327-0200; www.intercontinental.com.

JW MARRIOTT HOTELS & RESORTS

The most elegant and luxurious hotels carrying the Marriott brand name, JW Marriotts cater to upscale travelers. All have restaurants, fitness centers and spas, and 24-hour executive business centers. Guests over the age of 62 are eligible for a 15 percent discount on the regular room rates.
For information: 800-228-9290; www.marriott.com.

KIMPTON HOTELS

A unique collection of 39 European-style hotels with fine restaurants in major cities across the U.S. and Canada, Kimpton Hotels encourages people who are 55 or older to ask for the Young at Heart Rate when making reservations. It gives you a discount of about 10 percent off the published rates, and it's yours when rooms are available. If you reserve online, select "aarp" under the Special Rates section.
For information: 800-KIMPTON (800-546-7866); www .kimptongroup.com.

KNIGHTS INN

Clean, comfortable, and inexpensive, the Knights Inn properties across the U.S. and Canada give a 15 percent discount on room rates to members of AARP and all other guests who are 50 or older.

For information: 800-843-5644; www.knightsinn.com.

LA QUINTA INNS

With more than 375 properties in 33 states, La Quinta Inns are inexpensive and become even more so when you get your 10 to 30 percent senior discount. You'll get it if you are an AARP member or are at least 55 and can prove it. A full continental breakfast, free local calls, and high-speed Internet access are included.

For information: 800-531-5900; www.lq.com.

LOEWS HOTELS

This group of 20 hotels and resorts located in major cities in the U.S. and Canada has a senior rate for guests 62-plus that takes 10 percent off all rates.

Its Generation G program, offered all year, is a choice of packages created for grandparents and grandchildren on vacation together. One package is designed for teenagers and features suite accommodations, sports and cultural tours, spa treatments, and tickets to events. Another is targeted for adventurous kids age 10 or older, and the third is suitable for all ages and lets you customize your own itinerary. Because each of the hotels is located in a city with its own unique attractions, the packages vary but always include activities appropriate for both generations. At several of the hotels, a second room may be reserved at reduced rates.

For information: 800-23-LOEWS (800-235-6397); www .loewshotels.com.

LUXURY COLLECTION HOTELS

This small group of unique hotels, some centuries old, in 25 countries offers a discount of up to 50 percent off the published room rates to AARP members who make a 21-day, nonrefundable advance purchase with a Thursday, Friday, or Saturday arrival. Without the advance booking, the savings are 15 to 25 percent any day of the week. You may also sign up for complimentary membership in the Starwood Preferred Guest Program at the Preferred Plus Tier, earning points for frequent nights, upgrades, instant awards, and late checkout.

For information: 800-325-3589 or 877-778-2277; www .luxurycollection.com or www.starwood.com/aarp.

MAINSTAY SUITES

See Choice Hotels International. MainStay Suites offer accommodations designed for extended stays with kitchens, dining, and living areas. Most locations have swimming pools and exercise rooms. Complimentary breakfast is served weekday mornings.

For information: 800-4-CHOICE (800-424-6423); www .choicehotels.com.

MARRIOTT INTERNATIONAL HOTELS

Marriott's good deal for seniors is a simple 15 percent savings on standard room rates every day of the week for everybody age 62 or older. It's valid at all Marriott properties, including Marriott Hotels, Resorts and Suites; JW Marriott Hotels & Resorts; Courtyard by Marriott; Fairfield Inn by Marriott; Renaissance Hotels & Resorts; Residence Inn by

Marriott; SpringHill Suites by Marriott; TownePlace Suites by Marriott; and even Marriott Vacation Club International. Subject to availability, the discount is good for up to two rooms for an unlimited number of nights.
For information: 800-228-9290; www.marriott.com.

MASTER HOSTS INNS & RESORTS

See Red Carpet Inn. 800-251-1962; www.bookroomsnow .com.

MCINTOSH MOTOR INNS

At many of these economy inns in New Jersey, Pennsylvania, and Delaware, guests who belong to AARP are offered a 10 percent discount off the regular rates. Continental breakfast is included.
For information: 800-444-2775; www.mcintoshinns.com.

MERCURE HOTELS

Guests who are 55-plus can enjoy special savings when they stay at Mercure Hotels throughout France because they may bring along a companion of any age and get a double room for the price of a single. Breakfast for two is included. The offer is good every day of the year at all 285 hotels in the Mercure network.
For information: 800-637-2873; www.mercure.com.

MICROTEL INN & SUITES

At these independently owned economy hotels, all virtually identical, some properties offer a 10 percent discount to guests with AARP cards. Continental breakfast is included and so is a tenth night free.
For information: 888-771-7171; www.microtelinn.com.

MOTEL 6

Take advantage of a 10 percent discount off the room rates at any of these more than 850 pet-friendly economy budget motels in the U.S. and Canada by showing your AARP or CARP card. You may save more by going online to check out the periodic special deals.

For information: 800-4-MOTEL6 (800-466-8356); www .motel6.com.

OHANA HOTELS & RESORTS

Most of these moderately priced hotels and resorts are located in Waikiki, with a couple on the Big Island and Maui in Hawaii and two in Guam. They all offer a straightforward 30 percent off the published rates for anybody age 55 or over. But before you make your reservation, be sure to check out the Simple Saver rate available to everyone. It may be even cheaper, although unlike the senior rate, it does not allow for your choice of room type.

For information: 800-462-6262; www.ohanahotels.com.

OMNI HOTELS

Omni Hotels offers luxury accommodations with a wide range of amenities at more than 40 hotels and resorts throughout the U.S., Canada, and Mexico. All of its locations offer a 10 percent discount off the published room rates every day of the week, subject to availability, to guests who are 50 or sometimes 55. The Omni Royal Orleans in New Orleans, for example, has its "Leisure 55" program that gives 10 percent off the available rates to any leisure traveler who's at least 55.

For information: 800-THE OMNI (800-843-6664); www .omnihotels.com.

OUTRIGGER HOTELS & RESORTS

Travelers 55 and over get a nice deal on the regular room rates at all Outrigger locations in Hawaii, the Marshall Islands, Fiji, and Guam, where they qualify for discounts that range from 20 to 30 percent. In Australia, the senior discount is a straight 20 percent. But first check out Outrigger's Best Value rate for all ages, which may sometimes give you an even better deal, depending on the property and time of year. *For information:* 800-OUTRIGGER (800-688-7444); www .outrigger.com.

PAN PACIFIC HOTELS & RESORTS

Each of Pan Pacific's luxury hotels and resorts around the Pacific Rim is unique. Ranging from secluded island resorts to city hotels, most have special rates for guests who are at least 55 or 60. The offers, which differ from place to place, include senior rates at Yokohama and San Francisco and special senior packages in Bangkok, Kuala Lumpur, and Manila. To take advantage of them, always inquire about them when you make reservations. *For information:* 800-327-8585; www.panpacific.com.

PARADORES OF SPAIN

See Spain, Chapter 8.

PARK INN

Senior Breaks offers up to 25 percent off the standard rate for guests 55 and over in the U.S. and Canada and 65 and over in Europe. Or, at age 50, you have the option of choos-

ing the AARP member discount of 10 percent available at all Park Inns. Complimentary breakfast is included.
For information: 800-670-7275; www.parkinn.com.

PARK PLAZA HOTELS & RESORTS

A group of full-service downtown, suburban, and airport-convenient hotels, Park Plaza offers you its Senior Breaks discount of up to 25 percent off standard room rates at age 55 the U.S. and Canada, age 60 in Australia and Asia, and age 65 in Europe. At 50, you may choose the AARP discount of 10 to 25 percent instead, but first make sure it saves you more than Senior Breaks or the special "Internet saver" rate available to all ages. Discounts are offered all year, seven days a week, when rooms are available.
For information: 800-814-7000; www.parkplaza.com.

PASSPORT INN

See Red Carpet Inn. 800-251-1962; www.bookroomsnow .com.

POUSADAS DE PORTUGAL

See Portugal, Chapter 8.

QUALITY INNS, HOTELS & SUITES

See Choice Hotels International. This group of about 900 full-service lodgings all over the world offers a range of amenities in addition to the usual Choice Hotels discounts

GOOD DEALS IN RESTAURANTS

Many restaurants offer special deals to people in their prime, but in most cases you must seek them out yourself by reading the menu, asking at the restaurant, or watching the ads in the local newspapers. At some big chains, such as the International House of Pancakes, Kentucky Fried Chicken, Bickford's, Lyon's, Arby's, Applebee's, TCBY, and Wendy's, there's a recommended corporate policy of senior discounts or special senior menus. For example, your local Applebee's gives you a free Golden Apple card that's good for 10 percent off your meal if you are 55-plus, and Boston Market offers a 10 percent discount to seniors at all of its restaurants. Denny's has an anytime senior menu with smaller portions and smaller prices for diners over 50. Even your local Chinese restaurant might give you 5 or 10 percent off the bill.

Sometimes a senior discount is available anytime you decide to dine, but often it's good only during certain hours or as "early bird" specials before 5:00 or 6:00 P.M. The eligible age varies from 50 to 65, and occasionally a restaurant requires that you sign up for its free senior club that issues you a membership card.

In addition, a few hotel chains will give you a break on your meal checks when you eat in their restaurants. For example:

At participating **Hilton Hotels** restaurants in the U.S. and Canada, you're entitled to a 20 percent discount on dinners for two, hotel guests or not, if one of you is a member of Hilton's Senior HHonors Worldwide. For a list of participating restaurants, go to www.hiltonhhonors.com.

Doubletree Hotels & Guest Suites reduces the bill for food and nonalcoholic beverages in participating restaurants for 60-plus guests of the hotel.

Stop in at a company-owned **Burger King** before 10:30 A.M. and you'll get free coffee if you're a senior. Check yours out—if it's a participating location, you're in luck. Some McDonald's locations will do the same.

for seniors. A hot buffet breakfast, now available in many locations, is one of them.

For information: 800-4-CHOICE (800-424-6423); www .choicehotels.com.

RADISSON HOTELS & RESORTS

At Radisson Hotels in 59 countries, you'll always get a discount if you've reached a certain age. In the U.S. and Canada, that age is 50, when you're entitled to 10 to 25 percent off the standard cost of a room at participating locations. Sometimes Radisson's own Senior Breaks program gives you the best deal, but sometimes the AARP discount of up to 25 percent is better, and occasionally the any-age "Internet saver" rate (with its many restrictions) tops both of them. The two senior discounts cannot be combined. So our advice is to ask questions and be sure you're getting the lowest available rate and all possible included benefits, such as free breakfasts and upgrades at check-in, before making a reservation.

To get the Senior Breaks discount in Australia and Asia, you must be at least 60; in Europe, you must be 65. There's no club to join, but you must be ready to show proof of your age.

For information: 800-333-3333; www.radisson.com or www.radisson.com/aarp.

RAMADA INTERNATIONAL HOTELS

This upscale group of hotels and resorts offers its 60 Plus Senior Traveler Plan, which gives 10 to 25 percent discounts to travelers who are at least 60 or are members of a senior organization. That means you can get your privileges at age 50 by mentioning your membership in AARP. Be sure to ask for your discount when you are making reservations and be ready to show proof of age or your membership card at check-in. Reservations are recommended.
For information: 800-854-7854, www.marriott.com.

RAMADA LIMITED, INN, AND PLAZA HOTELS

Spend the night at a Ramada Limited, Ramada Inn, or Ramada Plaza Hotel, and you're entitled to a 20 percent discount off the regular rates with an advance reservation if you belong to AARP. If you're not a member but are over 60, you'll get 15 percent off at participating locations.
For information: 800-2-RAMADA (800-272-6232); www .ramada.com.

RED CARPET INN

Almost all of the independently owned, affordable, limited-service inns in the Hospitality International group have a senior discount for guests over the age of 50, a 10 percent discount on the room rates, subject to availability. Most include a complimentary continental breakfast and parking right in front of your door. Located off major highways and suburban byways throughout the U.S. and Canada, they include Red Carpet Inn, Passport Inn, Downtowner Inns, Master Host Inns, and Scottish Inns.

For information: 800-251-1962; www.bookroomsnow.com.

RED LION HOTELS & INNS

Mostly located in the western and midwestern states, Red Lion Hotels and Red Lion Inns give a 10 to 20 percent discount to members of AARP. Part of the WestCoast Family of Hotels, they range from upscale full-service hotels to small inns and all-suites properties.

For information: 800-RED-LION (800-733-5466); www .redlion.com.

RED ROOF INNS

If you belong to AARP, you will be eligible for a 10 percent discount off the regular rates at all of these pet-friendly budget motels across the country. You can often save even more money by checking out the "Red Hot Deals" on the website for current specials.

For information: 800-RED-ROOF (800-733-7663); www .redroof.com.

RENAISSANCE HOTELS & RESORTS

After your 62nd birthday, you qualify for a 15 percent discount on the regular room rates every day of the week, subject to availability. It's valid for up to two rooms for an unlimited number of nights at any of these upscale lodgings, part of the Marriott Hotel group, in the U.S. and Canada. Just ask for it when you make reservations.

For information: 800-468-3571; www.renaissancehotels
.com.

RESIDENCE INN BY MARRIOTT

These long-stay all-suite accommodations, complete with
kitchens and separate living areas, offer guests age 60 or over
a 15 percent discount on regular rates every day of the year
at participating locations. Complimentary continental breakfast, evening social hours, and free Internet access are usually
included.
For information: 800-331-3131; www.residenceinn.com.

RODEWAY INNS

See Choice Hotels International. Rodeway Inn features
Senior Rooms with bright lighting; grab bars in the bathroom; and large buttons on telephones, remote controls, and
alarm clocks. Complimentary continental breakfast is part of
the package.
For information: 800-4-CHOICE (800-434-6423); www
.choicehotels.com.

SANDMAN HOTELS

All located in western Canada, this small group of inns takes
about 25 percent off the regular room rates for guests age 55
or over, when space is available. Ask for the senior rate, or
better yet, sign up for the free 55 Plus Program that guarantees you'll get a significant reduction whenever you book
a room. Join by telephone or online.
For information: 800-726-3626; www.sandmanhotels.com.

SCOTTISH INN

See Red Carpet Inn. 800-251-1962; www.bookrooms now.com.

SHERATON HOTELS & RESORTS

All of the upscale Sheratons in 70 countries around the world offer you an outstanding break if you are a member of AARP. It's a discount of up to 50 percent off the published room rates when you book a stay that includes a Thursday, Friday, or Saturday arrival and make a nonrefundable reservation at least 21 days in advance. If you can't plan that far ahead, you can get the everyday senior discount of up to 25 percent off.

You are also eligible for complimentary membership in Starwood Preferred Guest program at the Preferred Plus tier, earning points for frequent nights, upgrades on rooms at check-in, instant awards, and late checkout, based on availability.

For information: 800-325-3535 or 877-778-2277; www .sheraton.com or www.starwood.com/aarp.

SHILO INNS

Shilo Inns, most located along major highways in western states, gives a 10 percent discount to AARP members and anybody else who is at least 62.

For information: 800-222-2244; www.shiloinns.com.

SLEEP INN

See Choice Hotels International. At these 400 or so hotels throughout the world, amenities include a complimentary continental breakfast and a discount for guests 50 and over.

For information: 800-4-CHOICE (800-424-6423); www .choicehotels.com.

SONESTA HOTELS & RESORTS

At its six U.S. properties—in Boston, Miami, and New Orleans—Sonesta gives 10 to 15 percent off the regular rates to members of AARP.

For information: 800-SONESTA (800-766-3782); www .sonesta.com.

SPRINGHILL SUITES BY MARRIOTT

Make a reservation at one of these all-suite, moderately priced hotels and, at age 62, you'll get a 15 percent discount on the regular rate for up to two rooms for an unlimited number of nights, when space is available. Included in the package are a complimentary continental breakfast and free local phone calls.

For information: 888-287-9400; www.springhillsuites.com.

ST. REGIS HOTELS

A small group of five-star luxury lodgings, these hotels offer a discount of up to 50 percent to members of AARP who make a 21-day, nonrefundable advance purchase with a Thursday, Friday, or Saturday arrival. Other members get a 15 to 25 percent discount any day of the week. All may join the Starwood Preferred Guest program at the Preferred Plus tier, earning points for frequent nights, upgrades on rooms, instant awards, and late checkout.

For information: 877-787-3447 or 877-778-2277; www
.stregis.com or www.starwood.com/aarp.

STAYBRIDGE SUITES BY HOLIDAY INN

Designed for extended stays, Staybridge Suites are residential-style hotels with amenities that include fully equipped kitchens, complimentary breakfast, and 24-hour business services with complimentary PC workstations and free Internet access. Members of AARP are entitled to a 10 percent discount any day of the year, subject to availability.
For information: 800-238-8000; www.staybridge.com.

SUMMERFIELD SUITES BY WYNDHAM

A collection of 38 upscale, all-suite properties, all of Summerfield's one- or two-bedroom suites have a full kitchen, a separate living room, and a private bathroom per bedroom. Included are a buffet breakfast and a social hour on weekday evenings. If you belong to AARP, you're entitled to a discount of 35 to 40 percent off the published nondiscounted room rates. If you join the free WyndhamByRequest program, you'll get benefits such as free Internet access, late checkout, and free local and long-distance phone calls within the U.S.
For information: 800-WYNDHAM (800-996-3426); www
.wyndham.com.

SUPER 8 MOTELS

One of the world's largest economy lodging chains, with nearly 2,100 independently owned motels throughout the

U.S. and Canada, Super 8 gives a discount of 10 percent off its regular rates to members of AARP, as well as everybody else over the age of 50. You must make advance reservations. *For information:* 800-800-8000; www.super8.com.

TOWNEPLACE SUITES BY MARRIOTT
Moderately priced all-suite hotels, TownePlace Suites caters to guests who plan extended stays. It offers townhouse exteriors, full kitchens, an outdoor pool, a 24-hour exercise room, free Internet access, and a welcome to your pet. And guests 62 and older get a 15 percent discount at participating locations for up to two rooms for an unlimited number of nights when space is available.
For information: 800-257-3000; www.townehousesuites .com.

TRAVELODGE HOTELS
All Travelodge brands—Travelodge, Thriftlodge, Travelodge Inns, Travelodge Hotels, and Travelodge Suites, almost 600 locations ranging from budget to full-service accommodations—have a nice, straightforward plan for older travelers in the U.S. and Canada. Members of AARP receive 15 percent off any time, any night, with advance reservations. Or there's 10 percent off when space is available for anyone over 50 who arrives with or without reservations.
For information: 800-578-7878; www.travelodge.com.

VILLAGER LODGES
Designed for extended stays, the amenities offered by the Villager chain—Villager Lodge, Villager Premier, and Hearthside by Villager—range from rooms with minikitch-

enettes to oversized suites with fully equipped kitchens and separate living and sleeping areas. These affordable, independently owned lodgings are found in about 100 locations in the U.S., Canada, and Mexico and give a discount of 15 percent to members of AARP and 10 percent at participating locations to all other guests age 60 or older. Advance reservations are required.

For information: 800-328-7829; www.villager.com.

W HOTELS

A group of intimate, upscale, downtown hotels with high-tech amenities for business travelers, fitness rooms, spa services, and stylish restaurants, W Hotels has 19 locations in major cities, including 5 in New York. As part of the Starwood family of hotels, they give members of AARP a discount of up to 50 percent off the published room rates when they make a 21-day, nonrefundable advance booking with a Thursday, Friday, or Saturday arrival. Without the advance paid reservation, members can save 15 to 25 percent any day of the week and may join the Starwood Preferred Guest program at the Preferred Plus tier, earning points for frequent stays, upgrades on rooms, instant awards, and late checkout.

For information: 877-946-8357 or 877-778-2277; www.whotels.com or www.starwood.com/aarp.

WELLESLEY INN & SUITES

This midpriced nationwide group of about 75 hotels, many designed for extended stays, gives a 15 percent discount on room rates and complimentary breakfast to members of AARP and CARP.

For information: 800-444-8888; www.wellesleyonline.com.

WESTCOAST HOTELS

At these upscale WestCoast Hotels in the western and midwestern states as well as Alaska, members of AARP get a discount of 10 to 20 percent off the best rate of the day. Many located on waterfront property, each of these full-service hotels and resorts is unique.

For information: 800-325-4000; www.westcoasthotels.com.

WESTIN HOTELS

Westin Hotels, a Starwood brand, offers substantial discounts of up to 50 percent off to members of AARP who book 21 days or more in advance and arrive on a Thursday, Friday, or Saturday. Otherwise there's a discount of 15 to 25 percent every day of the week, when rooms are available. In addition, members may join the Starwood Preferred Guest program at the Preferred Plus tier and receive free room upgrades, late checkouts, and points for frequent stays.

For information: 800-WESTIN-1 (800-937-8461) or 877-778-2277; www.westin.com or www.starwood.com/aarp.

WINGATE INN

Wingate Inns are new-construction, moderately priced hotels with free high-speed Internet access in every room and 24-hour self-service business centers. Other amenities include complimentary breakfast and exercise facilities. Wingate gives a 15 percent discount to members of AARP

with advance reservations and a 10 percent discount at participating properties to anybody who's 60 or more.
For information: 800-228-1000; www.wingateinns.com.

WYNDHAM HOTELS & RESORTS

Wyndham's offer to mature guests is generous and simple.
At most of these upscale, full-service properties—including Wyndham Luxury Resorts—throughout the U.S.,
Canada, Mexico, and the Caribbean, AARP members get 35
to 40 percent off the regular nondiscounted room rates
every day of the year, with some blackout dates. If you join
the free WyndhamByRequest program, you'll get benefits
such as free Internet access, late checkout, and local and
long-distance telephone calls within the U.S.
For information: 800-WYNDHAM (800-996-3426); www
.wyndham.com.

5

Alternative Lodgings for Thrifty Wanderers

I f you're willing to be innovative, imaginative, and occasionally fairly spartan, you can travel for a song or thereabouts. Here are some novel lodging options that can save you money and perhaps offer adventures in the bargain. Not all of them are designed exclusively for people over 50, but each reports that the major portion of its clientele consists of free spirits of a certain age who like to travel, appreciate good value for their money, and enjoy getting to know new people from other places.

For more ways to cut travel costs and get smart at the same time, check out the residential/educational programs in Chapter 13.

AFFORDABLE TRAVEL CLUB

Join this bed-and-breakfast club limited to people over 40 and you'll pay a pittance for accommodations, meet interesting people, and see new places. As members, you will act as hosts for fellow members, putting them up in your spare bedroom perhaps a couple of times a year and providing breakfast and a little of your time to acquaint your guests with the area. Visitors pay $15 for a single or $20 for a double per room per night for their stay, and $10 for each additional person. When you travel, you do the same.

There are currently about 1,300 member households in this club in 47 states and 30 countries offering accommodations ranging from simple bedrooms to suites and condos. For a membership fee of $60 a year, U.S. hosts receive a printed newsletter twice a year ($50 online) plus an annual directory from which you choose your own hosts and where others may choose you. Fees differ for hosts in Canada, Mexico, and overseas and for e-mail delivery. The club also sponsors a group tour at least once a year.

If you have a pet, you may want to take advantage of the club's house-sitting and pet-sitting service—members move into your house and care for your house and/or pets while you're on vacation, meanwhile enjoying a visit to your neighborhood in exchange and no money changes hands. *For information:* Affordable Travel Club, 6556 Snug Harbor Ln., Gig Harbor, WA 98335; 253-858-2172; www.affordable travelclub.net.

DEL WEBB'S SUN CITIES

The largest builder of active adult communities, Del Webb offers its Vacation Getaways program at many of its properties, with the details differing with place and season. These are low-cost, short vacation stays so you can sample the lifestyle to see whether you'd like to move in. Reservations are required. You'll stay in your own guest house for a few days, spend time with the residents, try out the facilities, play a round of golf perhaps, explore the clubhouses, and tour the model homes. At this writing, the rates range from about $250 for four nights to about $675 for a seven-day package in peak season.

The requirements are that one partner in a visiting couple must be at least 55 years old, no one in the group may be younger than 19, guests may stay no more than twice at the same location, and they must agree to meet with a sales representative during the stay.

For information: Del Webb's Sun Cities, www.delwebb.com.

EVERGREEN BED AND BREAKFAST CLUB

This bed-and-breakfast club, exclusively for people over the age of 50, was founded in 1982 and now has about 3,500 member families and 2,000 host locations in the U.S. and Canada plus many other countries. Whether a host home is elegant or simple, members pay only $10 for a single or $15 per couple for each overnight stay and bountiful breakfast. In return, they welcome members of the club into their own homes as often as they wish.

Twice a year the club publishes directories of members with relevant information about all of the host families and the special attractions of their areas. You then make your own arrangements for visits and pay the gratuities directly to the hosts. A quarterly newsletter provides the latest information. Annual club dues are $60 for a single and $75 for two.

An important aspect of this hospitality club is the opportunity for members to make new friends and perhaps travel together, as many members do.

ELDERTRAVELERS.ORG

If you're sociable, adventurous, 50 or more, and love making new friends, check out ElderTravelers.org, a website that helps match up potential guests with hospitable hosts all over the U.S., Canada, and several foreign countries. Travelers are hosted at no cost when they share their hosts' homes for short visits. Hosts enjoy the company of their guests from other places while showing them the local sights.

When you join the service (free at this writing), you may post information about yourselves, your home, hometown, interests, and accommodations, perhaps including photographs. You may then contact one another by e-mail and together make plans for a visit. The database can be searched by country, state, or city.

For information: ElderTravelers.org, 1615 Smelter Ave., Black Eagle, MT 59414; www.eldertravelers.org.

For information: Evergreen Bed and Breakfast Club, 201 W. Broad St., Ste. 181, Falls Church, VA 22046; 800-962-2392 or 815-456-3111; www.evergreenclub.com.

JENSEN'S RESIDENTIAL COMMUNITIES

If you are prospective buyers, you may stay free of charge for a couple of nights in your own fully furnished guest house at one of Jensen's three communities for adults over the age of 55. You'll have access to the clubhouse, the swimming pool, and all organized activities and have plenty of time to talk to the residents at the villages that are located in North and South Carolina.

For information: 800-458-6832; www.jensencommuni ties.com.

NEW PALTZ SUMMER LIVING

Think about spending a couple of summer months in the mountains, about 75 miles north of New York City. Every year, while the usual student occupants are on vacation, 140 furnished garden apartments are reserved for seniors in the village of New Paltz, near Mohonk Mountain and home of a branch of the State University of New York. The rents at this writing for the entire summer (from early June until late August) range from $1,500 to $3,300, depending on the size of the apartment. Living right in town next to the campus, you may audit college courses for free, attend lectures and cultural events, and take part in planned activities in the clubhouse. A heated pool and tennis court are in the complex. Buses travel to New York City frequently for those who want to go to the theater, and there are frequent day trips to places of interest.

For information: New Paltz Summer Living, 4 Southside Ave., New Paltz, NY 12561; 800-431-4143 or 845-255-7205; www.npsummerliving.com.

ROBSON COMMUNITIES

The Preferred Guest Program at Robson's five villages for "active adults" in Arizona and Texas offers prospective homeowners a three-night stay for two in your own house, with free rounds of golf, use of the recreational amenities, and a complimentary dinner with homeowners. You may use the clubhouse, swimming pools, tennis courts, spas, and golf courses. Of course, visitors must also spend a few hours talking with a salesperson.

The requirements for a visit are that one person in your party must be at least 40 and no one may be under 19. Current costs range from $149 to $279 for the package January through May with periodic specials in summer.

For information: Robson Communities, 9532 E. Riggs Rd., Sun Lakes, AZ 85248; 800-732-9949; www.robson.com.

SENIORS ABROAD

Seniors Abroad, celebrating its 20th anniversary, is a cultural exchange program for adventurous people over the age of 50. It pairs American travelers with host families for three- to four-week homestays in Japan or New Zealand and Australia. There, singly or as couples, visitors spend five or six days in the homes of several different families during the trip. In the U.S., host families do the same for foreign visitors from those same countries. Hosts are volunteers, and guests pay only for transportation, tours, hotels between stays, and other such expenses.

For information: Seniors Abroad, 435 Virginia Ave., Winchester, VA 22601; 540-722-4232.

US SERVAS

Servas, the oldest free hospitality exchange program in the world, is an international network of hosts and travelers who offer lodging to one another without cost as a way to promote friendship and understanding among people of diverse cultures. Through mutually arranged visits, members "share their lives, interests, and concerns about social issues."

With more than 14,000 hosts in 130 countries, Servas is open to "ambassadors of peace" of all ages who must provide two letters of reference and complete an interview before being accepted into the program. The cost is $50 a year for travel in the U.S. only and $85 for both U.S. and international travel.

For information: Send a #10 self-addressed, stamped envelope to US Servas, 11 John St., Room 505, New York, NY 10038; 212-267-0252; usservas.org.

WCI COMMUNITIES

The Preferred Guest Getaways offered at 24 of this developer's adult villages all over Florida are designed to show potential homebuyers what they're getting. Sign up for a getaway for a couple of days and you get lodging on-site or at a nearby hotel, access to all of the facilities and restaurants, discounted rounds of golf, and an escorted tour of the community. The cost, which varies widely depending on the location and the season, starts at $39 per night.

For information: 800-924-2290; www.wcicommunities .com.

WOMEN WELCOME WOMEN WORLD WIDE (WWWWW)

The goal of "5W," a hospitality exchange club with 3,000 members in 70 countries, is to promote friendship and understanding among women of different countries and cultures. Its members agree to welcome one another as guests in their homes for short visits without charge. In addition to publishing a list of members who provide descriptions of themselves, their interests, and their homes and hometowns, the club also schedules conferences and gatherings that are announced in its three newsletters a year. It is up to potential guests to make their own contacts and arrange their own visits. A yearly donation of $35 is requested to cover costs.

For information: 203-454-1609; www.womenwelcome women.org.uk.

HOME EXCHANGE FOR 50-PLUS

One way to go on vacation without seriously depleting your funds is to exchange homes with other adult travelers who live in a place you'd like to visit and who want to spend time in your house. No money changes hands, and you can save plenty on the cost of hotel rooms and perhaps even car rentals if you swap cars.

Although many exchange programs are ready to serve as house-swapping matchmakers, we know of only one that deals exclusively with people over the age of 50. Seniors Home Exchange provides listings of about 1,500 houses or apartments in the U.S. and Canada and 36 other countries around the world that may be traded for yours for a period of time to be mutually agreed on. Even motor homes and caravans are traded. The catch is that you must have access to the Internet, possess an e-mail address, and pay $65 ($90 Canadian) for a three-year membership or $100 ($150 Canadian) for a lifetime membership. Members of AARP and CARP pay only $45 for a three-year membership.

Any arrangement that suits both parties is encouraged—you may trade abodes simultaneously or exchange hospitality by visiting them at one time while they visit you at another. The trades need not come out even, including length of visits, size of homes, or amenities.

For information: Seniors Home Exchange, www.seniorshome exchange.com.

6

Beating the Costs of Car Rentals

Never rent a car without getting a discount or a special promotional rate. Almost all car-rental agencies in the U.S. and Canada give breaks to all manner of customers, including those who belong to over-50 organizations (see Chapter 20) or have reached a certain birthday. The discount that's coming to you as a senior member of society can save you some money, although short-term sales will almost always save you more. Refer to the membership material sent by the group to which you belong for information about your discount privileges.

It's almost impossible to sort out the confusing choices of rates, discounts, and add-on fees from the rental companies. To save money, you must shop around, compare costs, and make many decisions that can raise or lower your bill. In general, the best rates are to be found online. When applicable, add the senior discount for renters over 50. It may not amount to much, but it will help a little.

But, first, keep in mind:

■ Car-rental agents might not always volunteer information about senior discounts or special sales, so always ask about them when you reserve your car.

■ Don't settle for a senior discount or senior rate too hastily without investigating the possibility of an even better deal. Shop around yourself or ask your travel agent to find the *lowest available rate or package* at the time you are going to travel. Ask for the total price that includes all extra charges such as airport fees, taxes, and drop-off fees. Senior discounts are usually given on the full published rental rate. So special promotional rates—in other words, sales—or even weekend rates are almost always better, sometimes much better. On the other hand, if you can get the senior discount *on top of the lowest posted rate*, regular or promotional, that's the deal you want.

■ Book your car as far in advance as you can, especially if you are traveling during a holiday season. Generally, the later you book the more expensive it will be and the less likely you are to get the car you want. If you find a better rate that suits your needs closer to departure, you can rebook it.

■ Remember that weekly and weekend rates are less expensive than daily rates.

■ Read newspapers and magazines—especially those targeting over-50s. Look for ads for seasonal sales and clip out "value-added coupons" for additional discounts, cash savings, or upgrades. Sometimes you'll also get coupons in the mail from clubs, associations, frequent-flyer programs, and credit-card companies. Your travel agent might have some to offer too. But read the details carefully. Many of these specials cannot be combined with other promotional offers, such as senior discounts. And some may apply only to specific car sizes.

Most of the major car-rental companies offer weekly specials linked to those of the major domestic airlines. Remember to check them out if you are flying to the city where you will pick up your car.

Be especially cautious if you are planning a one-way rental because rates can be outrageously high for picking up a car in one city and returning it in another.

If you have access to the Internet, check the rental agencies' websites for special deals and last-minute offers. Most car-rental companies give a discount for booking online.

Before driving away in your rented car, inspect it for dents, scratches, or other damage. If you find any, ask the agent to sign a statement on the condition of the car and attach it to your rental agreement. That way, you won't be in danger of being charged for the damage on your return.

Ask if there is an additional-driver fee, and don't sign up for it if you don't need it or rent from a company that doesn't charge for additional drivers. If your spouse will be a second driver, rent from a company that allows both a husband and wife to drive at no extra cost.

When you reserve a car, always ask for a confirmation number. When you pick up your car, verify the discount or special rate *before* signing the agreement and ask if a better rate has become available since you booked.

When you call to ask about rates or reservations, always be armed with your organization's ID number and your own membership card for reference. Present them again at the rental counter when you pick up your car, and be sure to confirm your rate before signing the agreement.

■ Special savings might not be available at every location, so remember to check them out every time you make a reservation.

■ Don't purchase insurance you don't need. Review your personal auto insurance coverage and credit-card policy to determine if you require the optional loss/damage coverage offered by the rental companies. Your home-owner policy may cover your personal belongings on the road.

■ In the U.S., there is no maximum age for renting a car, but there are restrictions in other countries that vary by country and agency. One agency, for example, de-nies rentals to people over 65 in Greece and Northern Ire-land or over 75 in Ireland and Israel. Another restricts drivers over 60 in Malaysia or the Philippines. In the United Kingdom and Ireland, most agencies will not rent a car to a driver over 75. In addition, some overseas rental agencies impose special conditions for older drivers such as a doc-tor's letter certifying good health. So make your age clear when you make your reservation. Shop around, and also consider leasing a car, in which case age may not be an issue.

■ If you are traveling outside the U.S., don't wait until you arrive at your destination to arrange a rental. Book it here before you go because renting abroad is much more expensive. Remember to request your senior discount. Consult with your insurance carrier and credit-card com-panies to be sure you are covered overseas. Most per-sonal automobile insurance covers you only for driving in the U.S., and coverage may not include certain types of vehicles.

■ If you can drive a stick shift, you can cut the cost of a rental significantly. In other countries, automatic transmissions are not readily available and when they are, they are much more expensive.

ADVANTAGE RENT-A-CAR

Independently owned and managed, Advantage maintains locations in nine western states. It gives AARP members a discount of 10 percent off the regular rates every day of the year, charges no additional fee for a second driver, and provides roadside assistance. If you join the Advantage Frequent Rental club, you'll earn a free day when you've rented four times. Do it online and you need only two rentals for a free day.
For information: 800-777-5500; www.advantagerentacar .com.

ALAMO RENT A CAR

Alamo's offer to seniors who want to take to the road here and abroad is very simple—it's a discount of up to 10 percent, depending on the season and location, off the weekly or daily rates to anybody over the age of 50.
For information: 800-GO-ALAMO (800-462-5266); www .alamo.com.

AUTO EUROPE

If you rent a car from Auto Europe—a company that services more than 4,000 car-rental locations worldwide—you are guaranteed the lowest rates based on those of comparable car-rental companies. And, if you are 50 or over, you will also get a discount of 5 percent, sometimes even on promotional rates, on all rentals, including chauffeur drives and prestige sports cars. The same 5 percent discount applies to Eurail passes, now sold by Auto Europe, which may be combined with a car rental.

Short-term leases are also available from Auto Europe, which has partnered with Peugeot to lease factory-new cars for periods of more than 17 days. All short-term leases include unlimited mileage; insurance; 24-hour, English-speaking roadside assistance; and taxes. And, very important to many travelers, unlike car rentals that may be limited to drivers between the ages of 25 and 70, there is no maximum age requirement.

For information: 800-223-5555; www.autoeurope.com.

AVIS RENT A CAR

If you are a member of AARP, you'll get a discount of 10 percent off super value daily and weekly rates and 5 percent off weekend rates from Avis, a company with more than 4,700 locations in 160 countries. All rates include enhanced insurance coverage, unlimited free mileage at participating U.S. locations, and no charge for second drivers who are spouses but only if you note the discount ID number in your rental agreement. Occasionally Avis also makes bonus offers to 50-plus customers, such as a free tank of gas or free upgrades.

For information: 800-331-1800; www.avis.com.

BUDGET RENT A CAR

Budget takes 15 percent off the regular rates for customers 50 or over. But sometimes its best deals for mature travelers can be found on its website where it posts periodic Senior Savings for customers "who have logged a few more miles." These deals vary from city to city and change frequently.

For information: 800-527-0700; www.budget.com.

DOLLAR RENT A CAR

Join the free Silver Dollar Club if you are over 50 and you'll get a discount of up to 10 percent on most rentals, with unlimited mileage and no charge for additional drivers. You must make an advance reservation, request the special rate, and mention the customer discount number SR2000. If you want to be notified about special promotions and sales, sign up for the club's e-mail newsletter.

For information: 800-800-4000; www.dollar.com. You may join the club online or by writing to Dollar Rent a Car, CIMS #7070, 5330 E. 31 St., Tulsa, OK 74135.

ENTERPRISE RENT-A-CAR

Enterprise, the largest car-rental agency in North America, specializes in renting vehicles in neighborhoods "where people live and work." That means its 5,000 or so branches in the U.S. are located in big cities and small towns as well as at major airports. It offers a discount of 5 percent off the regular rental rates to members of AARP.

For information: 800-RENT-A-CAR (800-736-8222); www .enterprise.com.

EUROPE BY CAR

The company that invented short-term leases of factory-new European cars, Europe by Car is the only company in the U.S. that offers both Peugeots and Renaults for periods of more than 17 days. All leases include collision and theft insurance with no deductible, unlimited kilometers, and 24-hour emergency assistance. And if you are an AARP member, you'll get a discount of $20 to $200, depending on the car type and the length of time you keep the car.

On car rentals, you'll also get a deal, a 5 percent discount with unlimited mileage, and all of the other perks.
For information: 800-223-1516; www.europebycar.com.

HERTZ CAR RENTAL

Members of AARP and NARFE are eligible for savings at participating Hertz locations all over the world. They can get a discount of 5 to 10 percent off the weekly and weekend rates with unlimited mileage and enhanced insurance coverage. The discount ID number must be noted on your rental agreement.
For information: 800-654-2200; www.hertz.com.

KEMWEL

This car-rental broker, with multiple suppliers, offers a discount of 5 percent off any rentals to anybody over the age of 50 at any of its locations in 25 European countries. Ask for it when you make your booking whether by telephone or online. Kemwel also offers short-term leases valid for a minimum of 17 days and a maximum of 264 days on brand-new Peugeots, complete with nondeductible, fully comprehensive insurance; 24-hour roadside assistance; and unlimited mileage. Best of all, there is no maximum age limit for drivers.
For information: 800-678-0678; www.kemwel.com.

NATIONAL CAR RENTAL

If you belong to AARP or CARP, you will get a discount of 5 to 20 percent off the daily, weekend, or monthly leisure rates at all locations in the U.S. and Canada, and 5 to 10 percent in Europe and other international locations. You'll also get enhanced insurance coverage at participating locations. If you are not a member but are over 50, you'll still get a discount if you ask for it and produce proof of age.

For information: 800-CAR-RENT (800-227-7368); www
.nationalcar.com.

PAYLESS CAR RENTAL
Everybody over the age of 50 gets a straightforward 5 percent discount on the lowest applicable rate from Payless.
Just ask for it when you reserve a car by telephone or click
the "over 50" banner online. Sign up for the free Nifty Fifty
Program and you'll get monthly newsletters that inform you
of seasonal specials. Payless has about 1,500 locations in 60
countries.
For information: 800-PAYLESS (800-729-5377); www
.paylesscarrental.com.

RENAULT EURODRIVE
As an alternative to car rentals, Renault Eurodrive offers
short-term leases valid to drive in more than 30 countries for
a minimum of 17 days and a maximum of 6 months.
Designed for leisure travelers who reside outside of Europe,
the program gives you a new tax-free, fuel-efficient Renault
vehicle with unlimited mileage; comprehensive insurance
coverage with no deductible; an extensive service network;
and 24-hour, English-speaking road assistance. The 36 pick-
up and drop-off sites are located in nine European countries,
so you may pick up your car in one location and leave it in
another.

Leasing may be cheaper than car rentals, but, even more
important to many travelers, it has no maximum age
requirement, whereas car rentals are often limited to drivers between the ages of 25 and 70.
For information: 800-221-1052 or 212-532-1221; www
.renaultusa.com.

RENT-A-WRECK

This company, whose cars are not wrecks but three to five years old, claims to be 15 to 20 percent cheaper than the major car-rental agencies. Because all of its 400 locations across the country are independently owned, it is up to each one of them to set its own senior discount, but most give renters who are at least 50 or 55 years old a 5 to 10 percent discount off the regular rates. Cars are rented for round trips only and must be returned to their home locations.

For information: 800-535-1391; www.rentawreck.com.

THRIFTY CAR RENTAL

If you are over 55, Thrifty guarantees you a 5 to 10 percent discount on most standard rentals at all of its locations throughout the world. To get it, an advance reservation is recommended. On the Web, click on "Great Deals for Silver Years."

For information: 800-THRIFTY (800-847-4389); www .thrifty.com.

U-SAVE AUTO RENTAL OF AMERICA

U-Save Auto Rental, with about 300 locations in the U.S. and Canada—all independent franchises—caters to the off-airport or neighborhood market and provides rental cars directly to consumers or local businesses. Many of its locations offer discounts of 5 to 10 percent to drivers over 50, so ask when you call for a car.

For information: 800-272-8728; www.usave.net.

7

Saving a Bundle on Trains, Buses, and Boats in North America

Getting around town, especially in a city where driving is not a practical option, probably means depending on public transportation to get you from hither to yon. Remember that once you reach a particular birthday—in most cases, your 60th or 65th—you can take advantage of some good senior markdowns on trains, buses, subways, and, in some places, even taxis. All you need in most cases is a Medicare card, a Senior ID card, or your driver's license to play this game, which usually reduces fares by half. Although you may find it uncomfortable at first to pull out that card and flash it at the bus driver or ticket agent, it soon becomes very easy. Do it and you'll realize some nice savings.

And don't fail to take advantage of the bargains available to seniors on long-distance rail, bus, and boat travel as well.

RIDING THE RAILS

Just about every commuter railroad in the U.S. and Canada gives older passengers a break on fares, although you may have to do your traveling during off-peak periods when the trains are not filled with go-getters rushing to and from their offices. New York's Metro North, for example, charges anyone over 65 only half the regular fare for all trains except those arriving in Manhattan during weekday morning peak hours. On the New York subways and buses, too, you pay only half whether you pay in cash, tokens, or with a Reduced Fare MetroCard. In Washington, D.C., passengers who are 65 or more pay only 50 cents to ride the buses and half fare on Metrorail trains.

As for serious long-distance journeys, many mature travelers are addicted to the railroads, finding riding the rails a leisurely, relaxed, romantic, comfortable, economical, and satisfying way to make miles while enjoying the scenery.

So many passes and discounts on railroads are available to travelers heading for other parts of the country that sorting them out becomes confusing. But, once you do, they will help stretch your dollars while you cover a lot of ground.

See Chapter 8 for the best deals on transportation in foreign countries for travelers of a certain age.

ALASKA RAILROAD

Passengers over 65 are entitled to a reduction of about 35 percent on weekend fares during the winter months—late September through early May—between Anchorage and Fairbanks and anywhere else in between. You're encouraged

to take food and drink with you because there's limited food service on the train for this 12-hour journey.
For information: 800-544-0552; www.alaskarailroad.com.

AMTRAK

For the growing numbers of senior travelers who love to travel by train, Amtrak offers those 62 or over a 15 percent discount on the lowest available coach fares, including Explore America Fares, in the U.S. and on some Canadian routes, every day of the week. The discount is also available on the Acela Express and Metroliner Service on Saturdays and Sundays but does not apply to the Auto Train or sleeping accommodations.

Amtrak and Via Rail Canada have teamed up to offer the North America Rail Pass. It lets you travel to more than 900 destinations, with unlimited stopovers on the 28,000-mile rail system in the U.S. and Canada, for 30 consecutive days after the first day of use. You must travel in both countries using the pass. If you're at least 60, you are entitled to 10 percent off the regular adult fare. Buy the pass that's good during peak and off-peak seasons from either the company or a travel agent. You'll need advance reservations and you'll travel coach, although you may upgrade to sleeping accommodations or other higher classes of travel for an additional charge.

If you are over 50 but haven't yet reached the age of 60 or 62 to qualify for the privileges described here, and you *are* a U.S. military veteran, you can get the same 15 percent—occasionally even more—on Amtrak trains if you join Veterans Advantage, a service organization, for $23 a year.

The discount applies during off-peak hours on most trains throughout the U.S. except the Acela Express, Metroliner, Downeaster, and services between the U.S. and Canada.
For information: 800-USA-RAIL (800-872-7245); www .amtrak.com. For Veterans Advantage: 866-VET-REWARDS (866-838-7392); www.veteransadvantage.com.

ONTARIO NORTHLAND

This passenger railroad serving northeastern Ontario gives travelers over the age of 60 a 10 percent fare reduction any day of the year on the Northlander train running between Toronto and Cochrane. The same discount applies to the Polar Bear Express, a summer excursion line between Cochrane and Moosonee, and the Little Bear Train that runs

TRAVEL TIPS FOR A HEALTHY TRIP

The U.S. Department of State offers a long list of tips for older travelers to help you plan a safe and healthy trip to other countries. You can get this useful advice as a brochure by calling 202-512-1800 or by sending a check for $1.50 to Superintendent of Documents, Washington, DC 20420. You may also read it online (for information, go to www .travel.state.gov/olderamericans). Among the issues discussed: reviewing your health insurance policies and, if necessary, buying supplemental insurance; considering trip insurance in case you must postpone, cancel, or interrupt your trip; carrying extra copies of prescriptions; getting the appropriate immunizations; finding medical assistance; and dealing with medical emergencies abroad.

three times a week from Cochrane to Moosonee, returning the following day.
For information: 800-461-8558 or 705-472-4500; www .ontc.on.ca.

VIA RAIL CANADA

The government-owned Canadian railroad, which provides coast-to-coast passenger service, gives seniors 60 and over a 10 percent discount off any fare every day of the year, even on top of other special fares. For example, add this discount to a 25 percent reduction on off-peak travel that's available to all ages and good every day of the week. You'll end up with a 35 percent savings.

Via Rail's "Bring a Friend for Free" promotion is another perk for older travelers. Buy one economy ticket for the senior fare—10 percent off the standard adult fare—and you can bring along a companion of any age for free. If you'd rather ride in first class or in a sleeper using your senior discount, you'll receive a 75 percent discount on your companion's ticket, at least during some months of the year. Some fares, including those on the Quebec–Windsor corridor and on the Constellation between Montreal and Toronto, require a ten-day advance purchase.

At 60 you are also eligible to buy three rail passes at a 10 percent discount. The first is the Canrailpass, available for peak or off-peak travel and valid for 12 days within a 30-day period anywhere on VIA Rail's transcontinental system. You may get on and off the train as many times as you wish, stopping wherever you like along the way after reserving your space for all segments.

The second pass to offer a 10 percent senior discount is the Corridorpass. Sold year-round for first-class or economy-class seating, it gives you ten days of unlimited train travel within the Quebec City–Windsor corridor.

And last, the North America Rail Pass, a cooperative venture with Amtrak, allows you to explore North America by train, giving access to all Via Rail trains in Canada and almost all Amtrak trains in the U.S. at a 10 percent discount. It gives you 30 consecutive days of unlimited travel (no more than four one-way trips on any given route or segment) to more than 900 destinations in the U.S. and Canada. You get as many stopovers as you like, but reservations are required for all portions of your journey. You must travel in both countries to use this pass.

To keep posted on special offers for adults over 60, including contests to win weekend getaways and discounted admission prices at attractions throughout Canada, subscribe to Via Rail's free senior e-newsletter.

For information: 888-VIA-RAIL (800-842-7245). To subscribe to the senior e-newsletter: www.viarail.ca/seniors.

GOING BY BUS

Never, never board a bus without asking the driver whether there's a senior discount, because even the smallest bus lines in the tiniest communities (and the largest—New York City, for example) in the U.S., Canada, and abroad give seniors a break, usually 50 percent off at age 60 or 65. In Europe, your senior rail pass is often valid on major motorcoach lines as well, so always be sure to inquire.

CITYPASS: SEE THE SIGHTS FOR LESS

Visitors to Boston, New York City, Chicago, Hollywood, Southern California, Philadelphia, San Francisco, Seattle, or Toronto who take in several of the area's main attractions during their stay can save time and money with CityPass. It is a booklet of admission tickets to six of each area's most popular cultural attractions, cutting your cost by at least half the box office price if you use them all. An added benefit is immediate admission without standing in ticket lines.

Tickets may be purchased online, at any of the CityPass attractions in each area, or through a travel agent. The booklets are good for only 9 consecutive days (30 days in Hollywood, 14 in southern California) from the first day of use. *For information:* 888-330-5008 or 707-256-0490; www.citypass.com.

COACH CANADA

This bus line, which serves southwest Ontario and the Niagara Peninsula and runs between Toronto and Montreal, offers discounts of 10 to 25 percent to passengers over the age of 60. In cooperation with Greyhound Lines (U.S.), it also offers through service to Boston; New York; Washington, D.C.; and Chicago.

For information: Coach Canada, PO Box 1017, Peterborough, ON K9J 7A5; 800-461-7661 or 705-748-6411.

GRAY LINE WORLDWIDE

Gray Line is an association of about 150 independent sightseeing tour companies on six continents. Participating locations give members of AARP a discount of 10 percent on fares for half- or full-day sight-seeing tours. You must purchase tickets at a Gray Line terminal and present a valid membership card. Some Gray Line companies also give discounts to nonmembers if they are 55 or 60, so inquire before signing up for a tour.

For information: Call the Gray Line Worldwide office in your area or the corporate headquarters at 303-394-6920; www.grayline.com.

GREYHOUND CANADA

Here you'll get 10 percent off all regular fares, any day of the week, all year round, if you are a traveler over 62 with a valid ID. What's more, if you're accompanied by a companion and buy your tickets three days in advance, the companion travels for $15 one way. On the family fare, you get 10 percent off at age 62 and an accompanying child under 16 goes free.

The 10 percent discount also applies to the Canada Pass, good for unlimited travel, with as many stopovers within the country as you like for specified numbers of days, and to the CanAm Discovery Pass, which gives you the same privileges on all routes wherever Greyhound and participating carriers go within the U.S. and Canada.

But hold on. If you are planning to travel long distances within Canada and the U.S., Greyhound Canada offers an even better deal than you'll get using your senior discount. That's the Go Anywhere Fare that with a 7- or 14-day advance purchase lets you take the bus between any two destinations serviced by Greyhound Canada in Canada and the U.S.—no matter how far—for only $125 to $149 one way, $200 to $298 round trip (Canadian). No stopovers with this fare, however, and no additional senior discount. *For information:* 800-661-8747 or 403-265-9111; www .greyhound.ca.

GREYHOUND LINES

Greyhound gives passengers over 62 a 5 percent discount on any nondiscounted fare.

The 62-plus traveler can also take advantage of up to 10 percent discount on the North America Discovery Pass that gives you unlimited travel for varying numbers of days (from 7 to 60) to any U.S. destination with as many stopovers as you like. The pass comes in several versions. The Ameripass covers travel in the U.S., the Canada Pass covers Canada, and the CanAm Pass allows for travel in both countries. You'll get your senior discount on all of them. *For information:* Call your local Greyhound reservation office or 800-231-2222; www.greyhound.com.

ONTARIO NORTHLAND

On all Ontario Northland's scheduled intercity bus lines in northeastern Ontario (with connections to Toronto), passengers over the age of 60 are offered a 10 percent discount on the regular fare every day of the week. *For information:* Ontario Northland, 800-461-8558 or 705-472-4500; www.ontc.on.ca.

PETER PAN BUS LINES

All passengers 62 or over can get a 5 percent discount on all journeys aboard Peter Pan buses, but if they pay $5 for a Senior Saver Card, valid for a year and available at ticket

counters, the discount goes up to 10 percent. Peter Pan is concentrated mainly in the New England states.
For information: 800-343-9999; www.peterpanbus.com.

VOYAGEUR BUS LINES

If you're at least 62, you can take advantage of Voyageur's year-round discount of 10 percent off the regular adult fares with a three-day advance purchase. Not only that, but you may bring along a companion for $15 each way.
For information: www.voyageur.com.

GOING BY BOAT

ALASKA MARINE HIGHWAY

Traveling on the Alaska Marine Highway, also known as the Alaska Ferry, in the off-season is a bargain for foot passengers 65 and older. Between October and April, you sail for half the regular adult fare within Alaskan waters. The discount does not apply to vehicle or cabin space or a round trip on the same sailing to the Aleutian Islands. Sometimes in the summer, too, there are half fares for seniors on several of the smaller vessels. The message is always ask if a senior rate is available.
For information: 800-642-0066; www.ferryalaska.com.

8

Cutting Your Costs Abroad

he most enthusiastic voyagers of all age groups, Americans over 50—one out of three adults and more than a quarter of the total population—spend more time and money on travel than anybody else, especially when it comes to going to foreign destinations. It's been estimated that more than four out of every ten passport holders are at least 55 years old. And there's hardly a country in the world today that doesn't actively encourage mature travelers to come for a visit.

Because you are now being avidly pursued, you can take advantage of many good deals in other lands. Airlines, for example, often offer you fare reductions on domestic flights within the country or the continent. Railroad and bus systems in most European countries give seniors deep discounts that are especially valuable if you plan an extended stay in one place. Even ferries and cruise ships are often ready to make you a deal. This chapter gives you a rundown on these and other ways to cut your overseas holiday costs, especially if you are planning your trip on your own. For the U.S. and Canada, see Chapter 7.

But, first, keep in mind:

- Always ask about senior savings when you travel on planes, trains, buses, or boats anywhere in the world. Do the same when you buy tickets for movies, theaters, museums, tours, sight-seeing tours, historic buildings, and attractions. Don't assume, simply because you haven't heard about them or the ticket agent hasn't mentioned them, that they don't exist. Senior discounts are becoming more and more common everywhere, and you'll be amazed how much money you can save.
- Some countries require that you purchase a senior card to take advantage of senior discounts, but most require only proof of age, usually in the form of a passport.
- Always have the necessary identification with you and be ready to show it. Occasionally you may need an extra passport photograph.
- For specifics on a country's senior discounts, call its national tourist office here before you go.
- Your passport may be required along with your rail pass while you are in transit, so keep it with you.
- You must purchase most European rail passes in the U.S. or Canada at least 15 days before your departure. Any travel agency can do it for you, or contact Rail Europe, CIT North America, or DER marketing agencies, which

specialize in European rail passes. However, some national passes that are good only within one country's borders are not available on this side of the Atlantic and must be purchased there, usually at major railroad stations or airports. Have your passport handy. It's best to check out all your options before you make your plans. Don't buy a pass unless you know you'd spend at least the same amount on individual tickets.

- Although there are many European rail pass plans, only a few of them offer senior discounts to travelers age 60 or over. Details to come in this chapter.

- Ask about rail pass insurance when you buy your pass, just in case it is lost or stolen during your trip. You might want to seriously consider overall travel insurance as well.

- Major U.S. hotel chains, such as Radisson, Marriott, Hilton, Choice, and Best Western, offer senior discounts that almost always apply at their participating properties in other countries.

- Travel passes for sight-seeing trips are available in confusing profusion, and because many overlap and some must be purchased before you leave home, it's wise to check them out before you go. Contact the national tourist offices of the countries you plan to visit.

- Be sure your rail pass is validated at a railway ticket office the first time you use it, before boarding the train.

- Tourist passes usually cost older travelers the same as everyone else, but in most cases they are definitely worth buying. Among the best buys everywhere are the inexpensive, easy-to-use "city cards" available for many major

European cities. Usually good for one to four days, they give you free public transportation plus admission to the most important tourist sites. Many also offer discounts on tours, meals, theater tickets, cultural attractions, and shopping.

EUROPE BY RAIL

If you intend to pack a lot of train travel in Europe into your stay, rail passes can make the going cheaper and easier, especially if you travel with a companion or a group. Some passes are multinational, good for travel in more than one country. Others cover transportation within the borders of one country only. Many passes must be purchased here before you travel and are not available overseas, while others may be purchased only in the country that issues them, so it is extremely important to explore the possibilities well in advance of your departure. Always ask if there is a senior discount on the pass you want. Some passes give seniors a break, others don't.

Most rail passes are available in two versions: the *flexipass* permits travel for a specified number of days within a certain time period (such as any four days in one month); the *consecutive-day pass* is valid on any day within a certain period of time (such as 15 days in a row). Whichever you choose, you must have it validated at a railway station ticket office before you board the train the first time you use it.

If you're not planning extensive travel by rail, however, you may be better off buying regular train tickets with a senior discount. All you need to qualify as a senior in many

FINDING A DOCTOR OVERSEAS

Before you leave on a trip to foreign lands, it would be wise to send for the **International Association for Medical Assistance to Traveller's** (IAMAT's) list of physicians all over the world who speak English, have had medical training in North America or Europe, and have agreed to reasonable preset fees. When you join the free, nonprofit IAMAT, you will get a membership card entitling you to its prearranged rates, a directory of English-speaking physicians in 125 countries and territories, and advice on immunizations and preventive measures for many diseases including malaria. A packet of information about climate, food, water, clothing suggestions, and sanitary conditions in 1,450 cities is given to members who donate $25 or more.

For information: IAMAT, 417 Center St., Lewiston, NY 14092; 716-754-4883; www.iamat.org.

countries is your passport or other ID that proves you are at least 60; however, in the U.K. you need a British Senior Railcard, which gives you a third off on almost any ticket, and in France you must have a Carte Senior, which is good for a 25 percent discount on all rail tickets and even more (50 percent) on many off-peak trips. Later sections in this chapter have more information about your special privileges in foreign countries.

EURAIL PASSES

The traditional Eurailpass gives you unlimited first-class train travel on all the major railways of 18 European countries. It is valid on a continuous basis for periods of 15 days to three months. The Eurailpass Flexi provides 10 or 15 travel days in first class within a two-month period. And the Eurail Saver Pass is issued for two or more people traveling together and saves 15 percent per person. None of these passes is discounted for seniors, but all are definitely worth considering if you plan to cover many miles across many borders, especially since they also entitle you to free or discounted travel on many buses, ferries, steamers, and suburban trains.

Another option, the Eurail Selectpass, the most popular pass because of its flexibility, lets you choose three, four, or five adjoining Eurail countries and get unlimited first-class passage for 5 to 15 days within a period of two months. This one costs less per person when two or more people travel together using the Eurail Selectpass Saver.

All of these rail passes must be purchased *before* leaving North America as they are not sold in Europe. And remember that none of them give seniors a special break. Buy them from a travel agent or directly through the following agents. *For information:* Eurail Group, www.eurail.com. Rail Europe, 800-438-7245; www.raileurope.com. DER Destination Europe, 800-782-2424; www.DER.com. ACP Rail International, 866-9-EURAIL (866-938-7245).

EUROSTAR

The Channel Tunnel train, connecting London with Paris or Brussels, makes many round trips a day beneath the English Channel. You're eligible at age 60 for the senior fares that are about 25 percent cheaper than the regular adult fares on both first-class and standard tickets. The tickets are unrestricted and refundable, but because there is a limited number of discounted seats available on each train, you must book at least two months in advance. If you have a rail pass, ask about the passholder fare that might save you even more than the senior fare.

For information: Rail Europe, 800-438-7245; www.rail europe.com. Eurostar, 800-EUROSTAR (800-387-6782).

THALYS TRAIN

Thalys, the European high-speed rail network, with trains that connect Paris with more than 25 cities in four countries, gives a discount of over 30 percent on the cost of first- and second-class tickets to travelers 60 and older. Tickets may be booked three months in advance.

For information: Rail Europe, 800-438-7245; www.rail europe.com.

MULTICOUNTRY RAIL PASSES
BALKAN FLEXIPASS SENIOR

Buy it here and use it there for travel in Bulgaria, Greece, Macedonia, Romania, and the countries of the former Yugoslavia. At 60 or more, you may buy a first-class pass for all state railroads for up to 15 days within a one-month period for 20 percent less than the regular adult price. Bonuses include reduced prices on ferry crossings between Italy and Greece, 25 percent off on a one-day cruise in Greece, and discounts on the room rates at several hotels in the region.

For information: Rail Europe, 800-438-7245; www.rail europe.com.

SCANRAIL PASS 60+

Sold only on this side of the Atlantic, the Scanrail Pass provides unlimited travel in Denmark, Finland, Norway, and Sweden. If you're over 60, buy the Scanrail Pass 60+. It offers you the same privileges on second-class travel but for about 10 percent less than comparable adult passes. For more, see the Scandinavia listing later in this chapter.

For information: Rail Europe, 800-438-7245; www.raileu rope.com.

COUNTRY-BY-COUNTRY TRAVEL DEALS

AUSTRALIA

For special vacations in Australia designed for mature travelers from the U.S., check out "Plan Your Trip" on the website of the Australian Tourist Commission.

For information: Australian Tourist Commission, 800-333-0262; www.australia.com.

AUSTRIA

Women who are at least 60 and men at least 65 can purchase an official Senior Citizen Railway card for about $30 and travel around Austria at half fare on all trains and buses run by the federal government. That makes it a good deal for those planning many journeys within the country. You can get it at major rail stations in Austria.

On its daily nonstop service across the Atlantic to Vienna, Austrian Airlines gives a discount of 10 percent to passengers over 62 and a younger companion on all fares except for promotional seasonal sales. See Chapter 3.

The Vienna Card and similar city cards in other Austrian cities and provinces, including Salzburg, Linz, and Innsbruck, are very good buys. Sold for varied numbers of days, they give you unlimited travel on all public transportation—no more fumbling for the proper change—as well as free or reduced admission to museums, shops, attractions, and historic sites.

For information: Austrian National Tourist Office, PO Box 1142, New York, NY 10108; 212-944-6880; www .austria-info/us.

BELGIUM

If you are a 65-plus visitor to Belgium, you may travel between any two railroad stations within the country on Belgian Rail trains for the bargain rate of EUR 3. You must buy round-trip second-class tickets and make your return trip on the same day as your departure. Departures on weekdays must be after 9 A.M.; on weekends and public holidays, you may leave at any time.

Something else to remember is that most hotels in Brussels offer a big reduction on room rates on weekends and during the months of July and August when the staffs of many of the international organizations based there leave town.

For information: Belgian National Tourist Office, 220 E. 42 St., New York, NY 10017; 212-758-8130; www.visitbel gium.com. For Belgian Railways: www.sncb.be.

BERMUDA

February is Golden Rendezvous Month in Bermuda, when visitors over the age of 50 are treated to special cultural events and activities—some free—every day. For example, there are complimentary bus tours around the island and talks on the traditions, culture, and history of the island. Some hotels offer special packages and rates, and the Visitors' Service Bureau distributes a free ferry/bus token per person.

For information: Bermuda Department of Tourism, 800-BERMUDA (800-237-6832); www.bermudatourism.com.

BRITAIN

Bargains abound in the U.K., undoubtedly the most popular foreign destination for Americans. Senior rates and special privileges are offered almost everywhere, from railroads and bus lines to museums, theaters, swimming pools, and historic sites. Visitors over 60, for example, get good breaks on the cost of admission to Windsor Castle, Hampton Court, the Tower of London, Kensington Palace, Westminster Abbey, St. Paul's Cathedral, Kew Gardens, and many more favorite visitor destinations. So be sure to carry proof of age with you, although you won't need it at many London museums, such as the British Museum and Tate Modern, because everyone regardless of age now gets in free.

Mature theatergoers in London can buy tickets last-minute at half price or sometimes less at most major theaters simply by arriving at the box office after 6 P.M. for evening performances and about an hour before the curtain rises for matinees. Have your ID in hand and ask for "Senior Standbys."

Also, don't forget that Marriott, Hilton, Choice, Best Western, and other international hotel chains offer their senior privileges at most of their locations around the world, including the U.K. That means you can get a senior discount on the room rate almost everywhere you go.

For information: British Tourist Authority, 551 Fifth Ave., New York, NY 10176; 877-899-8391; www.travelbritain.org or www.maturebritain.org. Ask for the free guide, *Time to Travel*, for mature travelers.

Train passes. In Britain, where virtually every town may be reached by train, it pays to consider buying a rail card or rail pass that makes your travel cheaper. The British Senior Railcard, which currently costs £18 and is good for a year, will give you a 33 percent discount off the regular adult fare for almost any ticket, first class or standard, including promotions and excursions, in England, Scotland, and Wales. If you are at least 60 years old, you can buy it at any train station in those countries after completing an application and showing proof of age. It won't work on tickets for journeys made only within London or during the peak period on weekday mornings.

For information: www.senior-railcard.co.uk.

Another way to save on train travel is to buy a multiday rail pass that will cost, if you are 60 or more, about 15 percent less than younger adults must pay. The passes are not sold in the U.K. but must be purchased here before your departure. They can't be used in Ireland or on special excursion trains, but they do include service between London and its two international airports, Heathrow and Gatwick. With the passes, you may get on and off the trains along any route as often as you like. The price breaks for seniors apply on first-class tickets only, but if you're not looking for luxury, you might opt for the cheaper second-class adult pass available to all ages.

One of your choices is the BritRail Senior Flexipass, ideal for use on extended trips, hopping on and off as you like, throughout England, Scotland, and Wales. Get one for 4, 8, or 15 days (they need not be consecutive) for unlimited first-class travel within a two-month period. You will save about 15 percent off the regular adult rate. Although there's no price break for seniors on a second-class adult pass, it's an even cheaper way to travel.

Another option is the BritRail Consecutive Senior Pass, less expensive than the "flexipass" variety, which allows 4, 8, 15, or 22 days or a month of unlimited first-class travel on consecutive days in England, Scotland, and Wales.

For those who want to travel only in England, there are the new BritRail England Senior FlexiPass and the BritRail England Consecutive Senior Pass. These are less expensive than the others because they exclude Scotland and Wales, and entitle you to first-class seats for varying numbers of days.

Finally, the new BritRail Days Out from London Pass, with a senior version that costs about 15 percent less than the one for adults under 60, allows you to take day trips by train to destinations within reasonable reach of London, again for varying numbers of days.

With any of these rail passes, request the "family pass" if you will be traveling with children. For no extra cost, they allow one child age 5 through 15 to travel free with each adult pass holder. Additional children 5 through 15 may ride at half fare, while those under 5 are free.

For information: BritRail, 877-677-1066; www.britrail.net. Rail Europe, 800-438-7245; www.raileurope.com.

Travel passes. Several passes help you see the sights for less in Britain. The Great British Heritage Pass, for example, available to non-U.K. residents only, gives you unlimited free entry to nearly 600 historic houses, castles, Roman ruins, abbeys, and gardens in England, Scotland, Wales, and Northern Ireland. Buy it from your travel agent, BritRail, or Rail Europe before you leave home or from Tourist Information Centres in Britain. A 4-day pass (it is also available for 7 or 15 days or a month) currently costs about $35.

The London Visitor Travelcard, which must be purchased outside of Britain, gives you unlimited travel for

HEALTH COVERAGE ABROAD

The standard Medicare plan, with a few exceptions, does not cover medical care outside the U.S. Some Medicare HMOs do cover emergency procedures abroad but not routine care, and many of the available Medigap policies provide 80 percent, after a deductible, of the cost of emergency care incurred in the first two months of a trip outside the country. If you do not carry your own private health insurance that will pay the expenses incurred overseas, talk to your travel agent about temporary health insurance that will cover you for the length of your trip.

For information: Call 800-MEDICARE (800-633-4227); www.medicare.gov.

three, four, or seven consecutive days, in all zones or the central zone only, on London's buses and subways as well as many trains. The all-zones card includes transfer via underground from Heathrow Airport to central London.

On all BritRail packages from the U.S. to the U.K. that include air and hotels, travelers who are at least 60 years of age are entitled to a 5 percent discount. Be sure to ask for it.

And then there's the London Pass, which may be purchased for one, three, or six days. Use it for free admission to more than 60 attractions, museums, and art galleries in London. Buy it from Rail Europe or BritRail at Tourist Information Centres in London, or online at www.london-pass.com. Sorry, no senior discount on this pass.

For information: British Tourist Authority, 877-899-8391; www.visitbritain.com. BritRail, 866-BRITRAIL (866-274-8724); www.britrail.net. Rail Europe, 800-438-7245; www.raileurope.com.

A Scottish Explorer Pass gives you unlimited entry to over 60 of Scotland's historic attractions, including castles, abbeys, and distilleries. Buy it for 3, 7, or 10 days at a Tourist Information Centre or a Historic Scotland property or order it in advance at www.historic-scotland.gov.uk. Be sure to ask for the senior discount that takes about a third off the regular price.

The Welsh Historic Monuments (CADW) Explorer Pass, good for 3 or 7 days of unlimited entry to Welsh Heritage Properties, costs the same for all ages but is still a bargain. Pick yours up at a Tourist Information Centre in Wales.

DENMARK

When you buy tickets for the Danish State Railway system at any train station in Denmark, be sure to ask for the discount for passengers 65 and older. You get a 50 percent reduction on tickets every day, except Friday and Sunday and some holidays when the discount drops to 25 percent. For further information about the Scanrail Senior Pass that you can use on the railroads of Denmark, Finland, Norway, and Sweden, see the Scandinavia listing found later in this chapter.

When traveling by air, remember that SAS offers passengers over the age of 62 a 10 percent discount on most fares for flights from North America to Scandinavia and other destinations in Europe.

To make things easier and cheaper, be sure to buy a Copenhagen Card. Available at tourist information centers in the city, it is valid for 24, 48, or 72 hours of free or discounted admission to the major sights in and around town, plus unlimited free travel on all buses and trains in the metropolitan area. City cards are also available for Odense and Aalborg.

For information: Danish Tourist Board, 355 Third Ave., New York, NY 10017; 212-885-9700; www.visitdenmark.com.

FINLAND

Travel within Finland is discounted, sometimes steeply, for people 65 or over. Simply show proof of your age—your passport—at the ticket office, and you will get a 30 percent reduction on train tickets as well as motorcoach journeys covering at least 80 kilometers one way.

In addition, Finnair, the national airline, offers you, at 62, and a companion 10 percent off most published transatlantic fares and, at age 65, a discount of about 70 percent on domestic flights. See Chapter 3 for more details.

Although the Helsinki Card is not discounted by age, it offers substantial savings on a city tour and admission to museums, exhibitions, attractions, buses, trams, and metro and commuter trains within the city limits. Available at the airport, many hotels, and tourist offices, it is sold for periods of one, two, or three days. For information about the Scanrail Senior Pass for railroad travel in Denmark, Finland, Norway, and Sweden, see the Scandinavia listing later in this chapter.

For information: Finnish Tourist Board, PO Box 4649, Grand Central Sta., New York, NY 10163; 212-885-9700; www.gofinland.org.

FRANCE

Wherever you go in France, from museums to historic sites, movies and theaters to concerts, always ask whether there is a senior discount and you will be amazed how often you'll get one. Most Paris municipal museums, by the way, are free to everyone.

The privileges that come with age are especially good, however, when it comes to transportation. You are offered several choices. For example, simply by showing proof that you are 60 or more when you buy a ticket at a railway station, you will get the Decouverte Senior rate that gives you 25 percent off on all TGV rail services (except overnight accommodations) in first or second class throughout the entire country, except on trips entirely within the Paris Transport Region. You will get the same reduction on non-TGV mainline and regional rail services for travel during off-peak periods on tickets purchased at the train station.

If you plan extensive travel in France, you may prefer a Carte Senior, which costs about EUR 46. Valid for a year, again at age 60, it allows unlimited travel in first or second class at a 50 percent discount on some journeys in off-peak hours and a 25 percent discount on others, plus 25 percent off on some rail travel in 27 other European countries. This pass currently costs about $50 and requires a passport photo when you buy it at a major train station.

Finally, there is the France Seniorpass which costs you a little less at 60-plus than it does other adult travelers and must be purchased over here. It gives you any four days of unlimited first-class travel within a month and the option of buying up to six additional rail days.

For getting around in Paris, the Paris Visite Card, available for varying numbers of days, allows you to travel for free on public transportation. That includes the metro, buses (including shuttle buses to central Paris from the airports), the RER (fast trains between main stations), the tramway, the Montmartre Funicular, and all SNCF trains in the greater Paris region. You may buy it here or in Paris at metro or SNCF stations and tourist offices.

And here's something else to remember. Seniors are invited, along with the disabled and families with small children, to ride the elevator to the top of the Arc de Triomphe for a panoramic view of the city.

For information: French Government Tourist Office, 444 Madison Ave., New York, NY 10022; 410-286-8310; www

.franceguide.com. For the France Seniorpass, Rail Europe, 800-438-7245; www.raileurope.com.

GERMANY

Many restaurants in Germany have a *Seniorenteller*, a special menu that offers lighter fare in smaller portions at a lower cost for older guests. Ask to see it and also ask if there are discounts for seniors wherever you go. You'll find they are available in places such as department stores, hair salons, museums, and historic sites, and for other attractions such as day cruises on the Rhine. Even some hotels and spa resorts have them, especially in off-peak seasons.

If you plan to travel by train and are over 60, you may buy a BahnCard 50 Senior for about EUR 100 second class or EUR 200 first class at any railway station (have your passport with you). The card gives you 50 percent off on tickets wherever you go in Germany on the Deutsche Bahn. For a small additional fee, you can get a BahnCard Rail Plus that takes 25 percent off the regular adult fares in 28 European countries. If you are traveling with children between the ages of 6 and 11, a family BahnCard may be an even better deal. It gives you 50 percent off on your tickets plus a reduction of 25 percent for children.

Although there is no senior discount on the German Rail Pass, you can lower the cost by 25 percent for two people traveling together by using the German Rail Twin Pass, available here and in Germany.

For those who would rather travel by motorcoach, Deutsche Touring, a long-distance bus line that will transport you in comfort almost anywhere in Germany as well as to most other European countries, takes 10 percent off the price of all tickets for all passengers 60 or older. You can buy tickets through a travel agent, at DER travel agencies, on the Internet, or at railroad stations.

There is a 10 percent discount on most fares across the Atlantic Ocean to European destinations on Lufthansa for people 60 and older and companions over the age of 18. The same discount applies to domestic flights in Europe. See Chapter 3.

Finally, check out the city cards, now available at local tourist offices, railway stations, and hotels in most major cities for savings on transportation, tours, and admissions. *For information:* German National Tourist Office, 122 E. 42nd St., New York, NY 10168; 212-661-7200; www.come togermany.com. Deutsche touring, www.touring.de.

HONG KONG

In this bustling city, there are several ways to save money on transportation, assuming you are at least 65. The *Star Ferry* will take you free of charge on the eight-minute crossing from central Hong Kong to Kowloon, giving you a fabulous view of Victoria Harbor. You pay half fare on the Mass Transit Railway (MTR), the HYF Ferry to outlying islands, the Light Rail (LR), and the Kowloon-to-Canton Railway (KCRC). And on the famous Peak Tram, you are offered a discount of about 60 percent off the regular adult fare. Always be prepared with an ID, such as your passport.

Several museums, too, give seniors age 60 or more a break on admissions, charging only half the regular entrance fee.

The Meet the People program in Hong Kong costs nothing, requires no reservations, and schedules events every day of the week to introduce visitors to English-speaking specialists who share their knowledge of local traditions. Among the topics are tai chi, the rituals of tea, Chinese antiques, Cantonese opera, pearl appreciation, and even a ride on a Chinese junk. Pick up the weekly schedule at a Visitor Information Centre.

For information: Hong Kong Tourist Association, 800-282-4582 or 212-421-3382; www.discoverhongkong.com/usa.

JAPAN

To get around Japan on its fast and spotless railroads, there is no better deal than the Japan Rail Pass, although it offers no special senior privileges. It is available only to visitors to the country and allows unlimited travel on almost all Japan Railway trains and its affiliated bus and ferry lines for 7, 14, or 21 days. You must buy your pass from an authorized travel agent or the Japan National Tourist Organization before you go. You'll get an exchange order, which you must then trade for the pass in Japan at any JR Travel Service Center, including those at the Tokyo or Osaka International Airports and major railroad stations. Passes for regional travel are also available, some of which may be purchased here and others only in Japan. Check with your travel agent.

By the way, if you plan to travel by air within Japan, be sure to buy your tickets on this side of the Atlantic so you'll get the Visit Japan Fare offered only to foreign visitors. You will pay about 35 percent less than you would if you waited until you got there.

Three special programs are especially appealing to older visitors to Japan and are designed to make your trip more enjoyable. Welcome Cards, for example, are available in many cities or areas of the country, giving you discounts and special services at art galleries, museums, sight-seeing attractions, shops, restaurants, and transportation. Pick them up at tourist offices.

The Good Will Guide System (SGG) connects foreign travelers with local volunteers in 58 cities or towns who offer free guided tours. Brochures with details about the program are available at the Japan National Tourist Office or on its website.

The Home Visit System, another volunteer organization, offers you a chance to spend a few hours as a guest in a Japanese home in your choice of 14 cities. For these visits, applications and appointments are required and are not available from abroad. You can get information at local visitor centers in Japan.

For information: Japan National Tourist Organization, 1 Rockefeller Plaza, New York, NY 10020; 212-757-5641; www.japantravelinfo.com. Japan Railways, 212-332-8686; www.japanrail.com.

NEW ZEALAND

Travelers over the age of 60 qualify for a 30 percent savings on the standard fares on Tranz Scenic 2001 Ltd.'s train journeys any time of the year. Tickets must be reserved in New Zealand at Tranz Scenic travel centers in Auckland, Wellington, or Christchurch; at accredited New Zealand–based travel agencies; or by calling the toll-free number listed here.

In addition, the Interisland Line that sails between the North and South Islands offers a discount of up to 25 percent to travelers 60 or more.

If you're planning a long stay in New Zealand, a Seniors Card might be a good investment. Offered to foreign visitors as well as New Zealanders age 55 or over, it is a travel and shopping card that provides discounts and benefits from a wide range of participating businesses from hotels and restaurants to shops and services. It costs $24 for a two-year membership.

For information: Tourism New Zealand, 501 Santa Monica Blvd., Santa Monica, CA 90401; 866-639-9325; www .newzealand.com. Tranz Scenic 2001 Ltd., 0800-872-467 (in New Zealand only); www.tranzscenic.co.nz. Interisland Line, www.interislandline.co.nz. Seniors Card, www.ageconcern .org.nz.

NORWAY

In this beautiful country, you're entitled to half fare on buses and trains, any time, any place. For this break, however, you must be at least 67 and ready to prove your age with a proper ID. Younger spouses traveling with you get the same privilege.

At age 60, you can buy a Norway Rail Pass Senior and save about 20 percent over what younger adult travelers pay for the same three to eight days of unlimited second-class rail travel on trains operated by the Norwegian State Railways (NSB), plus a 30 percent reduction on the Flam Railway, for three days within one month with an option to buy five more. The pass must be purchased in the U.S. or Canada through your travel agent, or Rail Europe, as it is not available in Norway.

At age 67, you become eligible for a discount of up to $170 per person (except in June and July) on Norwegian Coastal Voyages that sail up the coast past myriad fjords to the Arctic Circle and back. What's more, if you belong to AARP, you may add another discount on top of that one— you'll get a reduction of $70 to $100 per cabin on all sailings year-round. See Chapter 10.

SAS, the Scandinavian airline, offers travelers 62 or over a 10 percent discount on most flights to Scandinavia and its other international destinations.

For information about the Scanrail Senior Pass to be used on railroads in Denmark, Finland, Norway, and Sweden, see the Scandinavia listing later in this chapter.

As for hotels, there are discounts for all of Scandinavia (discussed later in this chapter). In addition, check out the Norway Fjord Pass (www.fjordpass.com). It costs about $10 and offers discounts on rooms in hotels, guest houses, apartments, and holiday cottages.

As you should everywhere, ask if there is a senior discount wherever you go and consider purchasing city cards for Oslo and Bergen. They will provide free public transportation plus free or discounted admission at most museums, historic sites, and cultural attractions.

For information: Norwegian Tourist Board, 655 Third Ave., New York, NY 10017; 212-885-9700; www.visitnorway.com.

PORTUGAL

If you're over 65, there's hardly anywhere you can go in Portugal without being offered a senior discount of 30 to 50 percent off the regular price. So make a point of asking for it when you take a train or a bus and when you go to a museum, a national monument, a theater, a movie, and any-place else that charges admission.

If you're a mere 60, you can take advantage of a very good deal called the Golden Age Program which gives you a 35 percent discount on the regular rates for accommodations and breakfast for two at most of Portugal's famous pousadas. These are the historic government-run inns scattered around the country, many of them in former castles, monasteries, or palaces. The discount applies on Sunday through Thursday nights, with some exceptions, from April through October and sometimes other times of the year too. The catch is that rooms with the senior discount are limited, so book them far in advance.

There's also a Tourist Pass available for all ages, which offers free unlimited travel on Lisbon's transportation system. Sold at the airport and tourist information offices, a four-day pass costs about $10.

The Lisbon Card gives you the same access to the underground, buses, trams, and lifts, plus free entry into museums, monuments, and other sites. It also provides discounts on sight-seeing tours, river cruises, and theatrical events. Porto, Portugal's second-largest city, offers the Passe Porto with similar benefits.

And don't forget that TAP Air Portugal, the national airline, will give you (at age 62) and a younger companion a 10 percent discount on transatlantic flights. See Chapter 3 for more details.

For information: Portuguese National Tourist Office, 590 Fifth Ave., New York, NY 10036; 212-354-4403; www.portugal.org. For pousadas: Marketing Ahead, 800-223-1356; www.marketingahead.com.

SCANDINAVIA

Scandinavia—which includes Denmark, Finland, Norway, and Sweden—has many good deals for mature travelers. Here are some that are valid in all four countries. (Those that are unique to the individual countries are described under their own headings throughout this chapter.)

The Scanrail Pass 60+ costs tourists 60 or over about 10 percent less than what younger adults pay for 5, 10,or 21 days of unlimited rail travel in Sweden, Norway, Denmark, and Finland. You may travel second class anywhere within the four countries for 5 or 10 days within two months or for 21 consecutive days. Among the added bonuses: half fare on many bus lines and discounted prices on several hotel chains, some ferry crossings, and private railroads, including the Flam Railway in Norway. Reservations are occasionally required and always recommended. Buy the pass here before you go.

For information: Rail Europe, 800-438-7245; www.raileurope.com or www.scanrail.com.

You can also save money in the Scandinavian countries by purchasing hotel passes. For example, with the Nordic Hotel Pass, which costs half the regular price for those 60 or over, you can get discounts of up to 50 percent off the regular room rates at more than 120 first-class hotels that are part of Choice Hotels International.

Another pass, the Skanplus Hotel Pass (www.skanplus.com), gives you discounted rates at about 200 participating hotels throughout all four Scandinavian countries. Although for most travelers it's valid only May through September, it's good all year at some hotels for anyone who's turned 62.

SAS, the Scandinavian airline, gives passengers 62 and over a 10 percent discount on most fares between the U.S. and Scandinavia and its other international destinations. In Sweden and Denmark, it gives special fares for passengers who are 65 or older. See Chapter 3.

Finnair also takes 10 percent off most transatlantic fares for you at age 62 and your companion at any age. But on domestic flights within Finland, you'll get a spectacular discount—up to 70 percent off—at age 65, whether you buy your tickets here or in Finland. You must pay for your tickets within three days of booking. See Chapter 3.

And, finally, you should seriously consider buying city cards for free public transportation plus free or discounted entry to museums, historic sites, and cultural attractions. They can be purchased ahead of time in the U.S. or at tourist information offices, train stations, airports, and hotels in Scandinavia. The cities include Copenhagen, Odense, and Aalborg in Denmark; Helsinki in Finland; Oslo and Bergen in Norway; and Stockholm, Gothenburg, and Malmo in Sweden.

For information: Scandinavian National Tourist Offices, 655 Third Ave., New York, NY 10017; 212-885-9700; www .goscandinavia.com.

SPAIN

In addition to discounts for mature travelers at just about every museum, cultural event, and historic site in Spain, there is another good deal for visitors over 60. The Golden Days Promotion offers a 35 percent discount on the cost of a room and a buffet breakfast at most of the country's famous paradores.

These are government-owned inns, 87 in all, and many of them are former palaces, castles, convents, or monasteries located in the Spanish countryside. The special rates apply all year except in July, August, September, and Easter and Christmas weeks. Some paradores are available every day of the week; others only from Sunday to Thursday; and still others only on Friday, Saturday, and Sunday. There are limited numbers of rooms at the special rate, so make your plans far ahead. *For information:* Tourist Office of Spain, 666 Fifth Ave., New York, NY 10103; 212-265-8822; www.okspain.org. For paradores: Marketing Ahead, 800-223-1356; www.market ingahead.com.

SWEDEN

Travel by bus in Sweden is inexpensive and hassle-free. Besides, seniors get substantial discounts. Hop on a local bus in Sweden, and, if you're 65, you'll pay about 40 percent less than the regular fare. Travel on the express buses operated by Swebus Express, the country's largest long-distance bus operator with 300 destinations in Sweden, and you are offered a 20 percent discount starting at age 60.

For seeing the sights in the greater Stockholm area, consider buying the SL Tourist Card sold at tourist offices and kiosks. It's half price for seniors (about $12 for three days). With this card, you get free transportation on buses, local trains, subways, and ferry tours.

For information about the Scanrail Pass 60+ for travel in Denmark, Finland, Norway, and Sweden, see the Scandinavia listing earlier in this chapter.

SAS, the Scandinavian airline, takes 10 percent off the regular fares for passengers over 62 flying from this side of the Atlantic to SAS destinations worldwide. On flights within Sweden, the airline offers special senior fares, depending on the route, to passengers 65 and older. See Chapter 3.

And don't forget the city cards—the Stockholm Card, Gothenburg Card, and Malmo Card. These very good deals give you free or discounted transportation and admission to places you'll want to visit.

For information: Swedish Travel and Tourism Council, 655 Third Ave., New York, NY 10017; 212-885-9700; www .visit-sweden.com.

SWITZERLAND

The Swiss Hotel Association will provide, for the asking, a list of about 400 hotels in 160 cities and towns that participate in a program called "Season for Seniors." This program gives reduced room rates—sometimes discounted as much as 50 percent—to women over 62 and to men over 65. If two people are traveling together, just one must be the required age. The only catch is that in most cases the reduced rates do not apply during peak travel periods, including the summer months.

The Swiss Museum Passport is valid for an entire month of unlimited visits to about 180 museums. If you are a woman over 62 or a man over 65, you may buy it at a discount at participating museums and tourist offices in Switzerland.

Switzerland's national airline, SWISS, gives passengers 62 and over and a travel companion of any age a 10 percent discount on nonsale fares on flights from the U.S. to Europe. See Chapter 3.

For information: Switzerland Tourism, 608 Fifth Ave., New York, NY 10020; 877-794-8037 or 212-757-5944; www.my switzerland.com.

9

Trips and Tours for the Mature Traveler

Many enterprising organizations, tour operators, and travel agencies now cater exclusively to the mature traveler. They choose destinations designed to appeal to those who might have already "been there and done that," arrange trips that are leisurely and unhassled, give you congenial contemporaries to travel with and group hosts to smooth the way, and provide many special services you never got before. They also give you a choice between strenuous action-filled tours and those that are more relaxed. In fact, most of the agencies offer so many choices that the biggest problem is making a decision about where to go.

Options range from cruises in the Caribbean or the Greek Isles to grand tours of the Orient, sight-seeing excursions in the U.S., trips to the Canadian Rockies, theater tours of London, safaris in Africa, and snorkeling vacations on the Great Barrier Reef off Australia. There's just no place in the world where mature travelers won't go.

Among the newer and most popular trends are apartment/hotel complexes in American and European resort areas, as well as apartments in major cities. Here you can stay put for as long as you like, using the apartment or hotel as a home base for short-range roaming and exploring with the guidance of on-site hosts.

There are many choices, too, for the growing number of intrepid, energetic, and courageous members of the 50-plus population who prefer travel that is adventurous and unusual, perhaps even exotic. Many are described in this chapter along with the more traditional variety. Because they are planned specifically for the seasoned traveler, they usually offer some measure of comfort and convenience even in the wilderness, plus a leisurely pace that allows time for relaxation and independent exploration. Most important, they offer clean, comfortable accommodations, though sometimes rustic or spartan, and almost always a private bathroom.

ADVENTURE SOUTH

If you're looking for action, consider Midlife Adventures, a 13-day itinerary for those who are "too young to be called old, and too old to be called young." Offered by Adventure South in New Zealand, it is a tour of both North and South Islands with soft adventure activities including sailing, sea kayaking, walking, visits to volcanoes and glaciers, scenic flights, and visits with New Zealanders in their own homes. This company also plans bike tours and walking vacations.

For information: Adventure South, PO Box 33 153, Christchurch, NZ; www.advsouth.co.nz.

AFC TOURS & CRUISES

Specializing in escorted tours designed for mature travelers, AFC schedules trips to all the most popular destinations in the U.S. and Canada and some in other countries. Not only that, but if you live in southern California, where AFC is based, you will be transported free between your home and the airport. Many of the most popular tours are "unpack once," which means you stay in one hotel and take day trips from there. Domestic tours take you to such places as the national parks, Branson, Charleston, New York City, Savannah, the Pacific Northwest, and Washington, D.C. International adventures cover all of Europe. Other choices include cruises, steamboating, train tours, holiday tours, and grandparent trips. In other words, almost anything you want. Special for singles: if you sign up four months in advance and a roommate cannot be found to share your room, you need not pay a single supplement.

For information: AFC Tours and Cruises, 11772 Sorrento Valley Rd., San Diego, CA 92121; 800-369-3693 or 858-481-8188; www.afctours.com.

CIE TOURS INTERNATIONAL

An agency specializing in escorted vacations in Ireland, Northern Ireland, Scotland, Wales, and England, CIE offers motorcoach tours and fly/drive vacations, some of which come with a "55 and Smiling Discount." This means that on selected tours you get $55 per person off the cost of the trip if you are 55 or older and are among the first 15 people to book the tour on certain departure dates.

For information: CIE Tours International, 100 Hanover Ave., PO Box 501, Cedar Knolls, NJ 07927; 800-243-8687 or 973-292-3438; www.cietours.com.

COLLETTE VACATIONS

Collette Vacations has been around for more than 80 years, offering worry-free worldwide vacations to the mature traveler. Its escorted tours move at a relaxed pace, put you up in good hotels, and provide experienced tour guides to see that all goes well. But this agency offers other kinds of vacations too. For example, its "hub and spoke" programs feature multiple nights in one place—city stays, resort stays, castle stays—so you can settle down for a while without constantly climbing on buses and unpacking your bags at the next destination. Meanwhile, day excursions take you to see the sights.

Collette's independent travel packages, land-only or air-inclusive, let you customize your own trip in North America or Europe. You have hotel options at each destination, optional activities, and rental cars or train transportation if you want them.

If you are a member of AARP, you can save up to $100 per person on escorted tours and up to $50 on some independent packages.

For information: Collette Vacations, 162 Middle St., Pawtucket, RI 02860; 888-344-5578 or 401-727-9000; www.collettevacations.com.

ELDERHOSTEL

The educational tours from Elderhostel number in the thousands, all of them bargains for adults over the age of 55 (and younger travel mates). See Chapter 13.

For information: Elderhostel, 11 Avenue de Lafayette, Boston, MA 02111; 877-426-8056 or 617-426-7788; www .elderhostel.com.

ELDERTREKS

An adventure travel company that specializes in exotic, far-out adventures for travelers 50 and over (and companions of any age), ElderTreks takes small groups of no more than 16 participants to more than 50 destinations worldwide, from Argentina to Mongolia, Antarctica, and Tibet. Its programs are designed for people who enjoy physical activity and are rated from easy to challenging. Itineraries, however, are chosen with older trekkers in mind, so if you are in good condition, you'll fit right in. On ship-based adventures, the expedition ships are small to allow for more personal interaction and less impact on the environment.

Hotels are selected for comfort, location, charm, and the availability of private washrooms. Accommodations in primitive places may be the floor of a nomadic tent or beneath a canopy of trees, but you can always count on an air mattress. Guides, cooks, meals, and porters are part of the package.

There is no additional charge for single travelers willing to share a room.

For information: ElderTreks, 597 Markham St., Toronto, ON M6G 2L7; 800-741-7956 or 416-588-5000; www.elder treks.com.

FANCY-FREE HOLIDAYS

Geared for senior travelers, Fancy-Free's domestic escorted motorcoach tours, all originating in Chicago, include the usual favorite destinations such as Branson, New England, Alaska, Williamsburg, Asheville, New Orleans, and Washington, D.C. Its fully escorted overseas tours by air, motorcoach, or cruise ship include Ireland, England, Scotland, and Wales.

For information: Fancy-Free Holidays, 24 W. 500 Maple Ave., Naperville, IL 60540; 800-421-3330 or 630-778-7010; www.fancyfreeholidays.com.

50PLUS EXPEDITIONS

This company offers "adventure travel for people over 50" and specializes in exotic trips all over the world, from exploring the rain forest in Ecuador and the Amazon jungle to cruising in Antarctica, cycling in the Czech Republic or down the Danube in Austria, hiking in Borneo, riding elephants and going on game rides in India, and visiting Kenya and Tanzania.

These are small group tours composed of 2 to 16 people who are escorted by experienced local guides. All trips are graded for difficulty from easy to demanding, depending on the level of physical activity, elevation, and climate, and most allow for optional extensions.

For information: 50plus Expeditions, 40 Brisbane Rd., Toronto, ON M3J 2J8; 866-318-5050 or 426-749-5150; www.50plusexpeditions.com.

FUN & FITNESS TRAVEL CLUB

The aerobics cruises scheduled about once a month by this club for older adults take you on voyages in the Caribbean, along the Mexican Riviera, through the Panama Canal, to Bermuda, along the eastern U.S. shores and up to Canada, and even to Alaska. Every morning, on every cruise, there are morning water aerobics led by certified instructors, plus other forms of physical activities such as yoga, tai chi, deck walking, ballroom dancing, and chair aerobics throughout the day, all exclusively for club members traveling together. The club, which costs nothing to join and is especially popular among single seniors, has a current enrollment of about 2,000 members nationwide.

For information: Fun & Fitness Travel Club, 7338 Dartford Dr., Ste. 9, McLean, VA 22102; 800-955-9942 or 703-827-1014; www.fun-fitness.com.

GLOBUS & COSMOS TOURS

This affiliated pair of escorted tour companies, together the largest in the world, offers everything from traditional escorted tours everywhere in the world to more leisurely vacations that give you a few days in each city on your itinerary. All of the tours are designed to appeal to over-50 travelers who constitute the vast majority of their clients. The upscale escorted tours from Globus will take you to all seven continents of the world, including Antarctica and put you up in three- and four-star hotels.

A Globus specialty is a choice of Tour & Cruise Vacations that combine land tours and cruises. One trip, for example, takes you to Vienna for four nights and then on a Danube River cruise to Budapest and Bratislava.

The company's LeisureStyle Vacations feature two- or three-night stays per city and activities such as cooking classes, golfing, and wine tasting. The Independent City

Stays, here and abroad, offer a chance to independently explore with advice and assistance from a professional on-site host.

Cosmos specializes in vacations for cost-conscious travelers and offers traditional escorted motorcoach tours all over the world. By the way, if you are traveling alone and are willing to share a room, you'll get a roommate and pay no single supplement. Members of AARP can save $50 on any Globus or Cosmos Vacation.

For information: Globus & Cosmos Tours, 5301 S. Federal Circle, Littleton, CO 80123; 800-276-1241 or 303-797-2800; www.globusandcosmos.com.

GO AHEAD VACATIONS

Go Ahead Vacations specializes in educational escorted sightseeing trips. It caters to the 50-plus traveler with international tours that include everything from airfare to guided sightseeing, the entire journey accompanied by full-time local tour directors so you can experience the places you visit from the perspective of a native.

In addition to its escorted tours, Go Ahead also features walking tours, combination land and cruise tours, and independent city-stay vacations, all with pre- and posttour extension options.

By the way, you can travel free if you get ten other people to go with you on a Go Ahead tour to a foreign destination.

For information: Go Ahead Vacations, 1 Education St., Cambridge MA 02141; 800-242-4686 or 617-619-1000; www.goaheadvacations.com.

GOLDEN AGE FESTIVE HOLIDAYS

Another agency that caters to the 50-plus crowd, this one offers tours to everywhere from Wildwood (New Jersey), Myrtle Beach, Nashville, Maine, and New York to the national parks, Las Vegas, Europe, Greece, China, and Australia—plus plenty of cruises. All packages are escorted and include accommodations, meals, and just about everything else.

In addition, Golden Age offers an innovation—"drive-to tours" for individual travelers, allowing them to take advantage of group discounts that make the trips remarkably inexpensive. On these, all on the East Coast, you drive yourself to your destination—for example, Wildwood, Ocean City, Myrtle Beach, Newport and Mystic Seaport, Hilton Head, Williamsburg—and join others traveling on their own for meals, entertainment, and tours.

For information: Golden Age Festive Holidays, 5501 New Jersey Ave., Wildwood Crest, NJ 08260; 800-257-8920 or 609-522-6316; www.goldenagefestival.com.

GOLDEN AGE TRAVELLERS CLUB

An over-50 club that specializes in discounted cruises on major lines everywhere in the world, Golden Age also offers land tours from well-known tour operators. When you join the club ($10 single or $15 per couple a year), you receive a newsletter with listings of upcoming sailings. Other inducements are tour escorts and bonus points. Single travelers may choose to be enrolled in the Roommates Wanted list to help them find companions to share cabins and costs. For members in the San Francisco and Sacramento areas, there are one-day travel shows where you may meet fellow travelers and share a snack.

Especially intriguing to mature travelers are the agency's long-stay trips. On these, you stay put—for example, in Spain, Portugal, Guatemala, Australia, Costa Rica, or Argentina—at the same hotel for two or three weeks and, if you wish, take short side trips. The packages include air, hotel, and sometimes meals.

For information: Golden Age Travellers Club, Pier 27, The Embarcadero, San Francisco, CA 94111; 800-258-8880; www.gatclub.com.

GRAND CIRCLE TRAVEL

Grand Circle Travel, the first U.S. company to market international vacations for Americans 50 and over, caters to the older traveler and plans all of its trips exclusively for them. That means the trips are easygoing with longer overall stays, unhurried itineraries, and plenty of time to relax. Grand Circle specializes in four varieties of travel. Its classic and educational escorted tours take groups of mature travelers all over the world, accompanied by experienced guides who take care of everything. All you have to do is show up and keep your eyes open. Its extended vacations allow you to travel in a group but, at the same time, be an independent traveler. You stay up to two weeks in one, two, or three destinations such as the Costa del Sol, Sicily, or Thailand. You live in hotels or apartments, with meals, social activities, tours, and a program director included.

River cruises are another option, taking you on leisurely voyages throughout Europe aboard the company's own fleet of private river boats. And finally, the ocean cruise tours combine sailing the major seas with land-based stays for in-depth explorations of the ports of call.

All vacations offer pre- and posttrip extensions that allow travelers to see more while taking advantage of their already included airfare.

If you are a solo traveler, you may ask to be matched with an appropriate roommate to avoid the single supplement or choose a trip or certain departure dates when the supplement is waived.

Bonus: Organize a group of ten friends and relatives to travel with you on a GCT trip, and you go free. Refer a new traveler and you earn $100 in travel credit.

For information: Grand Circle Travel, 347 Congress St., Boston, MA 02210; 800-248-3737 or 617-350-7500; www .gct.com.

HORIZON & CO.

This Canadian company specializes in exotic luxury trips exclusively for travelers 55 and older. Its escorted groups are small and the cost covers everything from tips to luggage handling to sightseeing excursions. Its destinations, which range from desert palaces to the meandering tributaries of the Mekong Delta, currently include India, southern Africa, Vietnam, Costa Rica, Cuba, and Iceland. Horizon also offers extensive tours of Canada as well as many cruises and a few forays into the U.S. Its Classic Series of tours is designed to appeal to older travelers who want a leisurely paced, all-inclusive planned group travel experience. The Exploratory Series, on the other hand, caters to younger, more active travelers and features cultural themes with independent time built into the schedule.

For information: Horizon & Co., 160 John St., Toronto, ON M5V 2X8; 800-387-2977 or 416-585-9911; www.horizon-co.com.

HOSTELLING INTERNATIONAL USA

This international organization, formerly known as American Youth Hostels, offers low-cost lodging all over the globe to people of all ages. Membership for U.S. adults costs $28 a year, but if you are 55 or older, you pay only $18. You get a membership card, a free guide to hostels in the U.S., and a free map. For an added fee, you may order a guidebook listing more than 4,000 hostels in more than 60 countries, including about 100 in the U.S. In addition, you are entitled to hundreds of discounts on transportation, car rentals, restaurants, admissions, festivals, ski lifts, and more.

Lodgings are dormitory-style, women in one room, men in another, although some hostels also have private rooms for families, couples, and groups that may be reserved in advance. These include the Gateway City Hostels in eight of the country's major cities—New York City, Los Angeles, San Francisco, Miami Beach, Washington, D.C., Chicago, Seattle, and San Diego. All are centrally located and have program directors who arrange special activities—such as walking tours and cultural events—for their guests. Although most hostels are located in basic structures, some are in castles, former dude ranches, convents, lighthouses, base camps, or other exotic locations.

For information: Hostelling International USA, 733 15th St. NW, Washington, DC 20005; 202-783-6161; www.hiayh.org.

HOSTELLING INTERNATIONAL–CANADA

A network of hostels throughout the Canadian provinces, HI–Canada offers members of all ages an inexpensive night's sleep in a wide variety of places ranging from modern facilities to historic homes, and refurbished jails to log cabins in the Rockies. Located in all major gateway cities and also in remote locations, your accommodations—private or shared—cost an average of $15 (Canadian) a night. Membership for Canadian residents over 18 costs $35 (Canadian) per year and allows you to use any HI facility worldwide at a special discount. No senior discount here, but at these rates, who needs it?

For information: Hostelling International–Canada, 205 Catherine St., Ste. 400, Ottawa, ON K2P 1C3; 800-663-5777 (Canada only); www.hihostels.ca.

MAYFLOWER TOURS

Most of Mayflower's travelers are "55 or better," so the pace of its tours is leisurely and rest stops are scheduled every couple of hours. You travel by motorcoach, stay in good hotels or motels, and eat many of your meals together. The trips are fully escorted by tour directors who make sure all goes well. If you are a single traveler and request a roommate at least 30 days before departure, you'll get one or a room to yourself with no single supplement to pay. Tours go almost everywhere in the U.S., Canada, and the rest of the world, especially Europe, Asia, the South Pacific, and South Africa.

For information: Mayflower Tours, 1225 Warren Ave., Downers Grove, IL 60515; 800-323-7604 or 630-435-8500; www.mayflowertours.com.

OUTWARD BOUND

Outward Bound is famous for its rugged wilderness survival trips for young people and is aimed at building self-confidence, self-esteem, and the ability to work as a team. But it also offers short adventure courses specifically designed for adults, some for those over the age of 40 or 50, who seek to examine their goals or gain personal insights. Among the recent courses for these mature adventurers: sailing in the Florida Keys or along the coast of Maine and whitewater canoeing down the Rio Grande.

For information: Outward Bound, 100 Mystery Point Rd., Garrison, NY 10524; 888-882-6863 or 845-424-4000; www.outwardbound.org.

OVERSEAS ADVENTURE TRAVEL (OAT)

OAT's soft adventures, exclusively for travelers over 50, combine creature comforts with off-the-beaten-path experiences in exotic places all over the world, from the rain forests of Borneo to Botswana or the Galapagos Islands. Groups are small, with no more than 16 participants. The trips—rated from "easy" to "demanding"—move at a leisurely pace and offer many optional side adventures. You'll travel by minivan and lodge in accommodations ranging from five-star hotels to jungle lodges or spacious tents and sometimes use unconventional modes of transportation such as dugout canoes, camels, yachts, or your own two feet.

Among recent tours, always including round-trip air, from this affiliate of Grand Circle Travel have been excursions to such places as the Amazon rain forest, Peru, Morocco, Botswana, China, Tibet, Borneo, and Tanzania.

Solo travelers are not charged a single supplement if they are willing to share accommodations.

Bonus: get ten of your friends and relatives to travel with you on an OAT trip, and you go free. Refer a new traveler and you earn $100 in travel credit.

For information: Overseas Adventure Travel, 247 Congress St., Boston, MA 02210; 800-955-1925 or 617-350-7500; www.oattravel.com.

PLEASANT HOLIDAYS

Many of Pleasant Holidays' discounted vacation packages to resorts in many countries include airfare, hotel or condo room, and sometimes a rental car. The Makua Club for people over 55 gives you free room and car-rental upgrades and other amenities that are specific to each hotel. When you make a booking, mention your age and ask for your privileges.

For information: Pleasant Holidays, 2404 Townsgate Rd., Westlake, CA 91361; 800-448-3333 or 818-991-3390; www.pleasantholidays.com.

RIVER ODYSSEYS WEST (ROW)

ROW reserves a couple of whitewater river trips each summer exclusively for adventurous people over 50 who like to travel with others their own age. These Prime Time trips take you down Idaho's Salmon River or the Snake River on the Oregon border for five days, passing through four spectacular volcanic canyons. You travel in rubber rafts by day and sleep in tents at the edge of the river by night.

Mature travelers may also choose one of ROW's raft-supported walking trips in Hells Canyon or the Salmon River in Idaho. See Chapter 14 for details.

For its canoe trips on Montana's scenic upper Missouri River, ROW schedules a few five-day float trips for older adventurers. Following the trail of Lewis and Clark, you travel in comfortable 34-foot voyageur canoes carrying up to 14 passengers plus two guides. You'll float down the river, stopping to explore many historic sites along the way. At the end of the day, you'll stop at luxury campsites with tents set up in advance, eat five-course meals, try your luck at fishing, and tell stories around the campfire.

For information: River Odysseys West, PO Box 579-UD, Coeur d'Alene, ID 83816; 800-451-6034 or 208-765-0841; www.rowinc.com.

SENIOR TOURS CANADA

Canada's largest operator of escorted tours for the mature traveler, this company takes 50-plus tourists all over the world on leisurely vacations that range from tours of southern Italy to Florida spa holidays; Polynesian cruises; grand tours of Arizona or Japan; and stay-put vacations in Turkey, Portugal, or Palm Springs. You can choose among traditional tours, stay-put vacations, cruises, and bus tours. All are escorted and include everything from round-trip transportation (usually between your home and the airport) to airfare, meals, gratuities, luggage handling, guided tours, and health and cancellation insurance. In other words, no hassle.

For information: Senior Tours Canada, 225 Eglinton Ave. West, Toronto M4R 1A9; 800-268-3492 or 416-322-1500; www.seniortours.ca.

SOPHISTICATED VOYAGES

A sister company to Grandtravel, Sophisticated Voyages operates one or two upscale tours a year for older travelers who want a relaxed itinerary rich in cultural activities, outstanding meals, fine hotels, and plenty of free time. What they don't want are hassles, large groups, all-day bus rides, hurried breakfasts, and many events crammed into the day. Recent trips have included a ten-day Britain tour that combined five nights in London with three nights at Thornbury Castle in County Avon; and a two-week safari in Kenya where travelers stayed in elegant hotels, lodges, and tented camps.

For information: Sophisticated Voyages, 6900 Wisconsin Ave., Chevy Chase, MD 20815; 800-247-7651 or 301-986-0790; www.grandtrvl.com.

TRAFALGAR TOURS

After 50 years of taking Americans on tours all over the world, Trafalgar has now added a first-class tour program in the U.S. and Canada with more than a dozen regional itineraries. Catering to older travelers who want to see the sights without worrying about logistics and details, these escorted motorcoach tours include luxury coaches, first-class hotels or lodges, guided sight-seeing tours, gratuities, and most meals. Trafalgar also continues its overseas tours, both first-class and budget, to Europe, Britain, Australia, New Zealand, China, and South Africa. Traveling alone? You'll be matched with an appropriate roommate and won't be charged the single supplement.

For information: Trafalgar Tours USA, 29-76 Northern Blvd., Long Island City, NY 11101; 800-854-0103 or 718-685-3000; www.trafalgartours.com.

VALUE WORLD TOURS

An agency that specializes in river cruises, Value World Tours takes 10 to 20 percent off the cost of some sailings on off-peak departure dates for travelers over the age of 55. Cruises are mainly on inland waterways in Russia, Ukraine, central Europe, Egypt, and China, while hosted or escorted motorcoach tours go to many destinations in the same parts of the world. The two-week programs may be extended before or after the trips.

For information: Value World Tours, 17220 Newhope St., Fountain Valley, CA 92708; 800-795-1633 or 714-556-8258; www.vwtours.com.

VANTAGE DELUXE WORLD TRAVEL

Vantage features upscale, fully escorted group travel packages for mature travelers. These all-inclusive vacations include land tours, train trips, and both river and ocean cruises. Accommodations are always deluxe, and explorations are leisurely and relaxed, so there is plenty of time to savor the sights. All trips are led by tour directors who see to it that everything—from ticketing and baggage handling to check-ins, meals, and tips—is taken care of for you. Among Vantage's most popular tours are a Danube River cruise, a trip through the Panama Canal, a visit to China and the Yangtze River, an exploration of Ireland, and a tour through the countries of Eastern Europe. There are also longer, more exotic trips, including a deluxe around-the-world tour.

If you are traveling alone and want a roommate, a compatible companion will be found or you'll pay only half the single supplement on escorted land programs. On river cruises, you are guaranteed a roommate or the per person double-occupancy rate.

For information: Vantage Deluxe World Travel, 90 Canal St., Boston, MA 02114; 800-322-6677; www.vantagetravel.com.

VISTA TOURS

Another agency providing escorted tours almost exclusively for the mature set, Vista Tours plans leisurely trips with plenty of stops and ample time to enjoy the points of interest and relax too. You travel on comfortable motorcoaches with escorts who deal with the reservations, transfers, luggage, meal arrangements, and all other potentially problematic situations. Destinations, although mainly in the mainland U.S., also include Canada, Europe, and Hawaii. A highlight every year is a five-day trip over the New Year's holiday to California for the Pasadena Rose Parade and a New Year's Eve party with a big band and a celebrity show. If you're a woman who doesn't have a dancing partner or wants a better one, you may take your turn whirling around the

floor with one of the gentleman hosts who accompany the group.
For information: Vista Tours, 1923 N. Carson St., Ste. 105, Carson City, NV 89701; 800-647-0800 or 775-882-2100; www.frontiertours.com.

WARREN RIVER EXPEDITIONS

Warren River Expeditions offers many whitewater raft trips limited to adventurers over 50, plus two expeditions a year for grandparents and their grandchildren. All the trips take you down Idaho's Salmon River, the longest undammed river in the country—fast and wild in the spring, tame and gentle in late summer. You'll float through unique ecosystems, down the deep Salmon River Canyon, and through the Frank Church Wilderness Area, where you'll view the lush scenery and abundant wildlife. Planned as soft adventure trips for people who are not enthusiastic about camping out, the six-day senior trips, limited to 16 guests, put you up each night in comfortable rustic backcountry lodges. There's a 10 percent discount on all trips for those over 55 and 25 percent for children under 14.
For information: Warren River Expeditions, PO Box 1375, Salmon, ID 83467-1375; 800-765-0421 or 208-756-6387; www.raftidaho.com.

WEST COAST RAIL TOURS

If you love to ride the rails, check out the tours run by West Coast Railway Association, a nonprofit society dedicated to the preservation of Canada's railway heritage. The association restores, preserves, and maintains vintage railcars. Its unique excursions, one to nine days long, are escorted by experienced rail buffs and treat you to rail adventures in scenic and historic areas of Canada. On some tours, you eat and sleep on board; on others, you stop for meals and lodging along the way. Seniors, usually starting at age 60, get a small price break on almost all of them.

For information: West Coast Rail Tours, PO Box 2790 Stn. Main, Vancouver BC V6B 3X2; 800-722-1233 or 604-524-1011; www.westcoastrailtours.com.

10

Cruising the Oceans, Rivers, and Seas

Cruises have always appealed to the mature crowd. The majority of passengers on many sailings are over the age of 50, especially on longer voyages, and in fact, the longer the cruise, the older the passengers tend to be.

Whatever your age, never book a cruise without shopping around. Cruise rates have always been heavily discounted, but today anybody who pays the full sticker price (also called the brochure rate) should also be offered a chance to bid on the Brooklyn Bridge. Usually the best bargains come from travel agents who specialize in sea voyages or from cruise brokers who buy blocks of cabins and sell them at a discount. But the cruise lines offer special rates, too, on advance-purchase or last-minute bookings, intro-

TIPS FOR FRUGAL TRAVELERS

ThriftyTravelPortal.com is a free website that is a virtual encyclopedia of travel resources, tips, strategies, and information, all designed to help you find the safest, easiest, and cheapest ways to travel—from great deals for hotels and other accommodations to cruise bargains and the best airfare deals. Included are tips on using these and other resources, plus extensive trip-planning information. Best of all, a special section is devoted to the over-50 thrifty traveler. *For information:* www.thriftytravelportal.com.

ductory or off-season sailings, repositioning cruises, group bookings, and two-for-one deals.

A few cruise lines offer senior discounts all the time, and others offer them now and then. For information about special senior rates, check with your travel agent or the cruise line before booking your trip. Or consult with one of the special cruise agencies that deal in discounted fares on multiple cruise lines.

AVALON WATERWAYS

Sign on for a European river cruise and choose among six itineraries on a sleek and elegant river cruiser with an English-speaking crew, local guides, large staterooms, and European cuisine. You'll get a deduction of $50 per person on new bookings if you belong to AARP.

For information: 877-797-8789; www.avalonwaterways .com.

CARNIVAL CRUISE LINES

Carnival's occasional senior citizen rates can save you a considerable amount of money for trips on certain ships and departure dates if one occupant of your cabin is at least 55 years of age. To inquire about them, call your travel agent or the cruise line and mention the code CPSE or FPS2.

If you belong to AARP, you can save $100 per cabin on most seven-day or longer voyages or $50 per cabin on shorter trips to the Bahamas, Mexico, the Caribbean, the Panama Canal, Hawaii, or Alaska. Singles save half that much. If you are traveling alone, you may request a roommate and pay no single supplement if none is available.
For information: 800-CARNIVAL (800-227-6482); www .carnival.com.

CELEBRITY CRUISES

This premium cruise line, whose nine ships make voyages to Bermuda, Alaska, Hawaii, Mexico, the Caribbean, and South America, features frequent senior specials for passengers 55 and over. Watch for them on the website, or ask your travel agent to check them out for you.
For information: 800-437-3111; www.celebrity.com.

COSTA CRUISES

Make an early booking for a Costa Cruise using the advance-purchase Andiamo rate and, if one person in the cabin is 60 or over, you will save $50 per person or $100 per stateroom for inside or ocean-view cabins. Choose a veranda stateroom and you will save $100 per person or $200 per

cabin. So will friends traveling with you if they book at least two cabins at the same time you do, while children 17 and under sharing a stateroom with two adults can cruise for $199 to $299, depending on the length of the voyage.
For information: 800-332-6782; www.costacruise.com.

CRUISE WEST

Cruise West's small ships take only about 100 passengers and give you an up-close look at hidden coves, narrow waterways, and little ports on voyages to Alaska; British Columbia; the California wine country; Baja, Mexico; or Costa Rica and Panama. Members of AARP who are making new bookings can get onboard credits of $25 to $200 per person, depending on the length of the cruise, to be used for optional shore excursions, drinks, purchases in the gift shop, or even tips. Cruises vary from 3-night excursions to 12-night expeditions.
For information: 800-296-8307; www.cruisewest.com.

ELDERHOSTEL'S ADVENTURES AFLOAT

One of Elderhostel's most popular categories of learning vacations for its 55-plus members is its selection of cruises on the world's most spectacular waterways. Your education will take place aboard river barges, yachts, cruise ships, or even the *Queen Mary 2*. Choices can be made from dozens of voyages all over the world, from the Mississippi River to Scandinavia, the Aegean Sea, the Yangtze River, the Texas Gulf Coast, the Danube River, the Mediterranean, and across the Atlantic Ocean. International programs include airfare,

and all trips include tuition, field trips, meals, and accommodations. For more about Elderhostel, see Chapter 13.
For information: Elderhostel, 11 Avenue de Lafayette, Boston, MA 02111; 877-426-8056 or 617-426-7788; www.elderhostel.org.

HOLLAND AMERICA LINE

Holland America offers discounts to members of AARP, with savings of $200 per outside cabin on cruises and Alaska cruise tours of 10 days or longer; $100 on cruises of seven to nine days; and $50 on shorter voyages. Single travelers save half those amounts. The discounts can be extended to up to four staterooms for friends or family.
For information: 800-887-3529; www.hollandamerica.com.

MSC CRUISES

Staffed by English-speaking Italian crews, these premium-class cruise ships sail the Caribbean and South America January through April and the Mediterranean the rest of the year. If you belong to AARP, you can save $200 per cabin except on suites. Single passengers can save $100 per cabin.
For information: 800-666-9333; www.msccruises.com.

NORWEGIAN COASTAL VOYAGE

The 11-ship Norwegian Coastal Voyage fleet sails daily year-round along Norway's 1,250-mile west coast, passing myriad fjords and calling at 34 ports between Bergen and Kirkenes above the Arctic Circle. The voyage is a combination of a first-class cruise ship and a working ship that ferries local passengers and cargo between remote coastal towns and fishing villages with shore excursions by foot, bus, or snowmobile. On these unique cruise ships, which carry 312 to 675 passengers, you may choose an escorted or independent vacation.

Passengers age 67 or older get a nice break on the rates, a reduction of $95 to $170 per person, one way or round trip, depending on the date and length of the trip, any time of the year except in June or July. There is no single supplement in many categories of outside cabins on off-peak sailings.

Any time of year, however, AARP members receive additional discounts of $70 per cabin on 6-day one-way journeys and $100 on 12-day round-trip sailings. Other discounts apply to air-inclusive independent and escorted vacations. What's more, these discounts may be added to the off-peak discounts for 67-plus passengers.

For information: Norwegian Coastal Voyage, 800-323-7436 or 212-319-1300; www.coastalvoyage.com.

NORWEGIAN CRUISE LINE

Occasionally throughout the year, this cruise line offers senior fares for passengers 55-plus, usually amounting to a savings of about 15 percent off the regular rate. Ask your travel agent to find one for you, or visit the "specials" section on the website.

For information: 800-327-7030; www.ncl.com.

ROYAL CARIBBEAN INTERNATIONAL (RCI)

Check with your travel agent or the website to find out when this cruise line will be offering one of its periodic specials for passengers 55-plus and their cabin mates. They are available from time to time on all of its ships, depending on the availability of space. And, so you know what you're getting into, each shore excursion on RCI voyages is rated "mild," "moderate," or "strenuous."

For information: 800-327-6700; www.royalcaribbean.com.

SAGA INTERNATIONAL HOLIDAYS

The voyages of the *Saga Rose* and *Saga Pearl* are planned exclusively for travelers over the age of 50 (and spouses who must be at least 40). Both cruise ships are owned by Saga Holidays, a British tour company that caters to mature travelers, and sail from England. The *Saga Rose*, a 587-passenger ship with large public rooms and lots of open deck space, travels to the Mediterranean, making stops in France, Portugal, and Spain. Its other itineraries take you to Bergen, Norway, then up the coast into spectacular fjords; or to the Baltic Sea with ports of call in Sweden, Finland, Russia, Estonia, Germany, Denmark, and Norway. The routes of the smaller, more intimate 352-passenger *Saga Pearl* include lengthy voyages to Norway and the North Cape; the western Mediterranean with landings in Portugal, Morocco, Corsica, and Spain; or to Iceland by way of Ireland and Scotland.

For information: Saga International Holidays, 1161 Boylston St., Boston, MA 02215; 800-343-0273; www.saga .holidays.com.

GENTLEMEN HOSTS

Many cruise lines take a few gentlemen hosts along on their voyages to dance, dine, and go ashore on excursions with women passengers who haven't brought partners with them. The hosts are carefully chosen, unattached older men who have polished social skills and the ability to be charming no matter what. Especially important, they must be accomplished dancers in everything from the rumba and the waltz to the foxtrot, cha-cha, and swing. The screening procedure for hosts is stringent, and since there are many more applicants than positions, don't be surprised if you are not encouraged to apply. Hosts usually pay a small fee for every day at sea and sometimes their own airfare to and from the port city.

Crystal Cruises, whose worldwide cruises carry three or four "ambassador hosts" per trip, look for personable social hosts over the age of 65 who are great dancers and enjoy keeping older single women passengers entertained both on board and ashore.
For information: Entertainment Dept., Crystal Cruises, 2049 Century Park East, Ste. 1400, Los Angeles, CA 90067.

Cunard Line's cruises aboard the *Queen Mary 2* and the *Caronia* carry along four to ten friendly gentleman hosts between the ages of 45 and 70. Their job is not only to whirl around the dance floor with women who need partners but also to act as friendly diplomats who help passengers get to know one another. A knowledge of foreign languages is a plus.
For information: The Working Vacation, 12544 W. 159th St., Homer Glen, IL 60491; 708-301-7535; www.theworking vacation.com.

Holland America Line recruits retired professionals with good social skills to act as dance hosts on its long cruises and big band sailings. Usually two to six hosts go along on each trip.

For information: To Sea With Z, 19195 Mystic Pointe Dr., Aventura, FL 33180; 305-931-1026; www.toseawithz.com.

Merry Widows Dance Tours offers many cruises and land tours for single, widowed, or divorced women who were born to dance. Accompanying them on the trip are gentleman hosts, one for every four women, who are expert in both traditional ballroom and Latin dancing.

For information: Merry Widows Dance Tours, AAA Auto Club South, 1515 N. Westshore Blvd., Tampa, FL 33607; 813-289-5004.

Norwegian Cruise Line's sailings to many places around the world usually include at least two gentleman hosts on longer voyages.

For information: To Sea With Z, 19195 Mystic Pointe Dr., Aventura, FL 33180; 305-931-1026; www.toseawithz.com.

Radisson Seven Seas Cruises includes two male hosts on all voyages of its vessels the *Navigator* and the *Mariner*, and on some sailings of the *Diamond*. Their job is to act as social liaisons between the passengers and the staff.

For information: Sixth Star Entertainment, 21 NW 5th St., Fort Lauderdale, FL 33301; 954-462-6760.

Silversea Cruises has introduced gentleman hosts aboard all of its luxurious small ships. The hosts' job is to dance, mingle, and mix, making sure all guests have an enjoyable voyage.

For information: The Working Vacation, 12544 W. 159th St., Homer Glen, IL 60491; 708-301-7535; www.theworking vacation.com.

11

Intergenerational Adventures

I f you'd like to get to know your grandchildren (or children, nieces, nephews, young friends) better, take them on vacation. A trip with the kids or your adult children is a wonderful way to spend time together and share common interests, especially for far-flung families who seldom have a chance to enjoy one another's company. Whether it's a one-day tour of a nearby city or a week on a dude ranch, this is the kind of family togetherness that works. You can plan your own itineraries, maybe visiting places you both want to see, renting a cottage at the beach, or choosing a resort or cruise that offers special activities for the youngsters.

If you don't want the hassles and anxieties of traveling on your own with kids, you can do it the easy way by going with a tour company that specializes in intergenerational vacations. These are scheduled in the summer and during winter breaks when the children are out of school. The best of them are fully escorted by counselors, often schoolteachers on holiday. The tours, ranging from a visit to Washington, D.C., to a safari in Kenya, move at a leisurely pace suited to both generations with plenty of stops and time to relax and relate. Some are designed for children in a certain age range, while others accept all youngsters over 7 and up to 17 or 18.

By the way, consider taking a cruise together. Several cruise lines cater to children now, providing activities for all of them, from toddlers to teenagers. Besides, many ships have cabins that accommodate three or four passengers. These extra beds or bunks are often sold at very low rates, especially for children. And sometimes third and fourth passengers, children or otherwise, can go along absolutely free except for port taxes and extras.

Growing in popularity, too, are other multigenerational holidays such as adventures for mothers and grown daughters; hostelers and adult children; and whole families, including children, parents, and grandparents. If you're wondering why a growing number of organizations and companies and even hotels are now catering to grandparents, here's the reason. There are now about 60 million grandparents in the U.S., according to the AARP, with the number expected to rise to 80 million by 2010. The average age for first-time grandparents is 48, giving them plenty of time and energy to spend with the kids.

COUNTRY COTTAGES

Choose from among more than 10,000 private homes—from cottages to castles—in England, Ireland, Scotland, or

Wales, and take the kids along for a week or more. Country Cottages offers its Grandparents' Houseparty package that at certain times of the year costs about $100 a day per person, including round-trip air from New York and a rental car or minivan. In some seasons, it adds a small discount for grandparents and grandchildren. All of the properties are second homes equipped with linens, tableware, and cookware and have accessible caretakers to provide information or assistance.

For information: Country Cottages, Box 810997, Boca Raton, FL 33481; 800-674-8883; www.vacationeurope .com.

ELDERHOSTEL INTERGENERATIONAL AND FAMILY PROGRAMS

Elderhostel offers many multigenerational vacations. Its intergenerational programs are for members of two generations—adults and young people. Its family offerings are open to the entire family and may include grandparents, aunts, uncles, adult children, and grandchildren. In either case, there is a limit of one child per adult. Usually the youngsters must be at least nine years old, and sometimes they must be within a specified age range. Many of the activities in the programs are for the entire group, while others are limited to the adults or the children.

You may choose programs in the U.S.—many in the national parks—or in foreign countries such as Bermuda, Costa Rica, Greece, New Zealand, and Ireland.

For information: Elderhostel, 11 Avenue de Lafayette, Boston, MA 02111; 877-426-8056 or 617-426-7788; www .elderhostel.org.

EXPLORATIONS IN TRAVEL

Multigenerational weekend trips for mothers, daughters, granddaughters, aunts, and other female friends or relatives are scheduled occasionally by Explorations in Travel, a company that specializes in action vacations for women over the age of 40 (see Chapter 14). At least two generations should be represented, with one participant over 40 and the other 21 or older.

For information: Explorations in Travel, 2458 River Rd., Guilford, VT 05301; 877-257-0152 or 802-257-0152; www .exploretravel.com.

FAMILYHOSTEL

Sponsored by the University of New Hampshire and a cousin of Interhostel, FamilyHostel specializes in one- to two-week learning vacations for families—parents and/or grandparents with school-age children. Its all-inclusive summer vacations combine travel with an inside look at culture and history in this country and abroad, and its destinations include such places as England, France, Greece, Italy, and Costa Rica, as well as Alaska, Hawaii, California, New England, and Oklahoma.

Separately and together, adults and children enjoy workshops, recreation, sight-seeing adventures, and social activities that include visits with local families. The groups of intergenerational travelers, limited to five to ten families, are accompanied by university representatives and teachers from the U.S. and the host countries. Lodging is in three- or four-star hotels.

For information: FamilyHostel, University of New Hampshire, 6 Garrison Ave., Durham, NH 03824; 800-733-9753 or 603-862-1147; www.learn.unh.edu/familyhostel.

GENERATIONS TOURING COMPANY

With a wide array of upscale escorted tours for generations traveling together—some exclusively for grandparents and grandchildren, others for grandparents and/or parents and children—Generations Touring Company's goal is to create meaningful family connections and learning experiences for everyone. Each of its itineraries in the U.S. and other parts of the world from Mexico to Italy, China, Peru, and Antarctica are led by a travel manager, an educator-escort, and local guides. The tour price covers just about everything.

Certain departure dates are reserved for children ages 8 to 17, while others are limited to those 8 to 12 or 13 to 17. You have your choice of four types of experiences, depending on how much activity you're looking for, but all include plenty of adventures as well as opportunities for adults and children to spend time together and separately.

For information: Generations Touring Company, PO Box 20187, Seattle, WA 98102; 888-415-9100 or 206-325-2830; www.generationstouringcompany.com.

GRANDKIDS AND ME CAMPS

Take your grandchildren to camp for a weekend of fun and togetherness; that is, if you live within range of the twin cities of Minneapolis/St. Paul, Minnesota. Grandkids And Me Camps offers a couple of affordable three-day weekend camps each year that give you a chance to spend quality time together and enjoy one another's company. Exclusively for grandparents of all ages and children between the ages of 4 and 13, one is scheduled in the spring and another in the fall at Camp Icagawahn near Amery, Wisconsin, 75 miles from the Twin Cities. Activities include crafts, canoeing, hiking, bird-watching, singing, wagon rides, music, dancing, telling stories around the campfire, and old-fashioned hoedowns.

For information: Grandkids And Me Camps, 1764 Hampshire Ave., St. Paul, MN 55116; 651-695-1988; www.grand kidsandme.com.

GRANDTRAVEL

This company pioneered the notion of sending grandparents and their grandchildren off on vacations together. For grandparents of any age and children from 7 to 17, its tours go to many parts of the world, including London, Paris, New York, South America, Scandinavia, Greece, the national parks, the Pacific Northwest, Kenya, Southern Africa, Australia, and Italy. It even schedules a transatlantic crossing on the *Queen Mary 2*. If you want to travel on your own, the agency will also arrange a special tour just for your family group. You needn't be an authentic grandparent, either—aunts, uncles, cousins, godparents, and other surrogate grandparents are welcome. Its 5- to 15-day tours are deluxe, educational, and limited to groups of 20.

Tours, each designated for certain ages of children, are led by teacher-escorts and always include plenty of rest stops and opportunities for both generations to spend time alone with their own age groups. As part of the package, Grand-travel provides predeparture counseling to help you deal with any special concerns such as what to pack or how to deal with kids who miss their moms.

For information: Grandtravel, 1920 N St. NW, Washington, DC 20036; 800-247-7651 or 202-785-8901; www.grandtrvl.com.

LOEWS HOTELS

Generation G packages, designed for grandparents and kids, are available year-round at all Loews hotels and resorts in the U.S. and Canada. They vary by city and season, but all of them include accommodations, special activities, and a $10 phone card for the grandchildren to call home. See Chapter 4 for details.

For information: 800-23-LOEWS (800-235-6397); www.loewshotels.com.

RASCALS IN PARADISE

Specializing in family vacations for parents and children, Rascals in Paradise also invites grandparents and grandchildren to go along on its adventure trips to places such as Mexico and the Caribbean, the Bahamas, Europe, New Zealand, Thailand, Australia, the Canadian Rockies, Africa, the Galapagos Islands, Hawaii, Alaska, and ranches in the West. All group trips, three to six families per group, include escorts who plan activities for the older children and arrange baby-sitters for the little ones. This agency will plan independent vacations, too, as well as family reunions and other multigenerational celebrations.

For information: Rascals in Paradise, 1 Daniel Burnham Ct., Ste. 105C, San Francisco, CA 94109; 800-872-7225 or 415-921-7000; www.rascalsinparadise.com.

RIVERBARGE EXCURSIONS

Aboard the 198-passenger riverboat *River Explorer*, the only hotel barge traveling America's inland waterways, you'll chug along on a four- to ten-day excursion exploring the country on its famous rivers. You'll stop along the way to visit nearby towns, eat home-style meals on board, and enjoy regional entertainment. Pricing is all-inclusive, including tips. Even better, you can take your grandchildren on one of the barge's Grand Vacations, scheduled year-round, that invite children 12 and under to sail free when sharing your stateroom and older youngsters up to 18 to sail half price when staying in their own rooms.

By the way, if you are a teacher, active or retired, you can travel half price.

For information: RiverBarge Excursion Lines, 201 Opelousas Ave., New Orleans, LA 70114; 888-GOBARGE (888-462-2743); www.riverbarge.com.

SAGAMORE GRANDS CAMP

Spend a week with the grandkids (no parents allowed) at Grandparent-Grandchild Summer Camp held annually at the Sagamore Conference Center, the Vanderbilt family's former summer retreat in the Adirondacks. Children age four or older are welcome, as are teenagers. This popular program, scheduled for two sessions in July every year, is designed to foster the vital connections between generations and teach stewardship and respect for nature.

Mornings at camp are spent hiking, swimming, canoeing, biking, berry picking, and other activities. Afternoons you may choose swimming, crafts or music, or simply relaxing. In late afternoon, the grandparents meet to discuss their own issues while the children play games. Evenings, there are music shows, night hikes, square dances, campfires, and gala "talent shows."

Other intergenerational programs take place at the camp in August in cooperation with Elderhostel.

For information: Great Camp Sagamore, PO Box 40, Raquette Lake, NY 13436; 315-354-5311; www.sagamore .org/camps.cfm.

SENIOR WOMEN'S TRAVEL

Recently added to the roster of journeys by Senior Women's Travel, which plans trips exclusively for solo women travelers over 50, are its grandmother/grandchildren adventures. One, Adventures in Paris, is just for the girls, and it takes you and your school-age granddaughters on a one-week trip to Paris, with side trips to Versailles and Giverny. Others that include grandsons too are planned for Costa Rica or the northern national parks. All are scheduled in the summer.

For information: Senior Women's Travel, 136 E. 56th St., New York, NY 10022; 212-838-4740; www.poshnosh.com.

SIERRA CLUB

Among the famous outings of the Sierra Club, the largest grassroots environmental group in the country, are a few affordable summertime vacations for grandparents and their grandchildren. One, long an annual event, is a six-day stay at the club's Clair Tappan Lodge in Tahoe National Forest in California. The laid-back holiday is designed for people between the ages of 5 and 95 who may pick and choose among activities that include short hikes, fishing, lake swimming, a beach picnic, and a tram ride at Squaw Valley. Lodging and meals are part of the package.

Check with the club for information about more intergenerational vacations, a few of which are planned every year. Recent adventures, for example, have included a four-day river rafting adventure for grandparents and kids in Dinosaur National Monument in Utah and a multigenerational tour of Hawaii Volcanoes National Park on the Big Island of Hawaii.

Participants must be members of the club. If you consider yourself a senior, your yearly membership costs only $24, compared to $39 for other adults. Two seniors in the same household may join for $32 a year, compared to $47 for younger adults.

For information: Sierra Club Outing Dept., 85 Second St., San Francisco, CA 94105; 415-977-5522; www.outings .sierraclub.org/outings/national.

STRATHCONA PARK LODGE

With special programs in the wilderness for all manner of people, Strathcona Park Lodge includes intergenerational weeks throughout the summer for active grandparents and kids ages 9 through 14, one grandchild per grandparent. The Lodge, located on Vancouver Island and surrounded by snowy peaks and dense forests, specializes in wilderness courses and outdoor adventures. Activities for the two of you include canoeing, orienteering, rock climbing, learning survival techniques, natural history discussions, and camping out. Accommodations are in lodges, timber chalets, or waterfront cottages. Buffet meals are included.

For information: Strathcona Park Lodge, PO Box 2160, Campbell River, BC V9W 5C5, Canada; 250-286-3122; www.strathcona.bc.ca.

VISTA TOURS

The family tours offered by Vista are designed for children and their relatives, whether grandparents, parents, aunts and uncles, or otherwise. There are several different trips, ranging from 4 to 14 days, such as the Railroads of the Rockies, the Idaho and Oregon Trail, and the California National Parks. Activities are planned for the different generations separately and together.

For information: Vista Tours, 1923 N. Carson St., Ste. 105, Carson City, NV 89701; 800-647-0800 or 775-882-2100; www.frontiertours.com.

WARREN RIVER EXPEDITIONS

Take the grandkids down the Salmon River in Idaho on a raft trip run by Warren River Expeditions. On special summer trips reserved for grandparents and grandchildren, you'll float through canyons and forests, taking time to swim and kayak. You'll sleep in comfortable backcountry lodges, some quite rustic, along the river's edge and have plenty of exciting adventures on the big rubber rafts powered by expert oarspeople. At least two midsummer departures, with a 10 percent discount for those over 55 and 25 percent for children 14 and under, are reserved each summer for the two generations.

For information: Warren River Expeditions, PO Box 1375, Salmon, ID 83467-1375; 800-765-0421 or 208-756-6387; www.raftidaho.com.

12

Singles on the Road

If you're single, on your own again, have a partner who isn't the traveling kind and couldn't care less about seeing Venice, or simply like to travel independently, you can do it your way. Many people love to vacation on their own, never having to cater to anyone else's whims or demands about where to go, when to eat, how long to stay at the museum, or what time to go to bed. Others, however, find traveling solo to be a rather lonely business and would prefer not to wander around the world by themselves.

To encourage and accommodate the growing numbers of mature single travelers, an increasing number of tour companies, cruise lines, and clubs now cater to them. Some plan itineraries for the independents, while others organize singles group tours or schedule special departure dates specifically for solo travelers.

Most mix them with everyone else but try to match them up with a roommate so they can avoid paying a single supplement, the extra charge for the privilege of sole occupancy of a room or cabin. Another way to avoid paying more than paired people is to watch for the special deals when single supplements are waived altogether. These are usually offered on off-peak packages with space that may otherwise go unclaimed.

Going with a group provides ready-made companions and an organized travel plan. But if you don't want to go places by yourself even in a group, consider joining a matchmaker club that helps you find a fellow traveler who is also looking for someone with whom to share adventures and expenses.

Finally, one of the surest ways to enjoy a vacation on your own is to sign up for a trip that features activities that especially intrigue you, because you'll meet people who like the same things you do. Consider, for example, art tours, bike trips, golf schools, gourmet tours, tennis camps, language programs, or volunteer vacations.

TOURS FOR SOLO TRAVELERS

Most tour operators and agencies specializing in escorted trips for people in their prime will try to find you a same-sex roommate to share your room or cabin so you do not have to pay a single supplement. And, if they can't manage to find a suitable roommate for you, they will usually reduce the supplement or even cancel it. Some offer singles-only trips too. In any case, keep in mind that you'll hardly have time or opportunity to be lonely on the typical escorted tour run by these agencies. If you are planning an extended stay in just one location, however, you may have more need for company.

ALL SINGLES TRAVEL

Exclusively for the single traveler, All Singles Travel plans many trips a year for solos of all ages but always schedules at least one or two specifically for those over 60 who prefer traveling with other people around their own age. Many of its adventures are cruises, but there are land trips as well, such as tours to the Greek Islands, Iceland, the Rocky Mountains, and Costa Rica.

For information: TSW Singles Vacations, 800-717-3231 or 770-645-3241; www.allsinglestravel.com.

CONNECTING SOLO TRAVEL NETWORK

A club based in Canada, Connecting is a "solo travel network" that aims to keep its more than 1,500 single members—almost half of them over 50—in touch with each other, advising them on where to go, what to do, and how to enjoy their travel alone or with friends. Members pay a yearly fee of $35 (Canadian) or $28 (U.S.) for an informative bimonthly newsletter sent by e-mail; or if they prefer to have the newsletter delivered by regular mail, $50 (Canadian) or $45 (U.S.). Both versions offer access to other services, such as a constantly updated Singles-Friendly Travel Directory. The newsletter includes information on upcoming singles trips and cruises, including those reserved for "mature" travelers, unlimited free listings for members looking for compatible travel companions, reader recommendations, travel tips and tales, and a directory of travel companies that offer special accommodations or programs

MERRY WIDOWS DANCE TOURS

Designed for solo women from 50 to 90 who love to dance but don't have partners, **Merry Widows Dance Tours** runs many cruises every year to places such as the Caribbean, Southeast Asia, Alaska, Greece and the Mediterranean, and the Panama Canal. The trips range from 7 days to 18. Sponsored by the AAA Auto Club South, the cruises take along their own gentleman hosts, one professional dancer for every four women. Each woman receives a dance card that rotates her partners every night throughout the cruise, whether she's a beginner or a polished dancer. The men are also rotated at the dinner tables so everyone gets the pleasure of their company. You don't have to be a widow and you don't even have to know the cha-cha or even the waltz to enjoy these trips. If you are traveling alone and wish to avoid paying a single supplement, you will be assigned a roommate.

For information: Merry Widows Dance Tours, AAA Auto Club South, 1515 N. Westshore Blvd., Tampa, FL 33607; 800-955-1365 or 813-289-5004.

for singles. An added benefit: you may participate in the Hospitality Program, which recruits volunteers to spend time with visiting members from elsewhere.

For information: Connecting: Solo Travel Network, 689 Park Rd., Gibsons, BC V0N 1V7; 800-557-1757 or 604-886-9099; www.cstn.org.

GO SOLO TRAVEL CLUB

This club for "the mature and discriminating traveler without a partner" guarantees private rooms on all trips, domestic and overseas, and no single supplements for those traveling alone. And its guided group tours travel in their own private buses. A newsletter issued three times a year offers travel tips and announcements of upcoming tours that have recently included Ireland, Branson, Paris, San Francisco, Santa Fe, and Alaska. The annual fee of $35 is deducted from the cost of your first trip of the year.

For information: Go Solo Travel Club, Tallyho Travel, 92 E. Main St., Elmsford, NY 10523; 800-354-4484; www.go solotravelclub.com.

GOING SOLO TRAVEL CLUB

A club that caters to solo travelers, singles, or people whose spouses want to stay home, Going Solo costs nothing to join and will send you announcements of upcoming trips as they are scheduled. Members may be any age, but most are between 35 and 70. Located in Calgary, Canada, the club has many U.S. members and welcomes them all on its worldwide escorted tours to places like England, Africa, Guatemala, Belize, Mexico, and Turkey.

TRAVELING ON YOUR OWN

For those who travel without a companion, here's a website run by a long-time flight attendant and author that offers resources, safety tips, tour information, and other useful advice to help you happily go solo. It posts new solo-travel tips every month, publishes a free monthly newsletter, and provides a place to share opinions and recommendations.

For information: www.travelaloneandloveit.com.; 7210-D Adams St., Willowbrook, IL 60527; 630-654-1156 or editor @travelaloneandloveit.com.

You will be matched up with a roommate if you want one and wish to avoid the single supplement fee. Or bring your own roommate and share a room.

For more information: Going Solo Travel Club, 629 11th Ave. SW, Calgary, AB T2R OE1; 888-446-7656 (outside Alberta) or 403-298-3532; www.goingsolotravel.com.

O SOLO MIO SINGLES TOURS

A travel club for singles who like to vacation in groups, O Solo Mio welcomes members of all ages but designs some of its tours specifically for "late 40s-plus" who prefer traveling with other singles their own age. Members who pay a fee of $50 a year receive a quarterly newsletter announcing upcoming plans and may ask to be matched with a roommate to avoid paying a single supplement fee. The many tours and cruises vary every year, but recent destinations have included Nova Scotia and Prince Edward Island, Italy, China, the Greek Isles, Branson, and Mexico.

SPECIAL FOR SOLO DINERS

Check out **SoloDining.com** if you eat meals alone for pleasure or business whether in your own hometown or on the road. It publishes a bimonthly newsletter (mailed) and maintains a website (with a new solo travel section). Both of them are full of tips and strategies to increase your options and comfort as a solo diner.

For information: SoloDining.com, PO Box 2664, Carlsbad, CA 92018; 800-299-1079 or 768-720-1060; www.solodining.com.

For information: O Solo Mio Singles Tours, 160 Main St., Los Altos, CA 94024; 800-959-8568 or 650-917-0817; www.osolomio.com.

SENIOR WOMEN'S TRAVEL

Senior Women's Travel is for "active and adventurous 50-plus women with a passion for travel." Its upscale, small-group guided tours concentrate on food, history, art, music, and literature. They take you to Paris, Venice, Rome, Barcelona, and the Riviera, as well as plenty of fascinating places in the U.S.

Grandmother/grandchildren tours are recent additions. Adventures in Paris takes grandmothers and school-age granddaughters on whirlwind tours of Paris, Venice, or Florence during the summer vacation. Others scheduled for the summer take the boys along too, these going to places like Costa Rica or the northern national parks.

For information: Senior Women's Travel, 136 E. 56th St., New York, NY 10022; 212-838-4740; www.poshnosh .com.

SOLO'S HOLIDAYS

The U.K.'s largest singles tour operator, Solo's Holidays offers hosted group vacations for unattached people. Although it is based in England, it will happily take Americans and Canadians on tour all over the world, giving them a chance to talk, dine, dance, and share experiences with other lone travelers. All trips are divided into three groups, for ages 25 to 45, 28 to 55, and 40-plus, although sometimes the ages are mixed.

FOR WOMEN ONLY

Journeywoman.com is a free online resource for women travelers. Packed with female-oriented travel information, tips, advice, and stories designed to inform and inspire solo travelers of any age, it includes a special section for the "50-plus adventuress." Topics range from female-friendly cities around the world to culturally correct clothing, health concerns, safety advice, money-saving tactics, and much more. The site also allows you to sign up for a free quarterly e-newsletter that is full of travel tips and advice for women.

A sister site is HERmail.net, a free e-mail–based service that allows you to connect with other women all over the world who are ready to offer advice and assistance when you visit their cities or countries.

For information: www.journeywoman.com; 416-929-7654; and www.hermail.net.

For information: Solo's Holidays, 54-58 High St., Edgware, Middlesex HA8 7EJ, England; e-mail travel@soloholidays .co.uk; www.solosholidays.co.uk.

HOOK-UPS FOR SOLO RVers

RVers who travel alone in their motor homes or vans can hook up with others in the same circumstances when they join one of the groups mentioned on this and the next few pages. All of the clubs provide opportunities to travel together or to meet at campgrounds on the road, making friends with fellow travelers and having a fine time. According to a survey by the Travel Industry Association of America, more than half of RV travelers are 55 or older and retired, so they tend to take longer-than-average trips.

FRIENDLY ROAMERS

Founded by former members of Loners on Wheels, Friendly Roamers is open to everyone, couples as well as singles, so friendships and RV activities can be continued despite a change of marital status or travel arrangements. Membership gets you admission to all club events, such as rallies and campouts; a newsletter; and a membership directory. Annual dues are $10 plus a one-time registration fee of $5 for new members. Local chapters hold their own events and join the others as well.

For information: Friendly Roamers, c/o Herbert Ott, PO Box 3153, Paradise, CA 95967; 530-872-8702.

LONERS OF AMERICA (LOA)

LOA is a club for single campers who enjoy traveling together. Established in 1987, it currently has 29 chapters throughout the country and well more than 500 active members from their 40s to their 90s, almost all retired and widowed, divorced, or otherwise single. Many of them live year-round in their motor homes or vans, and others hit the road only occasionally. They camp, rally, and caravan together, often meeting at special campgrounds that cater to solo campers.

A not-for-profit, member-operated organization, the club publishes a biannual membership directory and a lively monthly newsletter that keeps its members in touch and informs them about campouts and rallies all over the country. The chapters organize their own events as well. Currently, dues are $40 a year plus a $5 registration fee for new members.

For information: Loners of America, Rte. 2, PO Box 2495 E, Elsimore, MO 63937; www.lonersofamerica.net.

LONERS ON WHEELS (LOW)

A camping and travel club for mature single men and women, Loners on Wheels is not a lonely hearts club or a matchmaking service but simply an association of friends and extended family who enjoy traveling, camping, RV caravaning, and camaraderie. With 68 chapters located throughout the U.S., Canada, and Mexico, LOW now has a membership of about 2,400 unpartnered travelers. The chapters schedule hundreds of campouts, rallies, and other events during the year at campgrounds, some of which are remote and cost little.

The club's newly acquired LOW-HI RV Ranch in Deming, New Mexico (which also serves as its headquarters), offers special rates for club members, two rallies a year, dances and games in the clubhouse, and occasional forays into Mexico. A monthly newsletter and an annual directory keep everyone up-to-date and in touch.

Annual dues at this writing are $45 U.S. and $54 Canadian, plus a onetime enrollment fee of $5.

For information: Loners on Wheels, PO Box 1060-WB, Cape Girardeau, MO 63702; 888-569-4478 or 505-546-4058; www.lonersonwheels.com. Ask for a free sample newsletter.

RVing WOMEN

Women travelers who take to the highways in recreational vehicles can get advice and support from RVing Women, a club with more than 4,000 female members. The group sponsors rallies, caravans, and other events across the U.S., Canada, and Mexico, plus weekend RV maintenance and driving classes in many locations around the country. Members pay an annual fee of $45 and receive a bimonthly magazine that covers topics such as safety, scams on the road, vehicle maintenance, and announcements of upcoming events and includes an annual directory of members.

For information: RVing Women, PO Box 1940, Apache Junction, AZ 85217; 888-55-RVING (888-557-8464) or 480-671-6226; www.rvingwomen.com.

S*M*A*R*T

A club for retired and active members of the U.S. and Canadian armed forces, Special Military Active-Retired Travel Club (S*M*A*R*T) provides social and recreational activities for its more than 3,000 members with "an avid interest in recreational vehicles." Through a network of 60 chapters, it provides seminars and workshops, assists military installations with the improvement of their campgrounds, and sponsors annual rallies.

The club offers several caravans a year in many destinations, including Arkansas, Tennessee, and several western states. It also tours Canada, Mexico, and Alaska, often in fully equipped rented RVs. A national muster, packed with activities, entertainment, seminars, and fellowship, is held every year.

To join, U.S. residents pay an initiation fee of $10 and then $30 a year per family; Canadian residents pay a $15 initiation fee and $35 dues per family, while associate members (disabled, former POWs, Medal of Honor recipients, surviving spouses of eligible members) pay a $10 initiation fee, then $15 a year.

For information: S*M*A*R*T, Inc., 600 University Office Blvd., Pensacola, FL 32504; 800-354-7681 or 850-478-1986; www.smartrving.net.

13

Learning After 50

ave you always wanted to speak Swedish; study African birds; examine Eskimo culture; learn to paddle a canoe or ski down a mountain; or delve into archaeology, international finance, horticulture, the language of whales, or great literature of the 19th century? Now is the time to do it. If you're a typical member of the over-50 generation, you're in good shape, healthy, and alert, with the energy and the time to pursue new interests. So why not go back to school and learn all those things you've always wished you knew? Many of us find it easier and cheaper than ever to go back to school.

Most states have reduced their state university fees for older learners to a mere pittance and, in addition, allow seniors to audit courses for free or close to it. For example, at the University of New Hampshire, state residents who are over 65 may take up to two courses per semester at no cost. At many colleges and universities in Texas, those 65 and over may enroll in up to six hours of college credit courses annually with no tuition. If you join California's Over Sixty Program, you'll pay only $3 a semester to earn credit toward a degree. And the University of Utah invites residents 62 and older to audit as many classes as they like for $25 per semester.

Many other colleges offer similar programs. To join the student population at an institution near you, call the admissions office and ask what the deal is for someone your age.

In addition, there are special programs as well as entire schools designed specifically for older students, many of them affiliated with the Institutes for Learning in Retirement (more information later in this chapter).

A growing number of retirement communities have also formed links with nearby colleges to offer special educational opportunities to their residents. Among them are the Kendel at Ithaca, New York, with ties to Cornell University and Ithaca College; and Oak Hammock, which is affiliated with the University of Florida at Gainesville.

Going back to class is an excellent way to generate feelings of accomplishment and to exercise the mind—and one of the best ways to make new friends. It doesn't always mean you'll have to turn in term papers or take excruciatingly difficult exams. Sign up for one class a week on flower arranging or Spanish conversation or a once-a-month lecture series on managing your money. Register as a part-time or full-time student in a traditional university program. Or take a learning vacation on a college campus. Do it *your* way.

You don't even have to attend classes to learn on vacation. You can go on archaeological digs, count butterflies, help save turtles from extinction, brush up on your bassoon playing, listen to opera, search for Roman remains in England, study dancing or Belgian cuisine, or go on safari in Africa.

CHAUTAUQUA INSTITUTION

For more than a century people have been traveling up to the shores of Lake Chautauqua, in southwestern New York, to a cultural summer center set in a quaint Victorian village nestled around a lake. The 856-acre hilltop complex offers a wide variety of educational programs, including summer weeks and off-season weekends designed for people over the age of 55. The 55-Plus Weekends and the Residential Week for Older Adults are filled up far in advance, so if you are interested, don't waste a moment before signing up.

Each 55-Plus Weekend has a specific focus, such as the U.S. Constitution, natural history, national politics, music appreciation, or trade relations with Japan. They include discussions, workshops, lectures, films, recreational activities, and evening entertainment, all led by professionals. Housing and meals are available in a residence hall with double rooms and shared baths.

The Residential Week for Older Adults is similar but longer and includes lodging and meals as well as admittance to other happenings at the center.

It's all quite cheap. The cost of tuition, room, meals, and planned activities for a Residential Week is currently $500, while a 55-Plus Weekend costs $40 for commuters or $175 with accommodations and meals.

For information: Program Center for Older Adults, Chautauqua, NY 14722; 800-836-2787 or 716-357-6250; www .ciweb.org.

CLOSE UP WASHINGTON

For a behind-the-scenes view of the nation's capital, sign up for one of Close Up's five- or six-night seminars for older adults in Washington, D.C. You'll visit Capitol Hill and the White House, attend classes on current events, study the presidents, exchange views with national political leaders, and gain insights on public policy. You'll stay at a comfortable hotel, and all meals, activities, in-town transportation, and perhaps a night at the theater are included in the modest fee. There's time for relaxation, conversation, social events, and theater in and around the city.

There are a few ways to participate. First, you can sign up with Elderhostel for a five-night program. Second, if you have a group of 35 or more participants, you can arrange for your own Lifelong Learning Series program in the nation's capital by calling the Close Up Foundation. The third way to participate is to join the Congressional Senior Citizen Intern Program, a one-week program for people 60-plus. You'll spend time in the Capitol Hill office of a member of Congress; engage in study visits to monuments, the Supreme Court, and/or a foreign embassy; explore key topics with members of Congress, journalists, lobbyists, and other policy experts; meet with a diplomatic official; and more.

For information: Close Up Foundation, 44 Canal Center Plaza, Alexandria, VA 22314; 800-CLOSEUP (800-256-7387); www.closeup.org/lifelong.htm.

THE COLLEGE AT 60

At Fordham University's The College at 60, you're welcome at a mere 50, despite its name. It offers you the option to take classes at leisure or become fully matriculated and pursue a college degree. Meanwhile, you learn in a community of peers.

As an enrolled student, you are entitled to a discount on courses in liberal arts at Fordham's Lincoln Center Campus. You pay half the regular university tuition to take the courses for credit and only half of that to audit. The 13-week courses are taught by university faculty. Included are a lecture series and the use of all college facilities. After taking four courses, you are eligible to enter the Fordham College of Cultural Studies at a 50 percent discount on tuition if you receive Social Security benefits.

For information: The College at 60, Fordham University at Lincoln Center, 113 W. 60th St., Room 301, New York, NY 10023; 212-636-6000; www.fordham.edu/collegeat60.

FEDERAL WEBSITE FOR SENIORS

FirstGov for Seniors (www.seniors.gov) is a website created specifically for older adults who are seeking information about government services. Maintained by the Social Security Administration, it helps users have secure and easy access to all government sites that provide services and benefits for seniors and also provides links to all federal agencies and agencies at the state and local levels in all 50 states. Still evolving, this site will eventually assist seniors with helpful services, resources, and information 24 hours a day, allowing them to complete applications and forms online and submit them electronically.

Currently the site offers information on consumer protection, education, health, legislation, computers, tax assistance, travel, volunteerism, and more.

COLLEGE FOR SENIORS

A membership program for those 50 or older, the College for Seniors is a component of the North Carolina Center for Creative Retirement at the University of North Carolina at Asheville. The courses, most of them taught by peer seniors, range from Chaucer to computers, foreign affairs to opera, and chemistry to tap dancing. The per-term fee for as many course, as you like is currently $56 to $112, depending on the season and the number of weeks involved. Added benefits include social events, travel programs, wellness clinics, exploration weekends, library privileges, parking decals, and access to the fitness center.

For information: College for Seniors, 1 University Hts., CPO #1660, UNCA, Asheville, NC 28804; 828-251-6384; www.unca.edu/ncccr.

ELDERHOSTEL

Elderhostel, the largest educational travel organization in the world, offers learning vacations for mature Americans, as well as some of the world's best bargains. Its remarkably affordable and infinitely varied short-term noncredit programs attract nearly 200,000 participants a year. All are hosted by a network of more than 3,000 educational and cultural sites, including colleges and universities, conference centers, state and national parks, museums, outdoor educational centers, and many others in all 50 states and more than 100 countries.

The only requirement for participation is that you must be 55 or older. An accompanying spouse or adult companion may be younger. No previous educational background is required, and there are no exams or grades and only occasional homework. The one- to four-week programs with classes on every conceivable topic are taught by the host institutions' faculty, staff, and local experts and include excursions and social activities.

Accommodations range from hotels or college dormitories to conference centers, cruise ships, barges, rustic cabins, and resorts. Meals are included. Most domestic programs last for five or six nights, while the overseas programs are planned for one to four weeks and include transportation. In addition to the longer programs, Elderhostel has added one-day and weekend excursions. The weekenders run Thursday or Friday evening to Sunday or Monday noon and take place in major American cities.

The many course offerings are listed in voluminous seasonal catalogs. You may also view them 24 hours a day, 7 days a week, on the Web at www.elderhostel.org, where you may search by subject, date, or location.

Many of the programs include sports and other outdoor activities such as canoeing, skiing, biking, rafting, golfing, and walking (see Chapter 14). The service programs (see Chapter 19) connect you to a wide variety of volunteer or-

ELDERHOSTEL SCHOLARSHIPS

Elderhostel offers a limited number of full or partial scholarships, to be used only in the U.S., for people who find the tuition costs of the programs beyond their means. Funds to cover travel costs are not included, and eligibility is determined upon completion of an application that includes a confidential questionnaire. Scholarship programs in Alaska and Hawaii are available only to residents of those states.

For information: Write to Elderhostel, 11 Avenue de Lafayette, Boston, MA 02111. Attention: Scholarships.

ganizations that provide significant services all over the world.

Elderhostel's Train Treks programs use trains as moving classrooms, combining rail travel with learning as you explore large expanses of territory, from Canada and the U.S. to China. The Adventures Afloat program uses ships as a way to visit and study remote places.

Intergenerational and family programs for members and their children or grandchildren are another option, along with many others. For a more independent experience, the City Highlights programs in foreign countries allow you an opportunity to explore on your own after information sessions with the group.

Elderhostel's Exploring North America programs feature on-the-move itineraries from the mid-Atlantic and the South to the Pacific, listed by geographic region and theme. Themes currently include American heritage, American landscapes, cultural arts, food and wine, houses and gardens, national parks, and signature cities. On these trips, you usually move from place to place, spending time in two or three locations, studying and exploring as you go.

And finally, there's the new Elderhostel Road Scholar program for adults of all ages that takes small groups for behind-the-scenes experiences in very special little-known places. Programs run from five nights to two weeks. More expensive than other Elderhostel excursions, the tours have less structure and more free time, and lodging in three- or four-star hotels.

For information: Elderhostel, 11 Avenue de Lafayette, Boston, MA 02111; 877-426-8056 or 617-426-7788; www .elderhostel.org.

INTERHOSTEL

Founded in 1984 by the University of New Hampshire, Interhostel was the first to offer educational travel programs for adults 50-plus—all-inclusive, one-week tours and cruises in the U.S. and two-week adventures packed with activities everywhere from New Zealand, Germany, France, and Canada to South America and Australia. Each program is hosted by a university or educational institution in the region you're visiting whose faculty and local experts lead the activities, sightseeing, and field trips.

On the overseas trips, you lodge in three- to four-star hotels, eat the local food, and get a first-hand look at the world, accompanied by a UNH faculty or staff member. The moderate cost covers airfare, accommodations, meals, tuition, ground transportation, and all of the activities from bus tours to boat trips and concerts. See Chapter 14 for Interhostel's walking tours abroad.

Recent programs in the U.S. have taken their 50-plus travelers (and spouses over 40) to the Southwest, New Orleans, Louisiana, New Mexico, Arizona, Hawaii, Alaska, and more.

The University of New Hampshire also offers Family-Hostel Learning vacations for grandparents and/or parents and school-age children. See Chapter 11.

For information: Interhostel, 6 Garrison Ave., Durham, NH 03824; 800-733-9753 or 603-862-1147; www.learn.unh.edu/interhostel.

NATIONAL ACADEMY OF OLDER CANADIANS (NAOC)

Based in Vancouver, the NAOC's mission is to involve Canadians over the age of 45 in lifelong learning and to help them keep pace with modern technology. It offers computer classes with "senior-friendly" courses. The membership fee is $17 (Canadian) a year or $10 for six months.

For information: National Academy of Older Canadians, 411 Dunsmuir St., Vancouver, BC V6B 1X4; 604-681-3767; www.vcn.bc.ca/naoc.

OASIS

OASIS is a nonprofit organization sponsored by the May Department Stores Company in collaboration with local hospitals, medical centers, government agencies, and other participants through a network of centers in 26 cities across the nation. Its purpose is to enrich the lives of people over 55 by providing programs in the arts, humanities, wellness, and technology and volunteer opportunities to its members. At its centers, OASIS offers classes ranging from French conversation and the visual arts to dance, bridge, creative writing, history, exercise, classical music, points of law, and prevention of osteoporosis. There are also special events such as concerts, plays, museum visits, lectures, and even trips and cruises. Membership is free.

For information: The OASIS Institute, 7710 Carondelet Ave., Ste. 125, St. Louis, MO 63105; 314-862-2933; www.oasis net.org.

SEMESTER AT SEA

A 100-day educational voyage around the world, Semester at Sea, academically sponsored by the University of Pittsburgh and administered by the Institute for Shipboard Education, takes more than 600 college students and about 60 "senior scholars" on a unique learning experience that is designed to advance the exchange of understanding and knowledge among cultures. The S.S. *Universe Explorer*, a former passenger ship refitted as a floating campus, circumnavigates the earth twice a year, visiting countries that have included Japan, China, India, Malaysia, Kenya, Brazil, Venezuela, Egypt, Israel, South Africa, Greece, Turkey, Vietnam, and Morocco.

While the college students earn credit hours toward an undergraduate degree, the older participants may audit classes or enroll for full credit, choosing from among 60 courses taught by faculty from various universities. Onboard courses range from anthropology and biological sciences to economics, fine arts, philosophy, political science, and religion. Lengthy stays in each port of call give students a chance to experience the peoples and cultures firsthand.

Amenities include an adult coordinator; entertainment; buffet-style meals; lectures; discussion groups; and guest scholars with expertise in local cultures, films, art shows, sports, and more.

In addition to the long voyage scheduled during the spring and fall, a new, condensed 65-day summertime Semester at Sea combines a smaller number of college students and seniors. From Vancouver, B.C., to Sitka, Alaska, then to Vladavlostok, Pusan, Shanghai, Hanoi, Keelung, and Osaka to Seattle, the group travels aboard the MTS *Explorer*, learning all the way.

For information: Semester at Sea, 811 William Pitt Union, University of Pittsburgh, Pittsburgh, PA 15260; 800-854-0195 or 412-648-7490; www.semesteratsea.com.

SENIOR SUMMER SCHOOL

In this program, you can spend two to ten weeks in the summer taking classes at your choice of seven college campuses in vacation locations: San Diego State University; University of Wisconsin at Madison; University of Pittsburgh at Greenburgh; Massachusetts College of Art at Boston; University of Judaism in Los Angeles; Appalachian State University in Boone, North Carolina; and Mount Allison University in New Brunswick, Canada.

The courses are college level but there are no grades, compulsory papers, or mandatory attendance. Accommodations and meals are in student residence halls. Sightseeing trips, excursions, classes, weekly housekeeping, and social activities are all part of the deal. While most students are in their mid-60s, people of any age are welcome to enroll. There are no previous educational requirements.
For information: Senior Summer School, PO Box 4424, Deerfield Beach, FL 33442; 800-847-2466; www.seniorsum merschool.com.

SENIOR VENTURES IN OREGON

Southern Oregon University in Ashland is where you can sign up for one- or two-week educational theater programs exclusively for people at least 50 years of age (and companions who may be younger). The summer programs coincide with Ashland's famous annual Oregon Shakespeare Festival, and classes are taught by actors, backstage professionals, and Shakespearean scholars. You stay on campus and eat your meals there. Added bonus: theater tickets to current productions. A few travel adventures, such as a Canadian theater expedition, are also offered.

For information: Senior Ventures, Southern Oregon University, 1250 Siskiyu Blvd., Ashland, OR 97520; 800-257-0577 or 541-552-6285; www.sou.edu/seniorventures.htm.

TRAVELEARN

The upscale learning vacations by TraveLearn take small groups of adults all over the world, putting you up in first-class or deluxe accommodations and providing local lecturers and escorts who are experts in their fields and in-country guides from cooperating universities and colleges in each destination. You'll learn through on-site lectures, seminars, meals with local families, visits to homes and workplaces, and field trips. Destinations include Ireland, Egypt, Kenya, China, Morocco, Greece, Italy, Turkey, South Africa, Costa Rica, Peru, Belize, Australia, and Central Europe. If you are traveling alone and wish to share a room with another single traveler, you are guaranteed the double rate if you register 90 days in advance, even if a roommate is not found for you.

For information: TraveLearn, PO Box 556, Hawley, PA 1848; 800-235-9114 or 570-226-9114; www.travelearn.com.

UNIVERSITY VACATIONS

Summer scholars may attend a range of six-day study programs, arranged by University Vacations, at prestigious institutions such as Yale, Princeton, University of Prague, Trinity College in Dublin, and Cambridge and Oxford universities in England. In-depth classroom lectures by university faculty are augmented by field trips, walking tours, excursions, and notable meals. Students live on campus or in nearby hotels and eat in fine restaurants. The programs are open to all ages but are largely attended by older students.

For information: University Vacations, 3660 Bougainvillea Rd., Coconut Grove, FL 33133; 800-792-0100 or 305-567-2904; www.universityvacations.com.

UTAH STATE UNIVERSITY SUMMER CITIZENS

Spend three months—May to August—at Utah State University in Logan where about 1,000 seniors participate in the Summer Citizens Program and choose from a variety of courses taught by university professors and local experts, attend cultural events, live in student housing, participate in recreational activities, and enjoy the pleasant temperatures.

An ID card that costs $80 is your ticket to the program and gets you into all parts of the campus from theaters to libraries, computer labs, exercise rooms, tennis courts, parking lots, and the swimming pool. You get a one- to three-week course free with the card, then pay $30 to $60 for others. Your housing may be on campus or off, and free shuttles and buses take you everywhere you want to go at the university or in the city. Housing costs range from $1,000 to $2,000 for the three months, depending on the amenities.

Three-week packages are also available for those with less time to spend getting smart.

For information: Summer Citizens Program, Utah State University, 5005 Old Main Hill, Logan, UT 84322; 800-538-2663 or 435-797-7573; www.summercitizens.com.

LEARN COMPUTER TECHNOLOGY

SeniorNet is a national nonprofit organization dedicated to teaching older adults how to use computers and understand computer technologies. It sponsors more than 240 local SeniorNet Learning Centers all across the country, staffed by volunteers, where members may take classes and use the facilities. Independent members participate through the organization's electronic community, SeniorNet Online.

To take the classes at a learning center, you must join SeniorNet for $40 a year, which gives you other benefits as well: a quarterly newsletter; discounts on computer-related books, software, and hardware; and invitations to national conferences and regional meetings.

Without cost, you can access SeniorNet Online, where you may join any of about 600 discussion groups and share information and opinions about everything from computers to politics, finance, news, social concerns, the arts, leisure, and health.

For information: SeniorNet, 121 Second St., San Francisco, CA 94105; 800-747-6848 or 415-495-4990; www.seniornet .org.

INSTITUTES FOR LEARNING IN RETIREMENT (ILR)

Another way to learn with a group of contemporaries is to join an ILR, a community-based organization of retirement-age learners for local people who commute to the program. Located in more than 300 communities across the U.S., most of these institutes are member-run under the auspices of a host college or university. Each is independent and unique, providing noncredit academic programs developed and often led by the members themselves. The institutes have an open membership for retirement-age students regardless of previous education and charge modest membership fees.

For a directory of ILRs, or information about starting a new program in your community, contact the Elderhostel Institute Network (EIN), which helps community groups set up their own learning programs.

For information: Elderhostel Institute Network, 11 Avenue de Lafayette, Boston, MA 02111; 877-426-8056 or 617-426-7788; www.elderhostel.org.

14

Good Deals for Good Sports

Real sports never give up their sneakers. If you've been a physically active person all your life, you're certainly not going to become a couch potato now—especially since you've probably got more time, energy, and maybe funds than you ever had before to enjoy athletic activities. Besides, you can now take advantage of some interesting special privileges and adventures offered exclusively to people over the age of 49.

ELDERHOSTEL

Many Elderhostel programs (see Chapter 13) include a wide selection of outdoor and sports activities for beginners as well as experienced athletes. Among the choices are golf, birding, walking and trekking, tennis, hiking, biking, sea kayaking, sailing, whitewater rafting, wilderness canoeing, skiing, snowshoeing, and trail biking.

For information: Elderhostel, 11 Avenue de Lafayette, Boston, MA 02111; 877-426-8056 or 617-426-7788; www .elderhostel.org.

EXPLORATIONS IN TRAVEL

Specializing in outdoor and cultural vacations for women over 40, Explorations in Travel's action-filled itineraries are geared for women with energy who love the outdoors and like to travel with contemporaries, leaving the men at home. Typical trips include inn-to-inn hiking and rafting in New England, wildlife-watching in Ecuador, cycling in Ireland, spotting butterflies in Mexico, cruising the canals in England, and exploring Namibia or the Florida rivers.

A few multigenerational trips are usually planned every year for mothers and daughters, grandmothers and grand-daughters, aunts, and other female friends and relatives. The rule is that one participant is over 40, the others 21 or over. *For information:* Explorations in Travel, 2458 River Rd., Guilford, VT 05301; 877-257-0152 or 802-257-0152; www .exploretravel.com.

GUNFLINT LODGE

On the shores of the Border Lakes in the highlands of northern Minnesota, Gunflint Lodge plans many wilderness adventures for older adventurers in the spring and fall. The Senior Packages put you up for four nights in a lakeside cabin with a fireplace, sauna, and hot tub. Included are dinners and all the hiking you want on miles of trails, plus unlimited horseback riding, canoeing, mountain biking, fishing, and motorboating. The equipment is included.

For information: Gunflint Lodge, 143 S. Gunflint Lake, Grand Marais, MN 55604; 800-328-3325; www.gunflint .com.

OVER THE HILL GANG (OTHG)

This is a club that welcomes fun-loving, adventurous people from 50 to 90-plus (and younger spouses or companions) who are looking for action and contemporaries to pursue it with. No naps, no rockers, no sitting by the pool sipping planter's punch. OTHG started as a ski club many years ago (see Chapter 15), but its members can now be found participating in all kinds of activities when the ski season ends. Recent trips have included fully escorted trips to ski areas in the West, Europe, and South America. Other options include whitewater rafting in Idaho, biking in Nova Scotia, hiking in Italy, and golfing in Ireland.

The club currently has about 6,000 members in 50 states and 14 countries and 13 regional "gangs" (chapters). Run by volunteers, each local gang decides on its own activities. If there's no chapter in your vicinity, you may become a member-at-large and participate in any of the happenings.

The annual membership fee ($50 single, $80 for a couple) brings you a quarterly magazine, discounts, information about national and chapter events, and a chance to join the fun. The local gangs, in which membership is optional, charge small additional yearly dues.

For information: Over the Hill Gang International, 1820 W. Colorado Ave., Dept. G, Colorado Springs, CO 80904; 719-389-0022; www.othgi.com.

BIKE TRIPS FOR 50-PLUS

Biking has become one of America's most popular sports, and people who never dreamed they could go much farther than around the block are now pedaling up to 50 miles in a day. That includes over-the-hill bikers as well as youngsters of 16, 39, or 49. In fact, some tours and clubs are designated specifically for over-50s.

CAPE COD BICYCLE ADVENTURES

A few of this company's many bicycle tours on Cape Cod during the warm months are planned exclusively for 50-plus bikers, covering about 30 miles a day on leisurely pedals through the cape's towns and dunes. You bike in a group with a guide to three different elegant inns in your five-night tour. Included are your bicycle, four dinners, all breakfasts, a boat tour, and a few lunches, plus a support vehicle that carries your luggage and stands ready to give you a lift if you want one.

For information: Cape Cod Bicycle Adventures, 2533 State Hwy., Wellfleet, MA 02667; 888-644-4566 or 508-349-8005; www.capecodbybike.com.

COMPASS HOLIDAYS

For a "cycling break" in the heart of England—the Cotswolds, Bath and Wiltshire, Cornwall, the Severn Vail, and the Lake District—look into the guided or self-planned biking tours from Compass Holidays. With a guide, you can ride for three days, for example, around Bourton-on-the-Water, or seven days in the Cotswolds, starting and ending in Cheltenham. You can also ride on your own with maps, planned accommodations, and luggage transfers on circular routes along quiet country roads from village to village near Bath or Malmesbury. Your luggage is transported for you. For bikers over 50, this tour company—which also schedules walking tours—offers a 10 percent discount if you take a seven-night tour and 5 percent when you book tours of two nights or more and mention this book. Take your own bike or rent one there.

For this company's walking excursions, see Walking Tours later in this chapter.

For information: Compass Holidays, Cheltenham Spa Railway Station, Queens Rd., Cheltenham, Gloucestershire GL51 8NP, UK; www.compass-holidays.com.

THE CROSS CANADA CYCLE TOUR SOCIETY

This is a bicycling club for retired people who love to jump on their bikes and take off across the countryside. Most of the club's members are over 60, with many in their 70s and 80s and only a few under 50. Says the society, "Our aim is to stay alive as long as possible." Now there's a worthwhile goal.

Based in Vancouver, B.C., with members—both men and women, skilled and novice—mostly in B.C., Ontario, and Alberta, but many in the U.S., it organizes many trips a year, all led by volunteer tour guides. Membership costs $30 single or $45 per couple per year and includes a monthly newsletter to keep you up-to-date on happenings. Several times a week, local members gather for day rides, and several times a year there are longer club trips to such far-ranging locations as South Africa, Germany, Switzerland, and U.S. national parks. Every few years a group of intrepid bikers pedals clear across Canada, an adventure that takes a few weeks to accomplish, with some members dropping in and out along the way. Many of the longer trips are tenting or camping tours, while others put you up in hostels, motels, or hotels.

For information: Cross Canada Cycle Tour Society, 6943 Antrim Ave., Burnaby, BC V5J 4M5; 604-433-7710; www .vcn.bc.ca/cccts.

ELDERHOSTEL BICYCLE TOURS

Elderhostel's famous educational travel programs include both domestic and foreign bicycle tours among its many offerings. These vary by the season and year and are all listed in the organization's frequent and voluminous catalogs. Recent programs in the U.S. have included six-day inn-to-inn pedals along the Erie Canal in New York, the northwest corner of Arizona, and the rolling hills of Texas. Lectures and sight-seeing excursions are included.

Bike tours in foreign lands are scheduled weekly from April through September in Canada, Denmark, England, Italy, Germany, Austria, France, and the Netherlands. Led by a guide and riding as a group, you cover 25 to 35 miles a day and learn about the culture and history from local educators and other specialists. Three-speed bikes are provided, as are breakfast, dinner, and accommodations in small hotels. The support van that travels with the group to carry the luggage and repair equipment will carry you as well if you decide that you can't possibly make it up another hill.

For information: Elderhostel, 11 Avenue de Lafayette, Boston, MA 02111; 877-426-8056 or 617-426-7788; www .elderhostel.org.

INTERNATIONAL BICYCLE TOURS (IBT)

The Fifty Plus Tour by IBT is planned for bikers over 50 who are not interested in pedaling up mountains but love to hit the road on two wheels. It takes you to Holland on leisurely eight-day rides along bicycle paths and quiet country roads on flat terrain through farmland, forests, islands, and small villages. You cover only about 30 miles a day, so there's plenty of time for sightseeing, snacking, shopping, and relaxing. You lodge in small hotels and dine on local specialties.

Although these are the only IBT tours specifically designated as 50-plus, most of the company's trips in Europe and the U.S. are geared to older riders.

For information: International Bicycle Tours, PO Box 754, Essex, CT 06426; 860-767-7005; www.internationalbicycle tours.com.

LAID BACK TOURS

To see New Orleans and its environs, check into Laid Back Tours, which send you out to see the world on your choice of bikes that include standard hybrids, mountain bikes, or two- or three-wheeled recumbent bikes and trikes that let you lean back in comfort while you pedal. Laid Back schedules several trips a year, anywhere from three hours to six days, just for people 50 and over. You'll pedal through the historic neighborhoods of New Orleans, along bayous and swamps, and the Mississippi River Levee Bike Path. Included in the tour is lodging and most of your meals, along with your bike.

For information: Laid Back Tours, 625 Hagan Ave., New Orleans, LA 70119; 800-786-1274 or 504-488-8991; www.laidbacktours.com.

OVER THE HILL GANG (OTHG)

This club, for energetic 50-plus adventurers whose main activity is skiing, schedules at least one group bike tour every year, usually in Europe along routes rated "easy" on gentle terrain. Bike during the day; sleep at small hotels along the way at night. See more information about the club and its activities earlier in this chapter.

For information: Over the Hill Gang International, 1820 W. Colorado Ave., Dept. G, Colorado Springs, CO 80904; 719-389-0022; www.othgi.com.

VBT BICYCLING VACATIONS

This venerable bike company, now an affiliate of Grand Circle Travel, an agency that specializes in travel for people over the age of 50, has tailored many of VBT's trips for the same fast-growing age group. Although challenging routes remain for those who want them, many of the itineraries in the U.S. and overseas are less demanding and their schedules more relaxed. VBT's biking vacations currently include a number of trips eminently suitable for older bikers who seek adventure without all that much physical stress, such as the Salzburg Sojourn, which takes participants on flat bicycle paths and easy descents in the Austrian Alps. Or a tour of Tuscany traveling along the coast on less-traveled roads.

For information: VBT, 614 Monkton Rd., Bristol, VT 05443; 800-245-3868 or 802-453-4811; www.vbt.com.

WANDERING WHEELS

This program, established in 1966, was created to work with local churches to provide long-distance bike tours for all ages and has since attracted people from all walks of life

SENIOR CYCLING

Exclusively for bikers over 50 who prefer to travel with congenial contemporaries, the bicycle adventures by Senior Cycling (a.k.a. Old Folks on Spokes) may do the job. You'll do the miles but at slower speeds than 20-somethings, taking time to enjoy the journey and make stops along the way. When overnights are required, you'll stay at local hotels or B&Bs and dine at local eateries. Trips range from local one- or two-day ventures out of the Washington, D.C., area to a seven-day spin along the Erie Canal from Buffalo to Albany in New York State. Other choices, for two to six days, include the Florida Keys, the Katy Trail in Missouri, Pennsylvania's Amish country, and the towpaths of the C & O Canal in Maryland.

The trips are rated for difficulty, with several featuring flat, easy terrain for rank beginners. Groups are small, from 6 to 12 participants, plus a guide and a support vehicle to carry luggage, lunch, and you, if necessary. Accommodations and most meals are included. Bring your own bike or rent one. *For information:* Senior Cycling, 37419 Branch River Rd., Loudon Heights, VA 20132; 540-668-6307; www.senior cycling.com.

and with various beliefs. Its trips include a 2,600-mile coast-to-coast ride every spring geared specifically for people who are middle-aged or older.

For information: Wandering Wheels, PO Box 207, Upland, IN 46989; 765-998-7490; www.wanderingwheels.org.

WOMANTOURS

Bicycle trips for women are the specialty of this group that schedules many trips suitable for older bikers with moderate terrain and easy mileage. Recent trips have gone to the Teton Mountains, the Canadian Rockies from Banff to Jasper, or the Vermont Champlain Valley. A van goes along with every group to carry the luggage, repair equipment, and give weary riders a lift. Exclusively for women over 50 is a much more ambitious 50-day, 4,250-mile trip through rural America from San Diego, California, to St. Augustine, Florida. Mileage averages 57 miles a day, mostly on fairly flat terrain, with one rest day per week. For this trip you'd better be in good shape!

For information: WomanTours, PO Box 746, Driggs, ID 83422; 800-247-1444 or 208-354-2652; www.womantours .com.

TENNIS, ANYONE?

An estimated three million of the nation's tennis players are over 50, with the number increasing every year as more of us decide to forgo sitting by the pool for a few fast sets on the courts. You need only a court, a racket, a can of balls, and an opponent to play tennis, but if you'd like to be competitive or sociable, you may want to get into some senior tournaments.

UNITED STATES TENNIS ASSOCIATION (USTA)

The USTA offers a wide variety of tournaments for players over the advanced age of 35, at both local and national levels. To participate, you must be a member ($35 per year). When you join, you will become a member of a regional section, receive periodic schedules of USTA-sponsored tournaments and events in your area for which you can sign up, get a discount on tennis books and publications, and receive a monthly magazine and a free subscription to *Tennis* magazine.

In the schedule of tournaments, you'll find competitions listed for specific five-year age groups: for men from 35 to 90-plus and for women from 35 to 85-plus. In addition, self-rated tournaments match you up with people of all ages who play at your level. If you feel you're good enough to compete, send for an application and sign up. There is usually a modest fee.

For information: USTA, 70 W. Red Oak Ln., White Plains, NY 10604; 800-990-8782 or 914-696-7000; www.usta .com.

USA LEAGUE TENNIS, SENIOR DIVISION

If you want to compete with other 50-plus tennis players in local, area, and sectional competitions, culminating in a national championship, join the Senior Division of the USA League Tennis program. Your level of play will be rated in a specific skill category ranging from beginner to advanced, and you'll compete only with people on your own ability level. You must join USTA ($35 a year) for the privilege and the details.

For information: USTA, 70 W. Red Oak Ln., White Plains, NY 10604; 800-990-8782 or 914-696-7000; www.usta .com.

VAN DER MEER TENNIS UNIVERSITY

Van der Meer Tennis University offers two- to five-day Seniors Clinics from September to May every year at its Van der Meer Shipyard Tennis Resort on Hilton Head Island.

Specifically for 50-plus players, beginning or experienced, the clinics provide more than 16 hours of instruction, including video analysis, tactics and strategies for singles and doubles, and match play drills, plus round-robins, social activities, and free court time. The goal is to improve your strokes and game strategy so you'll get more enjoyment out of your game. Discounted accommodations are available for participants, making a week's package quite inexpensive.

For information: Van der Meer Tennis University, PO Box 5902, Hilton Head Island, SC 29938; 800-845-6138 or 843-785-8388; www.vdmtennis.com.

WALKING TOURS

Walking tours have become remarkably popular among people of all ages but especially ours—those of us who are old enough to appreciate the close encounters with the world and its wonders that moving along at a leisurely pace on our own two feet allows. Among the many tour companies that plan walking tours are some that specialize in travel on foot for mature participants.

APPALACHIAN MOUNTAIN CLUB (AMC)

Every year this famous hiking club, the oldest conservation and recreation organization in the U.S., schedules a few inexpensive two- to five-day treks for people over the age of 50. You'll hike two to eight miles a day at an easy pace in New Hampshire's White Mountains or the Catskills in New York and sleep in a comfortable lodge at night, with plenty of time to savor the scenery and glimpse the wildlife.

Routes vary from year to year. Yearly membership fee in AMC for adults is $50 ($65 per family), but if you are 69 or over, you pay only $25.

For information: Appalachian Mountain Club, 5 Joy St., Boston, MA 02108; 617-523-0636; www.outdoors.org.

COMPASS HOLIDAYS

This company specializes in walking holidays in the English countryside, with or without a guide. You'll enjoy walks through quiet villages, bustling towns, and pastoral countrysides for three to eight days, covering only a few or many miles, stopping each evening at a small family hotel for local food and a comfortable night's sleep. If you are over the age of 50 and you sign up for a seven-night break, you'll get a 10 percent discount if you remember to mention this book. Compass also offers many bike tours in England.

For information: Compass Holidays, Cheltenham Spa Railway Station, Queens Rd., Cheltenham, Gloucestershire GL51 8NP, UK; www.compass-holidays.com.

ELDERHOSTEL WALKING & HIKING PROGRAMS

Both Elderhostel's domestic and international programs include walking and hiking tours for which you should be practiced walkers with energy and good health. Accompanied by guides, lecturers, and local specialists, the overseas walkers, carrying small day packs, cover 4 to 12 miles a day, rain or shine. You'll stay and dine mostly in small hotels, while lunch is taken en route. Educational programs are part of the package. Trekking trips are also on

Elderhostel's menu, taking you up to eight miles a day on footpaths in Nepal or Switzerland. For these you must be in even better physical shape and accustomed to vigorous exercise.

For information: Elderhostel, 11 Avenue de Lafayette, Boston, MA 02111; 877-426-8056 or 617-426-7788; www .elderhostel.org.

ELDERTREKS

On these trekking trips in the Far East, all of them for 50-plus travelers, you will hike overland on foot and, in many cases, sleep on an air mattress in a village house or a tent. The trips are rated for difficulty so you may choose one that matches your abilities. For more, see Chapter 9.

For information: ElderTreks, 597 Markham St., Toronto, ON M6G 2L7; 800-741-7956 or 416-588-5000; www.elder treks.com.

EXPLORE HOLIDAYS

A specialty of this Canadian company is its 50-plus Mountain Tours, fully catered and guided camping and hiking tours of the Canadian Rocky Mountains for adventurers over 50. Starting and ending in Calgary, the 10-day tours are scheduled in the summer months and take groups of no more than ten participants accompanied by two staff members to campsites in Kananaskis country and Lake Louise, where they settle down in large stand-up tents furnished with comfortable cots. Meals, served up by the cook, are eaten in a dining tent. Each day, there's a three- to five-hour hike deep into mountain passes and glacier-filled valleys.

For information: Explore Holidays, PO Box 607, 743 Railway Ave., Canmore, AB T1W 1P2; 403-609-4101; www .exploreholidays.com.

GUNFLINT LODGE

Among this outfitter's packages just for seniors are several hiking vacations that not only give you a chance to hike on wilderness trails in the forests of northern Minnesota along the shores of the Border Lakes but also include unlimited horseback riding, canoeing, mountain biking, fishing, and motorboating with all equipment supplied. Most trips are scheduled for spring or fall, the best time of year in these parts just below the Canadian border. You sleep in a lakeside cabin with a fireplace, sauna, and hot tub. Dinner is included.

For information: Gunflint Lodge, 143 S. Gunflint Lake, Grand Marais, MN 55604; 800-328-3325; www.gunflint .com.

INTERHOSTEL

If you love to amble along, taking a good look at the world, sign on for one of Interhostel's educational walking tours for people over 50. Foreign itineraries currently include vacations around Galway and Killarney in Ireland and Stirling and Edinburgh in Scotland. Itineraries in the U.S. include California, Colorado, Alaska, and more. Traveling from place to place by van, you explore on foot and cover perhaps three to five miles a day on gentle terrain that includes some hills and lodging in small hotels or student residences. See Chapter 13 for more about Interhostel's programs.

For information: Interhostel, 6 Garrison Ave., Durham, NH 03824; 800-733-9753 or 603-862-1147; www.learn.unh .edu/interhostel.

RIVER ODYSSEYS WEST (ROW)

If you love wilderness rivers but aren't into whitewater rafting (see Chapter 9), consider ROW's raft-supported walking tours along trails that follow the course of the Middle Fork of the Salmon River in Idaho or the Snake River in Hells Canyon on the Oregon border. Carrying only a day pack and led by a guide, you hike six or eight miles a day with plenty of time to smell the flowers and spot the wildlife. A cargo raft carries all the camping gear and your luggage as well as the food and other supplies, and a smaller support raft floats along at the group's pace to act as a sag wagon for tired walkers. When you arrive at camp each afternoon, the staff has already set up the roomy tents and the kitchen and has started cooking dinner, giving you time to relax, fish, or explore.

For information: River Odysseys West, PO Box 579-UD, Coeur d'Alene, ID 83816; 800-451-6034 or 208-765-0841; www.rowinc.com.

SILVER SNEAKER EXCURSIONS

Silver Sneaker walking tours, many of them exclusively for people over 50, are led by a couple of experienced outdoor adventure guides. In the U.S., their trips vary from weekends to 18-day adventures, including hikes from inn to inn in Vermont as well as walks on Rhode Island's beaches, in Sedona and the Grand Canyon in Arizona, on the coast of Maine, and around the famous resort city of Newport, Rhode Island. Abroad, they offer longer hiking trips in Wales or England's Cornwall as well as the Copper Canyon in Mexico, Bolivia and Peru, Ecuador and the Galapagos Islands, and Costa Rica.

For information: Silver Sneaker Excursions, 100 Worsley Ave., N. Kingstown, RI 02852; 401-295-0367; www.silver sneakerexcursions.com.

WALK YOUR WAY

Walk Your Way Into the Heart of England tours are designed for older walkers. These are 12- to 15-day tours off the beaten path in quaint and picturesque areas of Devon and Dorset, the Lake District, Yorkshire, or the Cotswolds in England, plus the islands and Highlands of Scotland and the villages of Ireland. Some walks are circular, beginning and ending in the same village, averaging five miles a day. Others are linear, covering eight to ten miles a day. The group is never larger than ten, lodging is in family guest houses or bed-and-breakfasts, and evening meals are eaten in local pubs.

For information: Walk Your Way, PO Box 231, Red Feather Lakes, CO 80545; 970-881-2709; www.walkyourway.co.uk.

WALKING THE WORLD

Anyone over 50 who loves adventure and is in good physical shape is invited to participate in Walking the World's explorations. These are 8- to 19-day backcountry treks, covering six to ten miles a day, that focus on natural and cultural history. On some trips, you'll camp out and, carrying only a day pack, hike to each new destination. On others, you will lodge in small country inns, hotels, or bed-and-breakfasts, setting forth on daily walks into the countryside. Groups are small, from 12 to 18 participants plus two local guides, and there's no upper age limit. No previous hiking experience is necessary.

Destinations include Arches and Canyonlands National Parks in Utah; Banff and Jasper National Parks in the Canadian Rockies; plus trips in Maine, Arizona, Newfoundland, Scotland, England, Norway, Wales, Iceland, Slovenia, Ireland, New Zealand, Hawaii, Tahiti, Peru, Ecuador, Costa Rica, and Italy.

For information: Walking the World, PO Box 1186, Fort Collins, CO 80522; 800-340-9255 or 970-498-0500; www .walkingtheworld.com.

BACKPACKING TRIPS
SIERRA CLUB

Every year, among this grassroots environmental organization's affordable outings, you'll find backpacking treks in the wilderness exclusively for physically fit hikers who are over the age of 50. The one-week trips are led by volunteers and change each year. Currently they include backpacking in the Sawtooth Mountains of Idaho, bunking in lodges and campsites; climbing, hiking, fishing, and camping in the South San Juan Wilderness Loop in Colorado; and backpacking in Klondike Gold Rush National Historic Park in Alaska, traveling by foot, narrow-gauge railway, and ferry from Skagway to the Canadian Yukon.

To participate you must belong to the club, but if you consider yourself a senior, your yearly membership costs you only $24, while other adults pay $39. Two seniors in the same household may join for $32 a year instead of $47.

For information: Sierra Club Outings, 85 Second St., San Francisco, CA 94105; 415-977-5522; www.sierraclub.org /outings/national.

NATURAL HISTORY TOURS
ELDERHOSTEL BIRDING PROGRAMS
Among Elderhostel's many outdoor programs are trips specifically designed for bird-watching in the field in Australia, Costa Rica, Ecuador, Iceland, Kenya, Mexico, Peru, and Norway. Here in the U.S. there are many Elderhostel programs that include this popular activity among their courses. *For information:* Elderhostel, 11 Avenue de Lafayette, Boston, MA 02111; 877-426-8056 or 617-426-7788; www .elderhostel.org.

FISHING AND CANOEING TRIPS
GUNFLINT LODGE
If you'd love to fish in a clear, cool lake, check out the four-night spring fishing packages offered just for seniors by Gunflint Lodge in the Border Lakes region of northern Minnesota. Also on the schedule is a three-night grandparent/grandchild fishing package, complete with a guide, boat, motor, and tackle, so the two generations can spend time together. You'll have a boat and motor ready and waiting for you, and if you want a change, you can go horseback riding, canoeing, hiking, or mountain biking as much as you like. See earlier in this chapter for more. *For information:* Gunflint Lodge, 143 S. Gunflint Lake, Grand Marais, MN 55604; 800-328-3325; www.gunflint .com.

SNOWMOBILE TOURS
SENIOR WORLD TOURS

Explore the winter wonders of Yellowstone National Park or the Black Hills of South Dakota aboard your own quiet, four-stroke snowmobile on a seniors-only seven-day adventure trip, which is limited to 16 participants age 50 or over. All tours travel on roadways already groomed for the use of park personnel—and never off-road, where snowmobiles can damage the environment. Included in the package are driving lessons, snowmobiles, fuel, boots, gloves, helmets, cross-country skis, meals, and trusty guides. No experience is necessary, but don't even think of going unless you enjoy the snow and are in good physical condition.

By the way, if you go with a companion who does not care to ride alone, you may choose a two-up machine that allows the two of you to travel tandem. Nonriders can go by snow coach.

On the Yellowstone National Park trip, you'll ride your snowmobile through the park to view the wildlife, geysers, hot springs, mountain passes, awesome views, and splendid scenery, overnighting in wilderness lodges and resorts. If you choose to ride in the Black Hills of South Dakota, your tour takes you to Mount Rushmore, Crazy Horse Memorial, on to Spearfish Canyon, Lead, and the gambling casinos of Deadwood. Choose the Montana itinerary and you'll go to a lodge in Whitefish to ride, ski, dogsled, iceskate, or kick back.

For information: Senior World Tours, 2205 N. River Rd., Fremont, OH 43420; 888-355-1686; www.seniorworld tours.com.

CROSS-COUNTRY SKIING

Many cross-country ski areas in the U.S. and Canada offer discounted trail passes to seniors, usually starting at age 62 or thereabouts, and some charge nothing at all at age 70 or 75. Among the latter are Bear Notch in Bartlett, New Hampshire; Lapland Lake in Northville, New York; Bohart Ranch in Bozeman, Montana; Stowe Mountain Resort in Stowe, Vermont; Mount Shasta in Mount Shasta, California; and Mount Washington in Courtney, B.C.

APPALACHIAN MOUNTAIN CLUB (AMC)

Famous for its hiking programs in New England, AMC also schedules several affordable cross-country skiing and snowshoeing courses for grown-ups every winter. The 50+ Cross Country Skiing for Beginners program gives you a chance to join a small group of peers for two nights at an inn in the Catskills or the White Mountains where you'll get accommodations, meals, and lessons on groomed trails. The 50+ Snowshoe Adventure is a similar program for beginners who want to learn the basics about navigating on top of the snow. To participate, you need to be in good physical condition and able to carry a full day pack. Members of the club are entitled to a 10 percent discount on the cost of these adventures. The annual adult membership fee for AMC is $50 ($65 for family) but only $25 for those 69 or over.

For information: Appalachian Mountain Club, 5 Joy St., Boston, MA 02108; 617-523-0636; www.outdoors.org.

GOLDEN GLIDES SILVER STRIDES

Bethel, Maine, a center of Nordic skiing, offers a remarkably inexpensive midweek Golden Glides Silver Strides package for cross-country skiers who are at least 50. Available Sunday through Thursday nights, it includes three nights lodging and breakfast at a choice of inns, cabins, or B&Bs; a three-day trail pass at any of three cross-country centers; use of the latest-model ski equipment; and a daily lesson or guided tour.

For information: Bethel Chamber of Commerce, 800-442-5826; www.bethelmaine.com/winteractivities.

SILVER SNEAKER EXCURSIONS

Every winter, Silver Sneaker Excursions adds a couple of cross-country skiing and snowshoe packages in Vermont to its list of adventures specifically for people over 50. For both beginners and intermediates, the packages include five nights, meals, and après-ski parties. All are led by experienced outdoor adventure guides.

For information: Silver Sneaker Excursions, 100 Worsley Ave., N. Kingstown, RI 02852; 401-295-0367; www.silver sneakerexcursions.com.

MOTORCYCLE HEAVEN

BEACH'S MOTORCYCLE ADVENTURES

If motorcycling is your passion and adventure is in your blood, look into the motorcycle tours offered by the Beach family who has been conducting cycling tours since 1972. All ages, including yours, may choose from a variety of trips in the Alps, Italy, and California. You must, of course, have a valid motorcycle license. Motorcycles are provided in your choice of available models and there is no mileage charge. A guide goes along with you, and your luggage is carried by a van. By the way, both bikes and automobiles are welcome on these tours, so if friends or family want to join you they may go along in a car.

You're on your own during the day, following a tour book that gives daily itineraries, road maps, distances, estimated en route times, business hours, sight-seeing ideas, good (and bad) roads, suggestions for activities, driving tips, and directions to the hotel of the night. The daily routing, pace, and stops are up to you. There are several riding options each day, so you may decide to cruise along or ride long and hard. Every evening, you'll meet the group and your guide at a hotel or family farm where you'll eat dinner that night and have breakfast the next morning.

For information: Beach's Motorcycle Adventures, 2763 W. River Rd., Grand Island, NY 14072; 716-773-4960; www .beachs-mca.com.

RETREADS MOTORCYCLE CLUB

Retreads, an association of 40-plus motorcycle enthusiasts with an average age of 60 and a few members in their 80s, get together for state, regional, and international rallies to talk cycling and ride together. Each state association and local chapter (there are more than 40 in Florida) also has regular get-togethers for short jaunts and socializing. Started as a correspondence club in 1969, Retreads has grown to more than 15,000 members—men and women—in the U.S., Canada, and several other countries. Annual contribution is $15 a year per person or $20 per couple. A club newsletter keeps members informed of the activities.

For information: Retreads Motorcycle Club International, 528 North Main St., Albany, IN 47320; 765-789-4070.

From November 1 to May 31: 4504 Pittenger Dr., Sarasota, FL 34234; 941-351-7199; www.retreads.org.

GOLF VACATIONS

GREENS FEES

Most municipal and many private golf courses offer senior golfers (usually those over 60 or 65) a discount off the regular greens fees, at least on certain days of the week. Take along identification and ask for your discount when you reserve a tee time.

AMERICAN SENIOR GOLF SOCIETY (ASGS)

More than 1,500 golfers over 50—average age 63—belong to ASGS, which sponsors recreational and competitive three-day, midweek golf holidays once or twice a month at highly rated courses all over the country. The holidays include accommodations, golf (including a 54-hole medalplay tournament), breakfasts, at least two dinners, and activities for nonplaying companions. Recent locations have included Pebble Beach Resorts in California; Kiawah Island, South Carolina; Banff Springs in Canada; and The Equinox in Vermont. Longer golf holidays are scheduled once a year to more far-flung locations such as Scotland and Portugal.

Membership in ASGS costs $35 a year or $75 for three years and includes dues for a nongolfing companion. It entitles you to a golf passport, free to three-year members and discounted for one-year members, with special discounts at golf courses and resorts; a newsletter; and a $50 gift certificate to use on your first event.

For information: ASGS, 1 Airport Pl., Princeton, NJ 08540; 800-504-2747 or 609-279-0024; www.asgs.net.

GOLF ACADEMY AT SEA PINES RESORT

Golfers over 50 will get a 15 percent discount on the three-day golf schools at the Golf Academy of Hilton Island at Sea Pines if they mention this book when they make their reservations. The three- or four-day school includes four hours of daily instruction from Class A PGA professionals each morning, followed by 18 holes of golf in the afternoon. Also included are on-course instruction, video analysis with a take-home tape, a personalized improvement manual, plus breakfast and lunch all three days.

For information: The Golf Academy at Sea Pines Resort, PO Box 5580, Hilton Head Island, SC 29938; 800-925-0467 or 843-785-4540; www.golfacademy.net.

THE GOLF CARD

Designed especially for senior golfers, the Golf Card entitles members to free greens fees at about 1,000 courses in the U.S. and Canada; up to half off the player's fees at many additional courses; and savings at 250 stay-and-play packages at more than 250 golf resorts in the U.S., Canada, the Bahamas, Jamaica, and the Dominican Republic. Current membership fees are $59 the first year and $75 a year thereafter. A subscription to *Golf Traveler*, a magazine that serves as a guide to the participating courses and resorts, is part of the package.

For information: The Golf Card, PO Box 7021, Englewood, CO 80155; 800-321-8269 or 303-790-2267; www.golfcard .com.

JOHN JACOBS GOLF SCHOOLS

Golfers over the age of 62 get a discount of 10 percent on the cost of golf vacations offered July through December at any John Jacobs Golf School. You'll learn how to improve your game while you play at some of the finest courses in the country. Most packages include lodging, breakfast and dinner, instruction, course time, greens fees, and cart. Commuter packages are available, too, at all 45 schools.

For information: John Jacobs Golf Schools, 7825 E. Redfield Rd., Scottsdale, AZ 85260; 800-472-5007; www.jacobs golf.com.

OVER THE HILL GANG (OTHG)

In the off-season when there's little or no snow for its members to ski on, this club for peppy people over the age of 50 always plans at least one group golf vacation every year at a well-known golf resort. See more information about the club and its activities earlier in this chapter.

For information: Over the Hill Gang International, 1820 W. Colorado Ave., Dept. G, Colorado Springs, CO 80904; 719-389-0022; www.othgi.com.

SENIOR GOLF ASSOCIATION OF AMERICA (SGA)

An association of amateur senior and super-senior golfers, SGA invites its members, all of them 50 or older, to travel to some of the best golf resorts in the country, stay in deluxe accommodations, and compete in friendly tournaments. Vacations include four nights' lodging and dinner reservations, three or four days of golf, plus banquets, award ceremonies, dances, cocktail parties, tours, shopping sprees, special events for nongolfing spouses, you name it. SGA handles all the details but you must provide your own transportation to the resort.

Tournaments at the resorts are based on your handicap and your age, with Senior (50+), Grand Senior (70+), and Legendary Senior (80+) championships and prizes. Annual membership costs $60 for an individual and $100 for a couple (one of you must be at least 50). Members must agree to abide by the "slow play" rules.

For information: Senior Golfers Association of America, 3013 Church St., Myrtle Beach, SC 29577; 800-337-0047 or 843-626-8100; www.seniorgolfersamerica.com.

SENIORS GOLF TOURNAMENT

Golfers over the age of 50, with a maximum handicap of 24 for men and 36 for women, can sign up for the Annual Seniors Golf Tournament held every winter at the Port Royal Golf Course on Bermuda's southwest coast. A special package includes five nights at the Pompano Beach Club, breakfasts and dinners, three rounds of golf, parties, and more.

For information: Pompano Beach Club, Bermuda Hotels, PO Box 78, Wayland, MA 01778; 800-343-4155; www.pompanobeachclub.com.

WATER AEROBICS
FUN & FITNESS TRAVEL CLUB

The aerobic vacations scheduled once a month by the Fun & Fitness Travel Club, a club for mature adults, feature water exercise classes every morning on every one of its cruises to places like the Caribbean, Alaska, the East Coast, and the Mexican Riviera, supplemented by other forms of daily physical activities, including yoga, tai chi, deck walking, ballroom dancing, and chair aerobics. The club—no dues required—is especially popular among single seniors. *For information:* Fun & Fitness Club, 7338 Dartford Dr., Ste. 9, McLean, VA 22102; 800-955-9942 or 703-827-0414; www.fun-fitness.com.

EVENTS FOR RAPID RUNNERS
FIFTY-PLUS LIFELONG FITNESS

This is not a club, although it occasionally sponsors athletic events for its over-50 members. It is an organization formed by exercise researchers at Stanford University as an exchange of information about fitness and its benefits for those who are 50 or more. Its members, from almost every state and several foreign countries, also serve as volunteers for ongoing studies of activities such as running, swimming, biking, and racewalking. Each is asked to contribute $50 a year, tax-deductible, to defray costs and receives a newsletter. The association sponsors many events throughout the U.S. but mostly in northern California. These include walks, runs, swims, bike rides, and seminars and conferences on aging.

For information: Fifty-Plus Lifelong Fitness Association, PO Box 20230, Stanford, CA 94309; 650-843-1750; www .50plus.org.

OVER-50 SOFTBALL

INTERNATIONAL SENIOR SOFTBALL ASSOCIATION (ISSA)

ISSA, an association that was founded to promote softball for men and women over the age of 50, conducts the World Championship Tournaments every year in Virginia for more than 300 senior teams. Players who are members of senior leagues and local softball associations all over the U.S. may join and so may individuals without affiliation. Members receive a master nationwide tournament schedule, the results of all national tournaments, and the rankings of all senior softball teams.

For information: ISSA, 9401 East St., Manassas, VA 20110; 703-368-1188; www.seniorsoftball.org.

NATIONAL ASSOCIATION OF SENIOR CITIZEN SOFTBALL (NASCS)

The NASCS is an organization composed of several thousand softball players and hundreds of teams in the U.S. and Canada, with a goal of promoting a worldwide interest in senior softball. To play ball on one of its teams, you must be at least 50 years old. There's no upper age limit, and both men and women are welcomed. NASCS runs qualifying tournaments for the annual Senior Softball World Series, when more than 125 teams from the U.S. and Canada compete in a major ballpark. A semiannual magazine, *Line Drive*, keeps members up-to-date on happenings here and abroad.

For information: NASCS, PO Box 1085, Mt. Clemens, MI 48046; 586-792-2110; www.nascs.org.

222 GOOD DEALS FOR GOOD SPORTS

SENIOR SOFTBALL-USA

This organization, the largest senior softball group in the world, conducts softball tournaments all over the country and organizes international tournaments as well, including the Senior Softball World Championship Games held in September. Anyone over 50, man or woman, in the U.S. and Canada may join for a $35 registration fee, and many thousands have. At age 75, you can get a lifetime membership for $35. Members get assistance finding teams in their areas and may subscribe to the *Senior Softball News*, which keeps them up-to-date on tournaments and other news. They are eligible to take part in an annual international tour that takes teams to play ball in foreign lands.

For information: Senior Softball-USA, 2701 K St., Ste. 101A, Sacramento, CA 95816; 916-326-5303; www.senior softball.com.

SOFTBALL WINTER CAMP

Softball Winter Camp is an annual event held every winter in Altamonte Springs, Florida (10 miles from Orlando). Older amateur players gather for five days to train, get batting and fielding practice, play eight umpired games, compete in a minitournament, join an exercise program, and socialize. Men of all ages and abilities participate, with wives invited to come along to enjoy the fun. Lunch every day, a couple of breakfasts, an awards banquet, an equipment bag, a team shirt, and a cap are included in the fee as are special hotel rates.

For information: Softball Winter Camp, Active Life Styles, 11465 Kanapali Lane, Boynton Beach, FL 33437; 888-335-3828; www.softballcamp.com.

SENIOR GAMES

HUNTSMAN WORLD SENIOR GAMES

Every October, about 7,000 athletes—men and women, 50 and over, from the U.S. and about 40 other countries—gather in St. George, Utah, for two weeks of competition in 20 individual or team events from basketball, mountain biking, golf, swimming, and tennis to track and field and triathlon, with skill levels from novice to expert. The registration fee (currently $79) includes participation in any of the athletic events and additional perks such as free health screenings, seminars on healthy living, receptions, band concerts, and ceremonial dinners.

For information: Huntsman World Senior Games, 82 W. 700 South, St. George, UT 84770; 800-562-1268 or 435-674-0550; www.seniorgames.net.

NATIONAL SENIOR GAMES ASSOCIATION (NSGA)

The NSGA is the organization that sanctions and coordinates the official senior games across the country. It sponsors the Summer National Senior Games/The Senior Olympics in odd-number years, attracting about 12,000 athletes over the age of 50 who compete in 18 sports. The Winter National Senior Games/The Senior Olympics, also held every other year, in even-number years, features competitions in alpine and cross-country skiing, curling, figure skating, ice hockey, and snowshoeing.

To compete in the national games, you must first qualify in authorized state competitions, which means you must be a medal winner in your age group or meet minimum performance standards in time and distance events.

For a free Qualifying State Games Directory, write to NSGA at the address given here or download it from the website. You'll find a representative sample of the games in the following pages.

For information: National Senior Games Association, PO Box 82059, Baton Rouge, LA 70884; 225-766-6800; www .nationalseniorgames.org.

STATE AND LOCAL SENIOR GAMES

Most states hold their own senior games once or twice a year and send their best competitors to national events. If you don't find your state among those listed here, that doesn't mean there's no program in your area—many are sponsored by counties, cities, and even local agencies and colleges. Check with your local city, county, or state recreation departments to see what's going on near you, or contact the NSGA for a free list. You can find it, too, on NSGA's website. You don't have to be a serious competitor to enter these games but merely prepared to enjoy yourself. So what if you don't go home with a medal? At the very least, you'll meet other energetic people and have a lot of laughs.

ARIZONA

If you are 50 or more, resident of the state or a visitor, man or woman, beginner or advanced athlete, you are invited to participate in the Arizona Senior Olympics held every year over about two weeks in February. Events include 29 sports from track to golf, biking, and swimming and are held in several venues in the Phoenix metropolitan area. Every two years you may compete in qualifying games for the national Senior Olympics. Festivities and medals are included.

Local senior games are also scheduled throughout the year in many Arizona cities, including Sierra Vista, Flagstaff, Prescott, and Tucson.

For information: Arizona Senior Olympics, PO Box 33278, Phoenix, AZ 85067; 602-261-8765; www.seniorgames.org.

COLORADO

The Senior Winter Games at the Summit take place each year during three days in the second week of February in Summit County. Anyone from anywhere who's over 50 and wants to compete against peers is welcome. Events include cross-country skiing, downhill slalom, speed skating, snowshoe races, biathlon, figure skating, and more, plus social activities. Age categories for the competitions begin at 50 to 54 and increase in five-year increments to 90-plus. A registration fee of $25 for state residents, $30 for others, allows you to participate in one event with $5 for each added event.

The summer Rocky Mountain Senior Games are held in Greeley the first week in June and include more than 20 competitions in sports ranging from basketball and racquetball to golf, softball, bowling, cycling, and tennis. A registration fee of $35 for state residents, $40 for others, includes admission to eight different events, continental breakfast, and snacks. To participate, you must be at least 50, and you can compete no matter where you're from.

For information: Senior Winter Games at the Summit, PO Box 1845, Frisco, CO 80443; 970-453-2461; or Rocky

Mountain Senior Games, 1010 6th St., Greeley, CO 80631; 970-350-9433; www.rmseniorgames.com.

CONNECTICUT

The Connecticut Senior Summer Olympics include not only competitive sports events but also a mini–health fair and many physical fitness activities. Residents of Connecticut and neighboring states who are 50-plus converge on the town of Southington on the first weekend in June for three days of events such as the 5,000-meter run, the 100-yard dash, the mile run, the long jump, swimming, bocci, and tennis. These summer games require a small entrance fee.

The one-day Connecticut Senior Winter Olympics, held in February, are open to anyone from anywhere who's at least 50 and an amateur. The games feature downhill, giant slalom, and cross-country skiing, as well as snowshoe races, and take place at Ski Sundown.

For information: Connecticut Senior Olympics, Nutmeg Senior Games, 290 Roberts St., E. Hartford, CT 06108; 800-528-4588; www.seniorgamesct.org.

FLORIDA

Since 1974, the Golden Age Games have taken place in Sanford every November. Today, they host more than 1,500 athletes for a week of 40 different competitions, plus ceremonies, social events, and entertainment. If you are over 50, you are eligible to participate regardless of residency. In other words, you needn't be a Floridian to compete for the gold, silver, and bronze medals in sports such as basketball, biking, bowling, canoeing, checkers, dance, swimming, tennis, triathlon, track and field, canasta, and croquet. There is an entry fee of $6 for the first event and $2 for each additional event.

For information: Golden Age Games, PO Box 1298, Sanford, FL 32772; 407-302-1010; www.ci.sanford.fl.us.

MISSOURI

The St. Louis Senior Olympics have become an institution in Missouri by now. A five-day event in May that is open to anyone who lives anywhere and is at least 50 years old, it costs a nominal amount and is action-oriented. No knitting contests here—only more than 70 energetic events such as bicycle races, 200-meter races, standing long jumps, golf, basketball, free throw, sprints, tennis (singles and doubles), and swimming.

For information: St. Louis Senior Olympics, JCC, 2 Millstone Campus Dr., St. Louis, MO 63146; 314-432-5700, ext. 3217; www.stlouisseniorolympics.org.

MONTANA

Men and women over the age of 50, from Montana or otherwise, are invited to participate in the Montana Senior Olympics, held every year in June. Events range from archery, bowling, and basketball to swimming, tennis, cycling, and track.

For information: Montana Senior Olympics, 2200 Bridger Dr., Bozeman, MT 59715; 406-586-5543.

NEW HAMPSHIRE

For a week in August, you can compete with your peers in the Granite State Senior Summer Games in Manchester, where you can choose from 15 sporting events ranging from swimming to tennis, track and field, shuffleboard, and table tennis. In alternate even-number years, these are qualifying games for the National Senior Games. Sign up if you are a man or a woman who is at least 50 and in good operating condition. The cost is minimal.

For information: Granite State Senior Games, 11 Stagecoach Way, Manchester, NH 03104; 603-622-9041; www.nhsenior games.org.

NEW JERSEY

Held once a year, the New Jersey Senior Sports Classic games feature more than 1,000 seniors competing in 21 competitive sports such as archery, golf, tennis, and track and field.

For information: SCAN Learning Center, Monmouth Mall, Eatontown, NJ 07724; 732-542-1326; www.scannj.com.

NEW YORK

The Empire State Senior Games, open to all New York residents who are 50 or over, are held in Cortlandt over four days in June. Winners may qualify for the National Senior Olympics. For a small registration fee, amateur athletes may compete in many events—swimming, bridge, basketball, softball, croquet, track and field, tennis, racewalking, cycling, and more. There are additional fees for golf and bowling. Participants are invited to social events each of the three nights.

For information: Empire State Senior Games, NYS Parks, 6105 E. Seneca Turnpike, Jamesville, NY 13078; 315-492-9654; www.empirestategames.org.

NORTH CAROLINA

After local games are held statewide, the winners travel to Raleigh for the North Carolina Senior Games State Finals and, perhaps, on to the national games. Most sports are on the agenda, plus an arts competition that celebrates artists in heritage, literary, performing, and visual arts. The state also sponsors the SilverStriders, a walking club for those 50 or better that gives its members logbooks for tracking progress, gifts and awards, and an annual report of their accomplishments.

For information: North Carolina Senior Games, PO Box 33590, Raleigh, NC 27636; 919-851-5456; www.ncsenior games.org.

PENNSYLVANIA

The Pennsylvania Senior Games "combine sports, recreation, and entertainment with fellowship." You can get some of each if you are a Pennsylvania resident who is 50 or older. The games are held over five days in July at Shippensburg University where you can get lodging and three meals a day at low cost. If you prefer to stay in a motel, you'll get a senior discount.

For information: Keystone State Games, PO Box 3131, Wilkes-Barre, PA 18773; 570-823-3164, ext. 7; www.key stonegames.com.

UTAH

The Utah Winter Games, open to everyone whatever their age, abilities, or home address, schedules more than 100 free clinics and events all over the state from November to

January in a variety of winter sports. It includes a free Senior Ski clinic at Brighton Ski Resort in late November, where skiers over 50 are invited for a day of instruction and fun.

The Utah Summer Games Foundation holds annual Olympic-style competitions every June in 41 events from archery to track and field, all of them open to amateur athletes of all ages and skill levels.

For information: Utah Winter Games, 2175 W. 1700 S., Salt Lake City, UT 84104; 801-975-4515; www.utahwinter games.org. Utah Summer Games, 351 W. Center St., Cedar City, UT 84720; 435-865-8421; www.utahsummergames .org.

VERMONT

If you are over 50 years old and an amateur in your sport, you are invited to participate in the Green Mountain Senior Games (GMSG). At the summer games, held throughout the summer months at several locations and at the three-day games at Green Mountain College in Poultney every fall, you may compete in sports ranging from golf and tennis to swimming, walking, softball, biking, basketball, and table tennis. The winter games are held in March and include cross-country and snowshoeing events.

For information: Green Mountain Senior Games, 131 Holden Hill Rd., Weston, VT 05161; 802-824-6521.

VIRGINIA

The Virginia Senior Games are an annual four-day event held each spring on a college campus, where older athletes compete to qualify for the U.S. National Senior Olympics— or just for the fun of it. It is a combination of social events and entertainment with sports competitions, open to anybody over the age of 50. Spouses are invited to come along and enjoy the hospitality, which includes parties, dances, tours of local sites, and other festivities. The fees are low; lodging and meals are cheap; and the sporting events are many, ranging from rope jumping, miniature golf, and riflery to swimming, running, and tennis for age groups from 55 upward.

For information: Virginia Senior Games, Virginia Recreation and Park Society, 6038 Cold Harbor Rd., Mechanicsville, VA 23111; 804-730-9447; www.vrps.com.

15

Adventures on Skis

ownhill skiing is one sport you'd think would appeal only to less mature, less wise, less breakable people. On the contrary, an astounding number of ardent over-50 skiers would much rather glide down mountains than sit around waiting for springtime. In fact, many of us ski more than ever now that we're older because we can go midweek when the crowds are thinner and get impressive discounts on lift tickets, especially after the age of 65. A lot of us, too, are taking up the sport for the first time. Ski schools all over the U.S. and Canada are reporting an increase of older students in beginner classes.

The truth is, you're never too old to learn how to ski or to improve your technique. Once you get the hang of it, you can ski at your own speed, choosing the terrain, the difficulty level, and the challenge. You can slide down cliffs through narrow icy passes or wend your way slowly down gentle slopes, aided by ever-improving equipment. You'll find clearly marked and carefully groomed trails and sophisticated lifts that take all the work out of getting up the mountain.

Besides, ski resorts are falling all over themselves catering to older skiers, offering discounts on lift tickets, cheaper season passes, and other engaging incentives. In fact, it is a rare ski area that does not give a substantial break to skiers over a certain age.

CLUBS FOR MATURE SKIERS

COPPER MOUNTAIN OHG

At Copper Mountain, members of the OHG, an independent snow-sports adventure club for people at least 50 and spouses of any age, ski in guided groups on Tuesdays, Wednesdays, Saturdays, and Sundays from mid-November to mid-April except for breaks during the major holidays. They gather for lunch and ski again in the afternoon, ending with an après-ski social for members and guests. Throughout the year, members organize potluck dinners, banquets, hikes, bike rides, golf outings, tennis tournaments, and other activities, and a monthly newsletter keeps members up-to-date on coming activities. Anybody may join or participate as a guest.

Membership dues are $225 for a single, $410 for a couple. For those who don't ski, a summer/social membership is offered for $50 a year. It includes the newsletter and all summer and social activities but does not include skiing with the gang.

For information: OHG, PO Box 3488, Copper Mountain, CO 89443; 800-458-8386 or 970-968-3059, ext. 60886; www.coppercolorado.com.

THE 100 CLUB

The 100 Club is open to couples whose combined ages total 100 years or more and singles who are 50 or older. Club members, beginners to experts, meet on the sundeck at Sunlight Mountain Resort in Glenwood Springs, Colorado, each Wednesday at 10 A.M. and Saturday mornings at the Ullrhof at Snowmaas during the season to ski together and stay for lunch. Guests are welcome. After the ski season ends, members get together for dinner, hiking, biking, or horseback riding. Cost for membership is currently $10 a year and includes a monthly newsletter.

For information: 100 Club, c/o Hal Sundin, 810 N. Traver Trail, Glenwood Springs, CO 81601; 970-945-0966.

OVER THE HILL GANG (OTHG)

OTHG is a club for energetic, fun-loving individuals and couples (one spouse must be at least 50) that schedules a wide assortment of guided ski trips every year in this country and abroad. Members—about 6,000, with 97 percent of them active skiers to date—are entitled to reduced rates for lift tickets, lessons, rentals, services, equipment, lodging, car rentals, dining, and transportation at nearly 100 of the top ski areas, in most cases, whether or not they are skiing with the club on their own.

The club's 13 regional "gangs," or chapters, in the U.S. run their own ski trips as well, and all members everywhere are invited to go along. At some ski areas, local and visiting members meet regularly to ski in small groups with similar ability, each group led by its own guide. At Steamboat, for example, they gather four days a week during the season. At Vail, they ski together on Mondays; at Breckenridge, on Tuesdays; at Winter Park, on Wednesdays; and at Keystone, on Thursday mornings. Out-of-town members and anyone else over 50 are invited to come along.

Members who reach their 70th birthday (and are willing to admit it) are part of the "Over 70 Gang," and members who have turned 80 are included in the "Over 80 Gang." They receive special shoulder patches and a discount on their next membership renewal or their next trip with the club.

When ski season ends, you may join OTHG for other activities including biking, rafting, hiking, and golfing (see Chapter 14).

Annual membership fee: $50 single, $80 per couple (three years for $125 or $190), plus chapter dues if you join a local gang.

For information: Over the Hill Gang International, 1820 W. Colorado Ave., Dept. G., Colorado Springs, CO 80904; 719-389-0022; www.othgi.com.

SENIORS ALPINE SKI CLUB

Based in Calgary, Alberta, this club for skiers 55 or older, run by volunteers, organizes affordable two- to four-day tours to major ski mountains as well as day trips via carpooling to world-class resorts within reach of the Calgary and Edmonton areas. When they're not skiing, members—who pay $20 per person per year—get a chance to attend biannual dinner dances and take part in a golf tournament. Although most members are residents of Alberta, the club has many participants from British Columbia and even the U.S. Six newsletters a year keep them informed about the club activities.

For information: Seniors Alpine Ski Club, 1725 10th Ave. SW, Calgary, AB, Canada T3C 0K1; 403-263-6167; www .seniorsalpineskiclub.com.

70+ SKI CLUB

The minute you hit 70, you're eligible to join the 70+ Ski Club for an annual fee of $10 ($15 for couples)—until you're 90, when you pay only a one-time $10 fee. Don't laugh. Among the approximately 18,000 registered members world-wide, 174 are over the age of 90 and almost 4,000 are between 80 and 90. Members get a selection of ski trips and special events every year at ski resorts throughout the U.S. and Canada and sometimes in Europe and South America. Hunter Mountain in New York hosts the club's annual meeting each March. Here the 70+ Ski Races have become such a popular event that contestants are divided into three age groups: men 70 to 80, women 70 to 80, and anyone over 80. Awards are presented at a gala party at the lodge.

Founded in 1977, the club has always promoted the interests of senior skiers, especially those on limited incomes. Today, largely as a result of its efforts, most ski areas give seniors free or half-price lift tickets.

Proof of age is required with your application to join the club, and you may not apply earlier than two weeks before your 70th birthday. Members receive a patch, a membership card, a periodic newsletter, and a directory of areas around the country that offer discounts or free skiing.

For information: 70+ Ski Club, 1633 Albany St., Schenec-tady, NY 12304; 518-346-5505; www.70plusskiclub.com.

SKIMEISTERS

A group of 55-plus skiers based in Denver, the SkiMeisters ski together at Colorado's Winter Park in small groups led by volunteer guides. They ski on scheduled Wednesdays, Thursdays, and Sundays from November to April. Guided cross-country ski days are included as well as group trips to other resorts. With 400 members and a waiting list, the club charges a onetime fee of $100, then $50 a year per person. Guests are permitted but they may ski with the club only twice during the season. To keep themselves busy when the ski season is over, members get together for biking, hiking, rafting, tennis, and golf.

For information: SkiMeisters, PO Box 620625, Littleton, CO 80162.

THE WILD OLD BUNCH

Skiers who frequent Alta in Utah are advised to search out members of the Wild Old Bunch, an informal group of long-time skiers who hang out together on the mountain and welcome anyone who wants to join them. There are no rules, no regulations, no meetings. The only requirement is that you must be over 55. The group grows haphazardly as members pick up stray mature skiers on the slopes. Lunch is usually at 11 A.M. on the deck of the midmountain Alps Inn.

For information: Look for the Wild Old Bunch on the slopes.

GOOD DEALS EVERYWHERE FOR SKIERS

The older you are, the less it costs to ski. There's hardly a ski area in North America today that doesn't give mature skiers a break. Many cut the price of lift tickets in half for skiers at age 60 or 65, and most stop charging altogether at 70, although a few—Alta and Powder Mountain in Utah, for example—make you wait until you're 80 to ski free. A few areas charge anybody over the age of 65 only $5 a day for lift tickets, and most make offers on season passes that are hard to refuse. Others plan special senior programs specifically for mature skiers.

To give you an idea of what's out there, here is a sampling of the special senior programs, workshops, and clubs in the states where downhill skiing is big business. This list does not include all areas, of course, so be sure to check out others in locations that interest you. Remember to carry proof of age with you at all times. The ski areas change their programs frequently, so while you can use the following information as a guide, you must do your own research too.

CALIFORNIA

Ski in California and you'll get good deals on lift tickets and season passes almost everywhere. Plus, there are some special programs designed especially for mature skiers, such as the following.

Every Thursday, Tahoe Donner offers skiers age 55 and over morning and/or afternoon clinics, a lift ticket, and lunch with top senior instructors. The cost at this writing is $25.

Donner Ski Ranch's deal for skiers 65 through 69 is a daily lift ticket for $5. Skiers 70 or older ski free.

At Northstar-at-Tahoe, the Golden Stars Workshop offers three days of instruction and camaraderie to skiers 65-plus. The program is for intermediate or advanced level skiers and includes a lunch, an après-ski party, a three-day lift ticket, and three hours of instruction daily. Current cost is $189 for seniors ages 65 to 69 and $135 for those 70 or more.

Royal Gorge Cross Country Ski Resort on Donner Summit schedules its Silver Streak Week every year, a week of specials for skiers 50 and older that offers reduced fees for trail passes and group lessons. You get a free trail pass for the entire season if you're 75.

Southern California's Mountain High has its Senior Days for 60-plus skiers on Wednesdays from 8 A.M. to 2 P.M. They include a lift ticket and two two-hour lessons. Up to age 69, the cost at this writing is $39 a day; at 70, it's only $25.

Adults, intermediate through expert, can take advantage of the Vertical Improvement Clinic, free with the purchase of a lift ticket morning and afternoon, any day they choose at Sierra-at-Tahoe. Although the clinic is not strictly for over-50 skiers, it attracts plenty of them.

At Heavenly Ski Resort, there are free four-hour workshops for skiers over 55. Mammoth Mountain offers three-day senior ski clinics.

Squaw Valley USA is offering a Just for Women Ski Clinic designed for women over the age of 50. The three-day clinic in January, which provides older women the chance to learn new technology, skills, and techniques, features women-specific coaching, stretching techniques, video feedback, workshops, and evening socials. The cost, currently $545, includes all activities, lunch, and lift tickets.

By the way, Squaw Valley, which reduces lift tickets for skiers over 65 and gives free rides to those over 75, offers $5 in Squaw Bucks valid all over the mountain to anybody hitting the slopes over the age of 85.

COLORADO

Every ski area in Colorado offers discounted lift tickets to seniors, some starting at 60, others at 65, and almost every ski area charges nothing at all to ski after you reach age 70. And many special programs, lessons, and clubs are especially designed for mature skiers.

Aspen Mountain offers skiers over 70 a season pass for $189 that allows unlimited skiing there and also at Snowmass, Ajax, Buttermilk, and Aspen Highlands.

At Breckenridge, two-day Silver Skiing Seminars in January and February for skiers over 50 of all abilities, taught by seniors, include lift tickets, lessons, video analysis, and a group dinner.

Breckenridge is the place where members of the local Over the Hill Gang, plus any other visitors 50 and over, get together on Tuesdays for a day on the slopes with their own guide.

It's Thursday mornings at Keystone for Gang members and visitors to ski with volunteer guides.

Also at Keystone, Senior Winter Games are organized by local skiers and held in February every year. Downhill skiing and skating events are held at K Resort.

At Vail, any skier over 50 is welcome to meet on Mondays and ski with OTHG members.

At Steamboat, led by local guides, they gang up on the slopes every day from Sunday through Friday during the season. Steamboat also gives skiers 65-plus a 20 percent discount on most ski programs.

Ski at Arapahoe Basin at 70-plus and you get a season pass for $30.

Join the Over the Hill Gang (OHG) at Copper Mountain and you can ski with volunteer guides on Tuesdays, Wednesdays, Saturdays, and Sundays; party with the members; and participate in other activities such as golf outings, bike rides, tennis tournaments, and social events.

The good news at Crested Butte Mountain Resort is that anybody 70 and over skis and snowboards free, while those ages 65 to 69 pay only half price for lift tickets. All 65-plus skiers also get 50 percent off group lessons and 25 percent off private lessons.

The 100 Club for singles over 50 or couples whose combined ages total 100 years or more meets Wednesdays at Sunlight Mountain Resort in Glenwood Springs and Saturdays at Snowmass.

At Powderhorn Resort, just show up any Tuesday morning during the season and join the Seniors Clinic, an informal group of mature skiers who ski together and work to improve their skills. The cost right now is $20 per lesson.

At Eldora, skiers and snowboarders 65 and older can participate in Senior Ski every Tuesday. Senior Days at Ski Cooper gives you a day lift ticket, free racing, and an après-ski party.

Every winter, Purgatory Resort in Durango schedules two one-week skiing and social events for skiers over 50. Called the Snowmasters Classic, each session, which currently costs $75, includes daily continental breakfast, two wine and cheese parties, and three half-day clinics. The clinics are chosen from the following subjects: shaped skis, powder skiing, racing, mogul skiing, and ski improvement. Participants get discounts on lift tickets, rentals, accommodations, food, and more.

The SkiMeisters ski together at Winter Park every Wednesday, Thursday, and Sunday from November to April. A membership club with a onetime fee of $100 and then an annual fee of $50, it has about 400 members and a waiting list.

IDAHO

Sun Valley's Prime Time, a week reserved for older skiers, is scheduled twice each winter. It includes seven nights' lodging, five days of lift tickets or a Nordic trail package, discount coupons, races, parties, special events, and a Big Band Buffet Dinner Dance. Skiers over 60 pay less for the package than those under 60.

Schweitzer Mountain's Prime Timers Club for skiers 55 and over is an informal club whose members ski together almost every day and get together for social gatherings on Thursday afternoons. In addition, there's a bargain senior ski week in March, the Snowmaster's Classic, a week of workshops, clinics, social activities, and race training for older skiers who are seeking to improve their technical abilities.

MAINE

At Sunday River, those who purchase the Perfect Turn Gold or Platinum Card and are over 50 may become members of the Prime Time Club. Members ski together every weekday at 10 A.M. and participate in many off-mountain field trips and parties too.

Shawnee Peak starts cutting costs for season passes at age 65, reduces them drastically at 70-plus, and charges skiers 80 and over $50.

MASSACHUSETTS

Ski every day all winter at Ski Butternut for only $99 if you've passed your 70th birthday, or pay $10 for a day ticket. At ages 50 to 69, you can buy a full-day lift ticket on any nonholiday Monday or Tuesday for $15.

At Jiminy Peak in Hancock, you may join the Silver Sliders every Thursday morning for coffee and a two-hour lesson. The six-week program is designed exclusively for people over 50, expert or novice, who want to perfect their technique of skiing or snowboarding.

MICHIGAN

The Silver Streak program at Crystal Mountain for skiers 60 or older offers free skiing when you book midweek lodging, excluding holidays. Other privileges for mature skiers include half price on lift tickets, cross-country trail passes, rental equipment, and group lessons, again excluding holidays.

At Caberfae Peaks Ski Resort in Cadillac, every Tuesday, Wednesday, and Thursday (except during the major holiday weeks) are Silver Streak Days, when anybody over the age of 50 is allowed to ski all day for only $15. In addition to the lift ticket, you will receive free rental skis and a one-hour lesson.

NEW HAMPSHIRE

It's a rare ski area in this state that does not offer older skiers an impressive break on lift tickets. Many also have special programs for senior skiers.

If you're 55 or more, you can join the Silver Streaks, a program for alpine skiers, cross-country skiers, and snowboarders, at Waterville Valley, paying an annual membership fee of $65. You'll get to ski or board the slopes with a guide several mornings a week and participate in races, clinics, and parties. Silver Streaks for cross-country skiers meets at the Nordic Center on Wednesdays to explore the White Mountain National Forest led by retirees from the U.S. Forest Service.

Attitash Bear Peak's T.G.I.F. (Thank Goodness I'm Fifty) program is a social club for senior skiers who meet every Thursday morning for coffee and a couple of hours on the slopes with an instructor. The cost is $90 for the season.

Loon Mountain's Flying 50s Plus meets every Thursday and Friday morning, except holiday weeks, for two-hour group skiing with friends and an instructor. Members pay $109 for the season.

At Cannon Mountain, Cannon Cruisers for skiers over 50 meets Monday mornings to ski for two hours with instructors at $10 per session or $79 for 10 sessions.

Skiers 50-plus get a lift ticket and lesson at Wildcat for $35 on nonholiday Tuesday mornings.

And at Mount Sunapee, Senior Cruisers for skiers and boarders age 65 and over meet on nonholiday Wednesday mornings throughout the season for skiing and socializing.

NEW MEXICO

Sign up for a Masters Ski Week at Taos Ski Valley if you are 50-plus and you get six consecutive mornings of instruction, all-day lift tickets for the week, and après-ski seminars.

NEW YORK

Skiers over 50 are invited to join the Senior Ski Program at Ski Windham for eight weeks of Tuesdays in January and

February. The purpose is to strengthen skiing skills, social-ize, and meet new people. Join for all eight weeks or by the day, if you prefer. What you get is morning coffee, guest speakers, two-hour morning and afternoon on-snow lessons, and a midweek nonholiday season pass to Ski Windham. For information, call 518-734-5070.

UTAH

Virtually all of Utah's ski areas give senior skiers reduced rates on lift tickets at 55, 60, or 65. Most others stop charging at 70—except Alta and Powder Mountain, where you must wait until you are 80.

By the way, don't forget to check out Alta's Wild Old Bunch that gets together informally to ski almost every morning. Anybody 55 or over is welcome to join the group on the slopes and then eat an early lunch at the mid-mountain Alps Inn.

At Snowbird, any intermediate or expert skier 62 or more may join the famous instructor Junior Bounous for a complimentary ski outing for a couple of hours on Tuesday mornings. If you like, you can continue to ski with him in the afternoon for more ski tips and instruction.

Sundance sells an all-day pass to seniors 65 or older for $12. Other adults pay $40.

As for Brighton Ski Resort, the Senior Workshop, a three-day program for "seasoned skiers" over 50, focuses on terrain, snow conditions, weather, conditioning, and moti-vation. It includes lessons and a lift ticket.

VERMONT

Vermont's ski areas were the first to cater to older skiers. It is highly unlikely that there are any resorts there that don't give seniors a decent break on lift tickets and season passes. Along with special rates, several areas offer special senior programs as well. Here's a sample.

Stratton Mountain's Trailblazers, open to skiers or snowboarders over 50 (and their partners), schedules activities for its hundreds of members almost every day of the week, starting with bridge or canasta on Mondays, snowshoe and cross-country activities on Wednesdays, recreational racing on Fridays, and après-ski parties whenever. Members may also participate in a special 50-plus ski clinic program that comes in two versions. The first, for full-time residents of the area, meets Monday, Wednesday, and Friday mornings (except on holidays) to ski in small groups with an instructor; the second is a weekend program that meets on Saturday mornings for 14 weeks. The basic membership fee is $25 a year per person, with an extra charge for participation in the ski clinics.

At Jay Peak, any skier 55 to 65 is invited to join Silver Peaks, a group that skis together every Tuesday. For $36, you are entitled to a day that includes your lift ticket, guide, coffee and doughnuts, and après-ski activities. Over 65, you may ski here any time for $12 a day and join the club on Tuesday too, if you like.

The Prime Time Club at Sugarbush offers skiers age 50 years and up, levels five to eight, a chance to meet, ski, and learn with a group of their peers. The club meets Tuesday and Thursday mornings for skiing on a variety of terrains.

Mount Snow's Prime-Time Seniors program, also for skiers and snowboarders 50 and over, meets once a week in February and March and offers clinics and a specialized video as well as resort savings.

The Silver Griffins at Bromley Mountain meet every non-holiday Monday through Friday for group skiing, clinics, fun races, picnics, and parties. Members of the group get preferred parking midweek and discounts on food, equipment, and lessons. The annual fee is $15.

Okemo's Trailblazers Program for intermediate and advanced adult skiers runs for a six-week series on Sunday mornings. Come as a single or put your own group of peers together. You'll meet in the morning for coffee and then ski with others of similar ability and pace with the guidance of a teaching professional. Skiers 65-plus get a half-price discount on group ski and snowboard lessons and a good break on lift tickets.

Members of Smuggler's Notch 55-Plus Club meet every Wednesday morning for coffee and bagels, then head to the slopes, finishing the day with a presentation from a guest speaker. Members 55 to 69 can ski on Wednesdays at 50 percent off the regular lift prices, while skiers over 70 ski free any time they wish. All members also get half price on rentals, group lessons, and cross-country trail fees on Wednesdays, as well as 20 percent on merchandise in the ski shop. If you want to join the club, the cost is $25 for the season.

WISCONSIN

Skiers over 55 get a lift ticket, day or night, Monday through Friday, for $10 at Cascade Mountain Ski Area in Portage.

16

Perks in Parks and Other Good News

All over the U.S. and Canada, enterprising officials in states, provinces, and cities have initiated some enticing programs designed to capture the imagination of the mature population. Often they are expressing their appreciation of our many contributions to society and simply want to do something special for us. And sometimes they are trying to attract us and our vacation dollars to their neighborhoods, having discovered that we're always ready to enjoy ourselves and know a good deal when we see one.

But, first, keep in mind:

- Before you set off for a new place, send ahead for free maps, calendars of events, booklets describing sites and scenes of interest, accommodation guides, and perhaps even a list of special discounts or other good things that are available to you as a person over 50. For state-by-state tourism information online, go to the website operated by the Travel Industry of America, www.seeamerica .org, and click on "Tour America Map."

■ Many states offer passes for admission to their state parks and recreation facilities for free or at reduced prices to people who are old enough to have learned how to treat those areas respectfully.

■ Following the section on national parks, you'll find information about state park passes and special events in many states. There may be other good deals that have escaped our attention, but those in this chapter are probably the cream of the crop.

NATIONAL PARKS

CANADIAN NATIONAL PARKS

The national parks and national historic sites throughout Canada charge modest entry fees for adults and take about 20 percent off those for visitors over 65. The same is generally true for provincial parks.

GOLDEN AGE PASSPORT

The Golden Age Passport is one of the best senior travel bargains around. Good for a lifetime, it costs only $10 for U.S. citizens or permanent residents who are at least 62 and gives free admission to all national parks that charge entrance fees, even the White House. An entire carload of family and friends, whatever their ages, also get in free when you enter a park with a per-car fee in a private vehicle, so one pass is enough if you're a couple or a group traveling together. Where a per-person fee is charged, your pass admits you, your spouse, and your children.

You'll also get a 50 percent discount on federal use fees charged for facilities and services such as camping, swim-

ESCAPEES CLUB

Escapees is a club dedicated to providing a support network for RVers, full-time or part-time, many of whom are on the far side of 50. It publishes a bulky bimonthly magazine filled with useful information for travelers who carry their homes with them; organizes rallies in the U.S., Canada, and Mexico; and hosts five-day seminars on RV living. Its almost 50 regional chapters also coordinate rallies and host get-togethers, and its Birds of a Feather (BOF) groups connect members who have common interests.

Benefits include a discount directory listing 800 commercial parks and campgrounds that provide 15 to 50 percent discounts to members, emergency road service, mail service, calling card service, vehicle insurance, and voice message service. After a $10 enrollment fee, the annual membership fee is $60 a year per family with a U.S. address.

The club has established its own CARE Center (Continuing Assistance for Retired Escapees), a separate RV campground where retired members can live independently in their own RVs while receiving medical and living assistance, housekeeping, and transportation services as needed.

For information: Escapees, Inc., 100 Rainbow Dr., Livingston, TX 77351; 888-757-2582 or 936-327-8873; www.escapees .com.

ming, boat launching, parking, and tours. It does not, however, cover or reduce special permit fees charged by concessionaires.

The passport is not available by mail or online but must be purchased in person, so pick yours up at the first park you visit or at a regional office of the National Park Service, the U.S. Forest Service, or the Fish and Wildlife Service. Your driver's license will do just fine as proof of age.

If you're under 62, what you need is the National Parks Pass, which costs $50 and is good for a year from the first time you use it. It gives you—and any accompanying passengers arriving with you in a private vehicle—free admission to any national park, forest, recreation area, monument, or wildlife refuge that charges an entrance fee. When a per-person entrance fee is charged, it admits you, your spouse, your children, and your parents.

Buy your National Parks Pass by mail, telephone, or online. If you belong to AARP, you can save $5 if you order it on the AARP website.

For information: National Park Foundation, PO Box 34108, Washington, DC 20043; 888-GOPARKS (888-467-2757); www.nationalparks.org or www.nps.gov/fees_passes.htm.

AARP PARK PROGRAMS

At several of the country's national parks and resorts, members of AARP can save up to 25 percent on lodging packages, tours, houseboat rentals, and outdoor activities, as well as 10 percent on purchases at some park gift shops. Check out the offerings at parks that include Denali National Park in Alaska, Olympic National Park in Washington, Shenandoah National Park in Virginia, Mesa Verde in Colorado, and Lake Powell in Rainbow Bridge National Monument in Arizona/Utah.

For information: AARP, 800-424-3410; www.aarp.org or www.aramarkparks.com/aarp.

GOOD DEALS FROM THE STATES

Virtually every state has a special senior rate for hunting and fishing licenses for people over a certain age (usually 65). Some states require no license at all for seniors, while others give you a reduced fee (usually half). Most require that you be a resident of the state in order to get these privileges. Most states also offer state park discounts to seniors, usually only residents, reducing or eliminating entrance fees and marking down camping rates. A few have other privileges to offer, such as shopping discounts. To check out the regulations and offers in your state or a state you are visiting, contact the state or local parks department or the state tourism office.

CALIFORNIA

At California State Parks, anybody 62 and over saves $2 on overnight camping fees and $1 on parking. Just show proof of age at the gate. And, for $10, seniors may buy a Limited Use Golden Bear Pass that gives them free parking between Labor Day and Memorial Day.

For information: California Parks and Recreation, 800-777-0369 or 916-653-6995; www.parks.ca.gov.

COLORADO

The Aspen Leaf Annual Pass entitles Colorado residents 62 and over to free year-round entrance to state parks any day and reduced fees for camping Sundays through Thursdays except on holidays. The pass costs $10 per year.

For information: Colorado Division of State Parks, 1313 Sherman St., Room 618, Denver, CO 80203; 303-866-3437; www.parks.state.co.us.

If you're at least 60 years old and live in Boulder, you're in luck. You may join the Gold Rush Club offered by Boulder Senior Services and take advantage of special savings at local businesses including some restaurants, and participate in many activities from classes to day trips and overnight adventures, special events, and wellness programs. You can join other members in monthly social get-togethers, tennis games, hikes, volleyball, strength training, yoga, water exercise, golf, and workouts, and get special rates on massage and reflexology. Membership costs $12 a year ($7 for a second member of the same household, who may be younger than 60).

For information: Gold Rush Club, Boulder Senior Services, 909 Arapahoe Ave., Boulder, CO 80302; 303-441-3148; www.boulderseniorservices.com.

CONNECTICUT

Residents of Connecticut who are over 65 get a free lifetime Charter Oak Pass that gets them into all state parks and forests plus Gillette Castle, Dinosaur Park, and Quinebaug Valley Hatchery for free. To get your pass, write to the address given and send along a copy of your current Connecticut driver's license.

For information: DEP, Charter Oak Pass, State Parks Division, 79 Elm St., Hartford, CT 06106; 860-424-3200; www.dep.state.ct.us.

FLORIDA

Orlando, one of the most popular destinations in the U.S. today, is visited by more than seven million mature travelers a year. To accommodate them, the Orlando Visitors Bureau offers a list of discounts for visitors age 55 or older at about 50 establishments in the area, including attractions, accommodations, and cultural sites. This list, however, is available only on the website that follows.

Whatever your age, be sure to acquire the free Orlando Magicard that's valid for up to six people, any age, and provides even more discounts. You may pick it up at the Official Visitor Center at 8723 International Drive or get it online.

For information: Orlando Visitors Bureau, 6700 Forum Dr., Orlando, FL 32821; 800-643-9492; www.orlandoinfo.com.

If you're a pair of "Senior Sweethearts," you qualify for special rates at many historic inns in St. Augustine, America's oldest city, for a two- or three-day stay from Sunday through Thursday during the months of January or June. Stay two nights and the second night is half price; stay three and the third night is free.

For information: 866-801-2990; www.seniorsweetheart.com.

To snowbirds spending the cold months in Panama City Beach, the Convention & Visitors Bureau offers its Winter Resident SunCard program. With it, seniors are entitled to complimentary coffee and doughnuts twice a month and can get discounts at participating area restaurants, hotels, attractions, and events. Stop by at the Visitors Information Center or call the number shown here.

For information: Panama City Beach CVB, 17001 Panama City Beach Pkwy., Panama City Beach, FL 32413; 800-PCBEACH (800-722-3224) or 850-233-5070; in Canada, 800-553-1330; www.thebeachloversbeach.com.

The thick little coupon booklet, *$1,000 Worth of the Palm Beaches for Free*, is not exclusively for visitors over 50, but it is included here because it offers many ways to save money in the off-season (April to mid-December), such as discounts, two-for-one deals, and complimentary offers on shopping, dining, sporting activities, and attractions.

For information: Palm Beach County Convention and Visitors Bureau, 1555 Palm Beach Lakes Blvd., West Palm Beach, FL 33401; 800-554-PALM or 561-233-3000; www .palmbeachfl.com.

HAWAII

Hawaii caters to the over-50 crowd, and there are discounts for almost everything, including hotels, golf courses, rental cars, and movies. If you live in Oahu and are 65-plus, take advantage of an offer from TheBus, the municipal bus system. This is a pass good for a year of unlimited travel on the island for only $30 or one month for $5. Or simply pay half fare (75 cents) after presenting your Medicare card to the driver when you board the bus. Yet another choice is the Visitor Pass, which is available for all ages and costs $15 for four days of unlimited travel.

For information: TheBus Customer Service, 811 Middle St., Honolulu, HI 96819; 808-848-5555; www.thebus.org.

INDIANA

The Golden Hoosier Passport admits Indiana residents over the age of 60 and fellow passengers in a private vehicle to all state parks and natural resources without charge. An application for the passport, which costs $12 a year, is available at all state parks.

For information: Indiana State Parks Dept., 402 W. Washington St., Indianapolis, IN 46204; 800-622-4931 or 317-232-4124; www.in.gov/dnr/parklake/fees.

KANSAS

If you're over 65 and a Kansas resident, show proof of age at the gate and you'll pay only half of the usual adult entry fee at all state parks. In addition, at the same age residents of the state no longer require a hunting and fishing license, although they must pay for special permits to hunt certain game.

For information: Kansas Department of Wildlife and Parks, 1020 S. Kansas, Topeka, KS 66612; 785-296-2281; www.kdwp.state.ks.us.

MAINE

Pick up your Senior Citizen Pass at age 65 and you will get free admission to all state parks and historic sites. The pass is available at no cost at any state park or by writing to the Bureau of Parks and Lands. Be sure to include proof of your age.

For information: Maine Bureau of Parks and Lands, State House Station 22, Augusta, ME 04333; 207-287-3821; www.state.me.us/doc.

MASSACHUSETTS

For just 50 cents, all seniors 60 and older may ride the Breeze buses and seasonal trolleys run by the Cape Cod Regional Transit Authority. The Breeze serves all major Cape Cod destinations, including Hyannis, Provincetown, Woods Hole, and Orleans. Residents of Cape Cod may also enroll in the dial-a-ride program, reserving in advance and paying $1.50 per ride plus 5 cents a mile for place-to-place transportation for any purpose.

For information: 800-352-7155; www.thebreeze.info.

You may fish and hunt for free in Massachusetts once you're 70 years old if you are a state resident, and if you're between 65 and 69, you'll pay less than other people for the privilege. A fishing or hunting license costs a younger adult $25 while a 64- to 69-year-old pays $16.25.

For information: Massachusetts Division of Fisheries and Wildlife, 508-792-7270; www.mass.gov/masswildlife.

MICHIGAN

You can get some good deals in Michigan if you are a resident who's reached the age of 65. These include a motor-vehicle permit for $5 a year that gets you into all state parks and a fishing or hunting license for $5.60 a year.

For information: Call the Department of Natural Resources at 517-373-9900; www.michigan.gov/dnr.

GOOD SAM CLUB

The **Good Sam Club** is an international organization of people who travel in recreational vehicles, mentioned here because the vast majority of those in rolling homes are over 50. Its goal is to make RVing safer, more enjoyable, and less expensive. Among the benefits are 10 percent discounts on nightly fees at more than 1,600 RV parks and campgrounds, plus more discounts on propane, parts, and accessories at hundreds of service centers.

The club offers a toll-free hotline, a lost key service, a lost pet service, trip routing, mail forwarding, a telephone message service, insurance, a magazine, and campground directories. Most important, it provides low-cost emergency road service anywhere in the U.S. and Canada, including Alaska. Social activities include Good Sam rallies and travel tours and cruises all over the world. And about 2,100 local chapters in the U.S. and Canada hold campouts and meetings and participate in local volunteer projects. Membership is $19 a year per family.

For information: The Good Sam Club, PO Box 6888, Englewood, CO 80155; 800-234-3450; www.goodsamclub.com.

MONTANA

Purchase a Resident Conservation license for $4 from the Fish, Wildlife, and Parks Department and, if you are a resident of Montana and at least 62, it includes licenses at no extra cost for seasonal fishing, warm-water fishing, and upland bird and waterfowl hunting. You will pay only half the usual fee for hunting deer and elk, as well as for overnight camping. Anyone of any age who arrives at the entrance gate to a state park in a car with Montana license plates is admitted without charge.

For information: Montana Fish, Wildlife, and Parks Dept., 1420 E. 6th Ave., Helena, MT 59620; 406-444-2535; www .fwp.state.mt.us.

NEVADA

In Carson City, you will strike silver without doing any digging—if you are over 50 and join the free Seniors Strike Silver Club. You'll get a list of discounts in town, plus a membership card to present as identification to participating lodgings.

For information: Carson City Convention & Visitors Bureau, 1900 S. Carson St., Carson City, NV 89701; 800-NEVADA-1 (800-638-2321) or 775-687-7410; www.carson -city.org.

NEW JERSEY

If you are at least 65, you may travel at half the regular fare anytime any day of the week aboard New Jersey Transit trains and buses. If you're only 62 to 64, you'll get the same deal but during off-peak hours—9:30 A.M. to 4 P.M. and 7 P.M. to 6 A.M. Either way, just show proof of age, such as a Medicare card or driver's license, or flash a Reduced Fare Card.

State residents who are at least 62 years of age are eligible for free senior citizen passes from the New Jersey Division of Parks and Forestry. With the pass, you pay nothing for admission and parking at all state parks, recreation areas, and historic sites. In addition, the Division of Fish and Wildlife reduces the cost of a fishing license by about half for those who are 65 to 69, while those at least 70 may fish for free. Hunting license fees are cut in half for seniors 65 and over.

For information: NJ Transit, 800-772-3606; www.njtransit.com. New Jersey Division of Parks and Forestry, 800-843-6420; www.njparksandforests.org. New Jersey Division of Fish and Wildlife, 609-292-2965; www.njfishandwildlife.com.

NEW YORK

Simply by presenting your current valid New York driver's license or a New York nondriver's identification card, you will be entitled to all of the privileges of the Golden Park Program for residents over the age of 62. The program offers, any weekday except holidays, free vehicle access to state parks and arboretums; reduced entrance fees at state historic sites; and reduced fees for state operated swimming, golf, tennis, and boat rentals. Just show your driver's license or ID card at the entrance of the facility.

For information: State Parks, Albany, NY 12238; 518-474-0456; www.nysparks.com.

At age 65, you can ride the commuter railroads and most bus lines in New York State by showing proof of age. You can also buy a reduced-fare MetroCard that entitles you to half fare on New York City's local buses and trains 24 hours a day and a fare of $1.50 on express buses between the hours of 10 A.M. and 3 P.M. Call for an application and instructions. By the way, a Fun Pass, good for a day of unlimited travel in New York City, may be purchased by anyone of any age for $4. Buy it in any subway station.

For information: New York City Transit Reduced-Fare Line, 718-243-4999; www.mta.nyc.ny.us.

OHIO

You are in luck if you live in Ohio because the minute you turn 60, you may sign up for a free Golden Buckeye Card that gives you discounts on prescription drugs and savings for such things as meals, entertainment, merchandise, and services at thousands of businesses all over the state. Some merchants offer daily discounts, some on certain days of the week, some during certain seasons of the year. Most Ohio residents receive their cards in the mail soon after their 60th birthdays, but if you don't get yours, call the toll-free number for the location of a sign-up site near you.

For information: Golden Buckeye Card Program, Ohio Dept. of Aging, 50 W. Broad St., 9th floor, Columbus, OH 43215; 800-422-1976 (in Ohio) or 614-466-5500; www .goldenbuckeye.com.

PENNSYLVANIA

In Pennsylvania, the Lottery Fund pays for many good things for seniors. Among them is free statewide transportation. Anyone 65 or older, resident of the state or not, can acquire a special identification card that gets him or her aboard scheduled buses, trolleys, subways, and commuter rail services without paying a cent. They must, however, travel off-peak: before 7 A.M., between 8 A.M. and 4:30 P.M., or after 5:30 P.M. on weekdays, and all day on weekends and designated holidays. Get the senior ID card from your local participating transportation company, then use it as a boarding card.

On the Southeastern Pennsylvania Transportation Authority (SEPTA) regional rail lines in the Philadelphia area, those traveling within Pennsylvania with a valid senior ID pay only $1 to ride the trains during the same non-peak weekday hours as above and on all weekends and holidays.

Another perk is the Shared Ride Program, also funded by the state lottery, which provides door-to-door transportation, usually by van, at a discount of up to 85 percent to anybody over 65 who requests it and makes an advance reservation.

For information: Call your local transit agency or the Bureau of Public Transportation, Pennsylvania Department of Transportation, PO Box 3151, Harrisburg, PA 17105; 717-783-8025; www.dot.state.pa.us. For SEPTA, 215-580-7478; www.septa.com.

PUERTO RICO

When you book accommodations at any of Puerto Rico's network of 24 small family-owned country inns called paradores (each one of which is different), be sure to mention that you are 65 or over and you will get 10 percent off the room rate as well as a flat rate of $30 for the third night of your stay.

For information: Puerto Rico Tourism Company, PO Box 902-3960, San Juan, PR 00902; 800-866-7827; www.goto puertorico.com.

You may travel free on the public buses in the San Juan metropolitan area if you are at least 75 and apply for a

Golden Program Pass. It's worth the paperwork if you are a resident or a visitor who plans an extended stay.

For information: Call 787-282-7115 or go to the Officina del Programa Dorado in the Terminal de Capetillo in San Juan.

SOUTH CAROLINA

Residents of South Carolina who are 65 or older must merely show their driver's licenses to get free admission at all state parks, plus half off on both the camping fees at all parks and the greens fees at Hickory Knob and Cheraw State Parks.

For information: South Carolina Department of Parks, Recreation, and Tourism, 1205 Pendleton St., Columbia, SC 29201; 803-734-0166; www.discoversouthcarolina.com.

TENNESSEE

Anyone over the age of 62, state resident or not, gets a 10 percent discount on food at park restaurants, cabins, and rooms at the Resort Park Inns. Tennessee residents over 62 pay no greens fees at state golf courses on Mondays. They are charged only 50 percent of the regular camping fees, while out-of-state 62-plus campers are entitled to a 10 percent reduction. Admission to all state parks is free, regardless of your age.

For information: Tennessee Parks and Wildlife, 401 Church St., LC Tower, Nashville, TN 37243; 800-421-6683; www.tnstatepark.com.

TEXAS

The Parkland Pass is free to all comers, residents of Texas or not, who are over the age of 65. If you turned 65 on or before August 31, 1995, the pass gives you free admission to state parks. If your 65th birthday was after that date, it admits you to the parks at half price. Pick up the pass at any park.

For information: Texas Parks and Wildlife, 4200 Smith School Rd., Austin, TX 78744; 800-792-1112 or 512-389-4800; www.tpwd.state.tx.us.

If you are a winter snowbird in Galveston, be sure to stop at the Galveston Island Visitor Information Center and sign up for a free Special Winter Texan ID card. It gives you discounts or specials at more than 100 businesses on the island, including accommodations, attractions, auto services, banking services, retail stores, restaurants, medical services, fishing charters, and golf courses.

For information: Galveston Island Visitor Information Center, 2428 Seawall Blvd., Galveston, TX 77550; 888-425-4753 or 409-763-4311; www.galvestoncvb.com.

UTAH

The Silver Card issued by Park City, an old mining town known for its great ski mountains, is a summer (June through September) program of discounts for visitors over 65. It provides 10 percent or more off at retail stores, attractions, and restaurants. Pick up your free ID card and an information packet at your hotel or the Park City Visitors Information Center.

For information: Park City and Visitors Bureau, 1910 Prospector Ave., Park City, UT 84060; 800-453-1360 or 435-649-6100; www.parkcityinfo.com.

VERMONT

Vermont residents age 62 or over can purchase a Green Mountain Passport for $2 from their own town clerk's office. It is good for a lifetime and entitles them to free admission to all state parks and state-sponsored events. Many local businesses offer discounts on merchandise and services to passport holders. In addition, residents 65-plus can get a lifetime hunting and fishing permit at a discounted cost.

For information: Vermont Dept. of Aging, 103 S. Main St., Waterbury, VT 05676; 802-241-2400; www.dad.state.vt.us. For hunting and fishing: Dept. of Fish and Wildlife, 802-241-3700.

VIRGINIA

Virginia offers many park passes just for those 62 and older. They include the Senior Lifetime Naturally Yours Passport Plus, good for parking and admission to state parks and discounts on facilities and equipment, which costs $100 but lasts for life; the Senior Parking Passport, $20, good for a year of parking and admission for your park of choice; and the Senior Park/Launch Passport that comes in various versions.

In this state that abounds with historic sites, you will find senior discounts almost everywhere you go. You will get them, for example, at Colonial Williamsburg, Busch Gardens, Mount Vernon, the Edgar Allen Poe Museum, and the Virginia Air and Space Center.

For information: Virginia State Parks, PO Box 1895, Richmond, VA 23218; 800-933-PARK (in Richmond, 225-3867); www.dcr.state.va.us/parks/passes. For historic sites:

Virginia Division of Tourism, 800-932-5827; www.vir ginia.org.

WASHINGTON

For $30, those 62-plus may buy an Off-Season Senior Citizen Pass that gives them free nightly camping or moorage in state parks from October 1 through March 31 and Sunday through Thursday in April.

For information: Washington State Parks, 7150 Cleanwater Lane, PO Box 42650, Olympia, WA 98504; 800-902-8500; www.parks.wa.gov.

WASHINGTON, D.C.

Senior theatergoers are in luck in Washington, D.C., because many theaters—including the Kennedy Center and the National Theater—offer them discounted tickets, sometimes even at half price. You may usually purchase your tickets in advance, but in some cases, you must wait until the day of the performance.

For information: Check with the theater that interests you.

If you're 65, you pay half price (currently 60 cents) to ride buses and subways in the nation's capital and the metropolitan area in Maryland and Virginia. For bus trips, you must show the driver a valid Metro Senior ID card or a Medicare card and photo identification with your address and date of birth. An alternative is a Metrobus Weekly Senior Pass that costs $6 and allows unlimited bus travel. You may purchase the cards at public libraries and Metro sales offices.

For traveling by subway, you require a specially encoded $10 Senior Fare Card to use as you enter and exit the system, allowing you to ride for half the regular adult fare. Apply for the card at Metro sales offices, Transit Stores, and some supermarkets.

For information: Washington Metropolitan Transit Authority, 202-637-7000; www.metroopensdoors.com.

WEST VIRGINIA

Everybody who turns 60 in West Virginia gets a Golden Mountaineer Discount Card, which entitles the bearer to 10 percent discounts from more than 600 participating merchants and pharmacies. If you don't receive a card in the mail from the state soon after your 60th birthday, you may apply for one at your local senior center or by calling 877-987-3646. Flash the card wherever you go and save yourself a few dollars.

West Virginia's state parks are free to everyone, no matter what age. Within the state parks, you are entitled (starting at age 60) to a discount of 10 percent on cabins and lodge rooms, camping fees, picnic-shelter reservations, and golfing greens fees. You'll also pay a lower fee for swimming. Be prepared to show proof of your age. West Virginia residents who are 62-plus get a 50 percent reduction on camping fees during the off-season.

For information: West Virginia Bureau of Senior Services, 1900 Kanawha Blvd. East, Charleston, WV 25305; 877-987-3646 or 304-558-3317; www.state.wv.us/seniorservices.

West Virginia Department of Parks, 1900 Kanawha Blvd., Charleston, WV 25305; 304-558-2764. Tourism hotline, 800-CALL-WVA (800-225-5982); www.callwva.com.

WISCONSIN

This state's residents who are over the age of 65 pay only half the annual fee for fishing and small-game hunting licenses and for the annual admission sticker that gets them into state parks. On a daily park pass, they save a dollar. Buy the stickers at the entrance to parking areas. Residents over 75 merely have to show proof of age to hunt or fish free.

For information: For hunting and fishing licenses: Wisconsin Department of Natural Resources, PO Box 7924, Madison, WI 53707; 877-945-4236; www.dnr.state.wi.us. For state parks admission stickers: DNR Parks & Recreation, PO Box 7921, Madison, WI 53707; 608-266-2181.

17

Back to Summer Camp

Maybe you thought camp was just for kids, but if you are a grown-up person who likes the outdoors, swimming, boating, birds, and arts and crafts—and if you appreciate fields and forests and star-filled skies—you too can pack your bags and go off on a sleepaway. Throughout the country, many camps set aside weeks for adult sessions, while others offer adult programs all season long. More and more adults are getting hooked on summer camp, and many wouldn't miss a year.

ASSOCIATION OF JEWISH SPONSORED CAMPS

You can renew your spirits by spending a week or two during the summer with other older Jewish men and women at one of the five adult camping centers operated by this association. All are inexpensive, and all but one serve kosher meals, put you up in lodges, and are located within a few hours of New York City. You'll be kept busy morning 'til night with activities and entertainment. The minimum age to be a camper is usually 55.

For information: Association of Jewish Sponsored Camps, 130 E. 59th St., New York, NY 10022; 212-751-0477; www .jewishcamps.org.

CHURCH-SPONSORED CAMPS

There are many adult camps and summer workshops sponsored by religious organizations—too many and too diverse to list here. One source of information is Christian Camping International, which publishes a directory of about 1,000 camps and conferences in the U.S.

For information: Christian Camping International/USA, PO Box 62189, Colorado Springs, CO 80962; 719-260-9400; www.cciusa.org.

ELDERHOSTEL

Many of Elderhostel's programs are a combination of camp and college. In this wildly successful low-cost educational program (see Chapter 13 for details), you can spend a week or two camping in remote scenic areas, enjoying all the activities from horseback riding to crafts, boating, campfires, and sleeping in a cabin or under the stars.

For information: Elderhostel, 11 Avenue de Lafayette, Boston, MA 02111; 877-426-8056 or 617-426-7788; www .elderhostel.org.

RV ELDERHOSTEL PROGRAMS

On these programs, you take along your own housing—a recreational vehicle, travel trailer, or tent—and stay on the host campus or at nearby campgrounds. Classes, usually held on the campus, are included, as are meals and excursions. On RV tours you join the group for classes, meals, and excursions but sleep on your own premises.

For information: Elderhostel, 11 Avenue de Lafayette, Boston, MA 02111; 877-426-8056 or 617-426-7788; www.elder hostel.org.

GRANDPARENTS/GRANDCHILDREN CAMPS

See Chapter 11 for summer camps and other vacations designed for grandparents and grandchildren who want to spend time together.

VOLUNTARY ASSOCIATION FOR SENIOR CITIZEN ACTIVITIES (VASCA)

VASCA is a nonprofit organization that offers scholarships to elderly low-income residents of New York City over the age of 55 to attend an adult camp for a week or two in the summer. Located in New York, New Jersey, Connecticut, and Pennsylvania, the seven camps, sponsored by nonprofit organizations and foundations, are small rustic country retreats, lakeside resorts, or big sprawling complexes. Two accommodate the disabled and the blind.

For information: VASCA, 108 W. 39th St., New York, NY 10018; 212-768-9166; www.vasca.org.

YMCA/YWCA

The Y runs many camps, most of them for children, but some also offer inexpensive weeks for adults. For example, the YMCA of the Rockies operates a resort, Snow Mountain Ranch, with a special program in mid-August for active adults over the age of 50 at its Camp Chief Ouray in Granby, Colorado. The High Point YMCA's Camp Cheerio, in the Blue Ridge Mountains of North Carolina, sets aside three weeks a year for campers over 50.

For information: Call your local YMCA or YWCA for information about camps in your area.

18

Shopping Breaks and Other Practical Matters

In this chapter you won't find suggestions for interesting vacation possibilities or unusual places to explore. Instead, you'll get useful information about benefits and services that could be coming to you simply because you are now sufficiently mature to take advantage of them.

SAVING MONEY IN STORES AND ELSEWHERE

All over the U.S. and Canada today, and increasingly the rest of the world, retailers now offer discounts and other special privileges to older customers. That's because they have come to realize that these huge numbers of consumers know the value of a dollar, are extremely fond of bargains, and usually have the will and the time to hunt them down. In fact, the

GOLDEN OPPORTUNITIES

Log on to seniordiscounts.com for a free website that lists thousands of local and national age-related deals all over the country, even in your own hometown. Name your city, state, or area code, then the business category—from restaurants to car-rental agencies, pharmacies, beauty salons, auto repair shops, movie theaters, and grocery stores—and you will get a list of businesses that offer discounts, along with addresses, telephone numbers, and maps to their locations.

For information: SeniorDiscounts.com, 1401 Central Ave., Albuquerque, NM 87104; 877-924-2023 or 505-924-2222; www.seniordiscounts.com.

older population has begun to expect reduced prices and to become loyal customers of the shops that offer them.

Stores and other businesses vary on the age at which you may take advantage of their special offers, but most start you off at 60. Some give you 10 or 15 percent off every day, others reserve one day a week or a month for their senior discounts, and still others schedule discount days sporadically. Even grocery stores are getting into the act and so are many specialty food stores. Most Kroger's, for example, will give you a 5 percent discount on your groceries on Wednesdays if you are at least 55. So will most Wild Oats Markets, which give you 5 to 15 percent off, sometimes only on certain days of the week.

Many pharmacies also have plans that will save you money. For example, if you are 55 or more, both Rite Aid and CVS give you a 10 percent discount on prescription drugs when you pay in cash. Longs Drugs, a group of drugstores in the western U.S., offers its Longs Senior Advantage program to customers at age 55 or 65 (depending on the state) who are not covered by insurance, saving them 10 to 50 percent on cash prescriptions. Eckerd's Senior Rewards Card allows 55-plus customers in Texas and Florida to earn 10 percent credit on all cash-paid prescriptions, the credit to be used toward the purchase of any merchandise in the store.

Even some major department stores, such as Lord and Taylor, occasionally feature senior savings days, when everything costs 10 or 15 percent less for customers over 60. Banana Republic gives older customers 10 percent off every day. Kohl's Department Stores schedules periodic senior days, always on a Wednesday and announced in local newspapers, when you get 10 percent taken off the cost of your purchases. Ross Dress for Less, with about 500 stores in 22 states, gives shoppers 55-plus the same 10 percent but does it every Tuesday. Many of Modell's sporting-goods stores take 10 percent off for seniors every day of the week.

But retailers aren't the only businesses that are willing to give you a break. Many beauty salons and barber shops, for example, offer senior discounts although, because they are usually individually owned, you must watch their ads or posted signs for the details. Plumbers, dry cleaners, and mechanics are among other local businesses with discounts. Even some car dealerships take money off for parts and service.

Fitness clubs usually knock off a small amount for new members who have reached a certain birthday. Gold's Gym, the largest chain of gyms in the world, takes 25 percent off monthly fees and 50 percent off the initial fee at most of its locations, while many company-owned Bally's Total Fitness Clubs deduct $50 to $100 from the initial cost of most

HELP FROM THE IRS

The IRS publishes a useful free booklet, *Tax Information for Older Americans* (Publication No. 554). Get it from your library or local IRS office or call 800-829-3676. You can also read it or download it—along with all tax forms and publications—from the IRS website: www.irs.gov.

memberships and 10 percent off the monthly fees for those 62 or over.

Most Jiffy Lube auto service centers offer a senior discount of 10 percent, and Midas Auto Service makes it a nationwide policy to take 10 percent off parts and service.

Even theme parks have a policy of admitting seniors— usually at age 55 or 60—for a little bit less than the going rate.

What all this means is that, wherever you go, it never hurts to ask whether there are good deals available to you.

GETTING HELP ON YOUR TAX RETURNS

Assistance in preparing your tax returns is available free from both the Internal Revenue Service and AARP.

The IRS offers Tax Counseling for the Elderly (TCE) for people over 60 and Voluntary Income Tax Assistants (VITA) for younger people who need help. Trained volunteers provide information and will prepare returns at thousands of sites throughout the country. Watch your local newspaper for a list of sites in your area or call 800-TAX-1040 during tax season, January 2 to April 15. Or consult your local tele-phone directory under "U.S. Government, Internal Revenue Service" to find a convenient IRS office where walk-in tax assistance is available.

Another route is to enlist the services of AARP's free and confidential Tax-Aide Service from February 1 through April 15 at thousands of sites nationwide. Trained volun-teers answer questions and help low- and moderate-income members of AARP with their tax returns. They will even go to your home if you are physically unable to get to a site. To locate a Tax-Aide office in your area, call 888-227-7669, call your regional or state AARP office, or visit AARP online at www.aarp.org/taxaide. Have your membership number and zip code handy and also your calendar, as an appointment is required. Off-season, this program provides online tax counseling.

HOW TO FIND ELDER SERVICES

For contact information about local services for older adults in your state and local area, such as senior centers, home health services, housing, transportation, legal assistance, or adult day care centers, call the **Eldercare Locator** at 800-677-1116 or go online to www.eldercare.com. This is a nationwide governmental resource that can help you con-nect with agencies close to home that provide services to seniors and their families. Call between 9 A.M. and 8 P.M. (eastern time) Monday through Friday and explain the prob-lem. Be prepared to provide the name, address, and zip code of the person needing help, as well as a brief description of the assistance you are seeking.

FOR MEDICAL EMERGENCIES

If you have a chronic medical condition, drug or food allergies, or special needs such as a surgical implant, or if you take medications on which your life depends, consider joining MedicAlert, an emergency medical information service that is especially useful when you're traveling. Members wear metal bracelets or neck chains engraved with their personal ID number, key medical facts, and the telephone number of the 24-hour Emergency Response Center. In an emergency, attending medical personnel can call for essential medical information. MedicAlert will also call your family contacts to notify them of your situation.

The cost is $35 to enroll, then $20 a year thereafter. Members may update their records as often as necessary at no extra charge.

For information: MedicAlert, 2323 Colorado Ave., Turlock, CA 95382; 800-633-4298 or 209-668-3333; www.medic alert.org.

SAVING ON AUTO AND HOMEOWNER INSURANCE

Among the nice surprises waiting for you on your 50th or 55th birthday is the possibility of paying less for your automobile and homeowner insurance. So try to take advantage of your age when you shop for a new policy or renew an existing one.

Mature drivers get breaks because, as a group, they tend to be cautious drivers, much more careful than the younger crowd, having shed their bad habits such as speeding and reckless driving. And, although older drivers total more accidents per mile, they drive fewer miles, have fewer serious accidents, use their seat belts, usually don't operate their cars to commute to work every day in rush-hour traffic, and tend to stay off the roads at night and in bad weather. Therefore, statistically, they have fewer serious accidents per driver than other risk categories do, at least until they are 75, when medical conditions—especially deteriorating vision—may start to kick in, increasing the risk of problems on the road.

An additional discount—usually 10 percent—applies on some of your automobile coverage in most states when you successfully complete a state-approved defensive-driving course. Among the programs is AARP's 55 Alive Driver Safety Program (call 888-227-7669 for information), an eight-hour classroom refresher that specifically addresses the needs of older drivers with physical and perceptual changes that affect their driving. Open to both AARP members and nonmembers at a current cost of $10 per person and taught by volunteers, the course is given locally all over the country. Defensive-driving courses are offered by other groups, including local high schools and AAA.

Homeowners over a certain age are also considered better risks for insurance claims than younger people because they spend more time at home where they can keep an eye on things and take care of their property. So some companies offer them reductions on premiums.

Although discounts are wonderful and we all love to get them, they aren't everything. Always shop the bottom line when you buy insurance. You may be able to save hundreds of dollars just by shopping around, but you should know what you are getting for your money. If one company charges higher premiums for comparable coverage and then gives you a discount, you have not profited. Get quotes from at least three insurers, going over your list of drivers, vehicles, and specific coverage needs.

Be sure to ask for the discounts that may be coming to you because agents don't always volunteer this information. In addition to your age-related discount, ask about others. Some insurers offer discounts for insuring more than one car on the same policy, clean driving records, antitheft devices, low mileage, more than one policy with the same company, and longtime coverage. And watch out for policies that bump up your costs again when you turn 70.

Remember that insurance regulations and the possibility of age-related discounts differ from state to state as well as company to company. That means you must do your homework to find out whether savings are in your future.

BENEFITS FROM BANKS

Almost all banks today offer special incentives and services to their older customers, often starting at age 50. These include privileges such as a low minimum-balance requirement; free checking, traveler's checks, and safe-deposit boxes; elimination of monthly service charges; reduced fees for cashier's checks or money orders. Some banks even throw in discount eyewear and pharmacy service, accidental-death insurance, social activities, group excursions, seminars, and newsletters.

Bank and state regulations differ, so it pays to be a comparison shopper to make sure you're getting the best deals available in your community.

LEGAL ASSISTANCE

FREE LEGAL SERVICES

The AARP Legal Services Network (LSN) is designed to give AARP members and their spouses easy access to qualified attorneys in their own communities for free 30-minute initial consultations on the telephone or in person. In addition to dispensing advice, the participating attorneys will provide basic services such as simple wills, powers of attorney, and living wills for low flat fees and give a 20 percent reduction on their usual rates for more complicated services.

For a list of participating LSN attorneys in your area, call 800-424-3410 or write LSN Fulfillment, PO Box 100084, Pittsburgh, PA 15233. Or look in your local Yellow Pages in the Associations, Attorneys, or Lawyers sections under the heading AARP-Legal Services Network. Another alternative is to visit the LSN website at www.aarp.org/lsn.

LOCAL SENIOR AGENCIES

Call on your local area senior agency, which is required by law to provide some legal assistance to older citizens. Yours may help you untangle some puzzling legal problems or at least tell you what services are available to you. Or contact your local bar association for information about referrals or pro bono programs. The National Academy of Elder Law Attorneys (520-881-4005 or www.naela.com) will also help you find an attorney who specializes in working with older clients and their families. Remember to ask about a living will, a health-care proxy, and a health-care power of attorney, all of which you need.

SENIOR LEGAL HOTLINES

For a list of toll-free telephone numbers of senior legal hotlines that offer free legal advice over the phone to anyone over 60, visit the website www.seniorlaw.com/hotlines.htm. The nonprofit hotlines, staffed by attorneys, are available in 20 states and can also make referrals for additional assistance.

Volunteer for Great Experiences

I f, perhaps for the first time in your life, you have time, expertise, talent, and energy to spare, consider volunteering your services to organizations that could use your help. Plenty of significant work is waiting for you, and more and more older Americans are volunteering as a way of finding fulfillment both before and after retirement. If you are looking for a good match between your abilities and an organization that needs them, take a look at the programs described here, all of them specifically seeking the experience and enthusiasm of older adults.

You can also visit www.seniorcorps.org, the website of Senior Corps, the umbrella organzation for three federal volunteer programs—RSVP, Foster Grandparents, and Senior Companions. Here you can search for volunteer opportunities by your zip code and interests.

But, first, keep in mind:

■ When you file your federal income tax, you may be allowed to deduct unreimbursed expenses incurred while volunteering your services to a charitable organization. You may be able to deduct program fees and reasonable costs for transportation, parking, tolls, meals, lodging, and uniforms. You may not be able to take off all of your travel expenses, meals, and lodging, however, when you spend a significant amount of personal or vacation time before, during, or after a service program, or if you get benefit from your service, such as academic credit.

CARIBBEAN VOLUNTEER EXPEDITIONS (CVE)

You can do valuable and meaningful work in the Caribbean helping local agencies to preserve the architectural heritage of the islands. Caribbean Volunteer Expeditions (CVE) takes volunteers there for a week at a time where you spend the mornings working on archaeological digs or documenting historical plantations, windmills, and other structures. Afternoons are free for explorations of the island and visiting museums and historic sites. Volunteers pay their own airfare and costs for housing and food, although sometimes lodging costs are reduced or even free. No need for architectural expertise but, if you have it, it will be appreciated.

For information: CVE, Box 388, Corning, NY 14830; 607-962-7846; www.cvexp.org.

ELDERHOSTEL SERVICE PROGRAMS

Elderhostel Service Programs tap the experience and expertise of older adults (55 or over) in short-term volunteer projects in the U.S., Canada, and other countries of the world. Teams of hostelers are paired with nonprofit organizations for a wide variety of service activities, from historical preservation to teaching English to natural-resources conservation, working with children with special needs, participating in archaeological research, and even helping to build affordable housing. No special skill or experience is required, and training is provided on the job. A 55 or older volunteer may be accompanied by an adult who is younger.

Many institutions and organizations—far too many to list here—collaborate with Elderhostel to put mature Americans, retired or not, to work for one to three weeks per session. These are hosted by such diverse groups as Habitat for Humanity, Oceanic Society Expeditions, the U.S. Forest Service, Global Volunteers, Appalachian Mountain Club, Hole in the Woods Ranch, Grand Canyon National Park, and many more.

The fee you pay to participate varies with each program and includes full room and board, equipment, social and cultural events, and airfare for services overseas.

For information: Elderhostel, 11 Avenue de Lafayette, Boston, MA 02111; 877-426-8056 or 617-426-7788; www .elderhostel.org.

EXPERIENCE CORPS

The Experience Corps, part of the Americorps network of national service programs, recruits older adults to serve as tutors and mentors to inner-city children in urban public elementary schools. Although it began only in 1995, it now runs programs in cooperation with local community organizations in many cities around the country. Volunteers,

WORKING FOR THE ENVIRONMENT

EASI (Environmental Alliance for Senior Involvement) is a nonprofit coalition of about 300 public and private environmental organizations that tap the talents, expertise, and enthusiasm of older adults and put them to work on projects that protect and improve the environment in their own communities. Volunteers in every state and many foreign countries may put in as much time as they wish on such projects as water-quality monitoring, forest management, pollution prevention, community gardens, brown-fields revitalization, and hazardous-waste disposal.

For information: EASI, PO Box 250, Catlett, VA 20119; 540-788-3274; www.easi.org.

many of whom are retired professionals and must be at least 55 years old, receive training in early childhood education and literacy. They may work half-time or part-time or on an episodic, as-needed basis and do not require special previous experience.

For information: Experience Corps, 2120 L St. NW, Washington, DC 20037; 202-478-6190; www.experiencecorps .org.

FAMILY FRIENDS

A national program sponsored by the National Council on Aging, Family Friends recruits volunteers over the age of 55 to work in many locations around the country with children with disabilities, chronic illnesses, or other problems. The volunteers act as caring grandparents, helping the families in whatever ways they can, mostly dealing with children, perhaps foster children or adoptees, at home but occasionally in hospitals, homeless shelters, or Head Start centers. They are asked to serve at least four hours a week and commit themselves to the program for at least a year. Volunteers are reimbursed for expenses incurred.

The local projects are funded by the federal government; corporations; foundations; and local, county, city, or state governments.

For information: Family Friends Resource Center, 301 D St. NW, Washington, DC 20024; 800-424-9046 or 202-479-6675; www.family-friends.org.

FOSTER GRANDPARENTS

Foster Grandparents serve as extended family members to children with special or exceptional needs. They provide emotional support to children who have been abused or neglected, mentor troubled teenagers and young mothers, care for premature infants and children with physical disabilities and severe illnesses, and tutor children who lag behind in reading. Volunteers must be 60 or older and have limited incomes. They serve 20 hours a week in schools, hospitals, correctional institutions, day care facilities, and Head Start centers in their own neighborhoods.

For this, they receive—in addition to the immense satisfaction—modest tax-free stipends to offset their costs, some meals during service, reimbursement for transportation, an annual physical examination, and accident and liability insurance while on duty.

For information: Contact your local Foster Grandparents program or the Corporation for National Service, 1201 New York Ave. NW, Washington, DC 20525; 800-424-8867; www.seniorcorps.org.

JEWISH NATIONAL FUND (JNF) CAARI PROGRAM

Each winter, the Jewish National Fund's CAARI (Canadian American Active Retirees in Israel) program sends a group, made up of retired adults age 50 and above, to Israel to participate in an interactive educational program that ranges from 2 to 10 weeks in length. The group meets Israelis of all ages, learns about the current situation firsthand, and experiences life through Israeli eyes. The participants attend lectures, tour the country, and volunteer in schools, hospitals, community agencies, and JNF's forests.

For information: JNF CAARI Program, Missions Dept., 42 E. 69th St., New York, NY 10021; 888-JNF-0099 (888-563-0099); www.jnf.org/caari.

NATIONAL EXECUTIVE SERVICE CORPS

This nonprofit organization performs a unique service. It helps other nonprofit organizations solve their problems by providing retired executives with extensive corporate and professional experience to serve as volunteer consultants. Its services are offered in five basic areas—education, health, the arts, social services, and religion—and the assistance covers everything from organizational structure and financial systems to marketing and funding strategy. Volunteers' expenses are covered.

For information: National Executive Service Corps, 120 Wall St., New York, NY 10005; 212-269-1234; www.nesc.org.

NATIONAL PARK SERVICE

You can put in as many hours as you like, every day, once a week, or full-time for a week or even a few months, helping out at the country's national parks and wilderness areas when you enlist in the National Park Service's Volunteers in Parks

(VIP) program. VIPs are not exclusively people over the age of 50, but a goodly portion of them are older people with time, expertise, talent, and a love for wildlife and wild places. You will not be paid for your hard work but may get reimbursed for out-of-pocket expenses, and other expenses are usually tax-deductible.

The job possibilities are myriad, depending on the park you choose. Some parks would like you to assist archaeologists or botanists in their research; others need you to help maintain and restore trails, drive a shuttle, make wildlife counts, act as guides, patrol the trails, work the computers, or act as campground hosts.

For information: Contact the VIP coordinator at the national park where you would like to volunteer and request an application. Or write to Volunteer Coordinator, National Park Service, 1849 C St. NW, Ste. 3045, Washington, DC 20240; 202-513-7140; www.nps.gov/volunteer.

NATIONAL TRUST WORKING HOLIDAYS

Britain's National Trust, which oversees historic and environmental treasures in the U.K., invites volunteers from all over the world on its low-cost Working Holidays in England, Wales, and Northern Ireland. Their job is to lend a hand for one or two weeks at a time performing such tasks as restoring historic buildings, maintaining footpaths, digging at archaeological sites, repairing dry stone walls, doing conservation surveys, herding goats, or even helping with office work. Most Working Holidays are open to anyone over 18, but some of them—the Oak Plus Projects—are reserved exclusively for energetic volunteers age 50 or over.

For most holidays, your accommodations will be converted dormitory-style farmhouses, cottages, or apartments, or you may find lodgings of your own. Work is paced to allow ample time to relax, take in the local sights, or go for a stroll. All meals are included, although you may be asked to take a turn cooking dinner. The current cost for a one-week stint is £60 to £75.

For information: National Trust, Rowan Kembrey Park, Swindon, Wiltshire SN2 8YL, England; www.national trust.org.uk/volunteering.

PEACE CORPS

It may surprise you to learn that the Peace Corps is a viable choice for idealists of any age. There is no upper age limit for acceptance into the Peace Corps, and since its beginning in 1961, thousands of older volunteers have brought their talents and experience to almost 100 countries all over the world. To become a volunteer, you must be a U.S. citizen and meet basic legal and medical criteria. Some assignments require a college or technical-school degree or an experience equivalent. Married couples are eligible and will be assigned together. Service is typically for two years after three months of training.

What you get in return for your hard work is the chance to travel; an unforgettable living experience in a foreign land; basic expenses; housing; plus technical, language, and cultural training. You will also have the opportunity to use your expertise constructively in fields such as agriculture, business, environment, health, education, and community development.

For information: Peace Corps, 1111 20th St. NW, Washington, DC 20526; 800-424-8580; www.peacecorps.gov.

SENIOR ENVIRONMENTAL EMPLOYMENT (SEE) PROGRAM

The SEE Program, administered by the U.S. Environmental Protection Agency (EPA), establishes cooperative agreements with six national organizations to recruit qualified people 55 and over to help with environmental problems. The recruits, who work on a temporary part-time or full-time basis in EPA offices or in the field, are paid by the hour in jobs ranging from secretarial and clerical work to highly specialized technical and scientific positions. All are designed to assist the agency in protecting and/or cleaning up the environment.

For information: U.S. EPA, Arial Rios Blg., SEE Program, 1200 Pennsylvania Ave. NW, mail-code 3650A, Washington, DC 20460; 202-564-0420; www.epa.gov/epahrist/see/brochure.

RSVP (RETIRED AND SENIOR VOLUNTEER PROGRAM)

RSVP matches the interests and skills of men and women over the age of 55 with a diverse range of volunteer activities in their own communities. Volunteers—who may serve anywhere from a few to more than 40 hours a week—may choose to tutor children, renovate homes, teach English to immigrants, plan community gardens, deliver meals, make hospital visits, work in day-care centers, assist victims of natural disasters, or do whatever their own communities need. They are not paid but may receive reimbursement for meals and transportation.

For information: Contact your local or regional RSVP office or Corporation for National Service, 1201 New York Ave.

NW, Washington, DC 20525; 800-424-8867; www.senior
corps.org.

SENIOR COMPANIONS

Senior Companions provide assistance and friendship to
older adults who are frail, have disabilities, or have serious
or terminal illnesses and have difficulty with daily living
tasks, helping them to live independently in their own
homes or communities. Volunteers must be 60 or older;
meet certain income eligibility guidelines; and serve 20
hours a week, usually 4 hours a day Monday through Friday. Although they are not paid, they receive a modest tax-
free stipend, reimbursement for transportation, some meals
during service, on-duty accident and liability insurance,
monthly training, and an annual physical examination.

For information: Corporation for National Service, 1201
New York Ave. NW, Washington, DC 20525; 800-424-8867;
www.seniorcorps.org.

SERVICE CORPS OF RETIRED
EXECUTIVES (SCORE)

A national organization, SCORE offers free counseling for
fledgling small businesses by working and retired executives
with expertise in a range of areas, including finance, management, and marketing. Its volunteers serve as mentors in
one-on-one counseling, computer counseling, seminars, and
workshops. SCORE currently has a membership of about
10,500 men and women and 389 chapters all over the
country.

For information: Contact your local U.S. Small Business
Administration office or SCORE, 409 Third St. SW, 6th floor,

Washington, DC 20024; 800-634-0245 or 202-205-6762; www.score.org.

FORTY PLUS

Offices in 20 cities throughout the U.S. comprise **Forty Plus**, a nonprofit cooperative of unemployed executives, managers, and professionals, men and women, who have earned at least $40,000 a year. Their objective is to help members conduct effective employment searches and find new jobs. There is no paid staff. The members do all the work and help pay expenses. They must commit themselves to attend weekly meetings and spend at least two days each week working at the club and assisting others in their search for work.

In return, members are assisted in examining their career skills and defining their goals, counseled on résumé writing and interviewing skills, helped to plan marketing strategy, and given job leads. They may also use the premises as a base of operations, with phone answering and mail service, computers, and reference library.

Forty Plus currently maintains offices in New York City and Buffalo, New York; Oakland, San Diego, San Jose, and Los Angeles (with a branch in Laguna Hills), California; Fort Collins, Colorado Springs, and Lakewood, Colorado; Columbus, Ohio; Dallas and Houston, Texas; Murray, Ogden, and Provo, Utah; Philadelphia, Pennsylvania; Bellevue, Washington; Washington, D.C.; St. Paul, Minnesota; and Honolulu, Hawaii.

For information: Addresses of locations and descriptive materials are available from Forty Plus of New York, 470 7th Ave., Ste. 403, New York, NY 10018; 212-947-4230; www.fortyplus-nyc.org.

SERVICE OPPORTUNITIES FOR OLDER PEOPLE (SOOP)

SOOP, sponsored by the Mennonite Mission Network and other organizations, provides a way for older people of all persuasions to contribute their experience and skills in 23 locations throughout the U.S. and Canada. You may sign up for five weeks or up to six months, living at the site and working to help others in need in whatever way you can, from teaching, building, and child care to homemaking, farming, and administering. Once you decide on the kind of work and time commitment you prefer, you make plans with a location coordinator for your assignment and housing. Volunteers usually pay for their own travel, food, and lodging.

For information: Mennonite Mission Network, 500 S. Main St., Elkhart, IN 46515; 574-294-7523; www.mennonitemission.net.

SHEPHERD'S CENTERS OF AMERICA (SCA)

An interfaith, nonprofit organization of older adults who volunteer their skills to help seniors in their communities, SCA has about 100 centers in the U.S. Supported by Catholic, Jewish, and Protestant congregations as well as businesses and foundations, the centers operate many programs designed to enable older people to remain in their own homes as active participants in community life. They also encourage intergenerational interaction. Centers offer such in-home services as Telephone Visitors, Family Friends, Meals on Wheels, Handyhands Service, and Respite Care, all provided mostly by volunteers. Programs at the centers include other services, day trips, classes, and courses as well as support groups and referrals. Membership is open to anyone over the age of 55.

For information: Shepherd's Centers of America, 1 W. Armour Blvd., Ste. 201, Kansas City, MO 64111; 800-547-7073; www.shepherdcenters.org.

SIERRA CLUB

The Sierra Club, the environmental organization, plans some of its famous "outings" exclusively for people over the age of 50. Several of them each year are volunteer service programs that give you a chance to team up with rangers and park service personnel to help out with research projects or the maintenance of wilderness areas. The one-week stints are inexpensive, labor-intensive, and sociable, with time allowed for sightseeing and relaxation. You must get your-

---

JOB PROGRAM FOR OLDER WORKERS

Senior Community Service Employment Program (SCSEP), a federally funded program, recruits unemployed low-income men and women over the age of 55, assesses their employment strengths, and places them in paid jobs in community-service positions. At the same time, the enrollees begin training in new job skills and receive such help as counseling, physical examinations, group meetings, and job fairs while the agency tries to match them with permanent jobs in the private and public sector. If you qualify and are looking for a paying position, this agency is worth a try.

For information: SCSEP, NCOA, 300 D St. SW, Ste. 801, Washington, DC 20024; 800-424-9046 or 202-479-1200; www.ncoa.org. Or contact your local, county, or state Office for the Aging.

self to and from the site you've chosen, but other expenses are included in the fee that ranges from about $250 to $500 per week. You may choose your location and the type of work you want to do, such as trail building in the mountains near Aspen, Colorado; restoring gardens and planting trees in New York City's Riverside Park; rehabilitating the nature trail, painting, and repairing fences at Channel Islands National Park in California; and inventorying songbirds or removing exotic alien plants at Bryce Canyon National Park in Utah.

Membership in the Sierra Club costs you less if you are a senior—$24 a year instead of the $39 for younger adults. Two seniors in the same household may join for $32 a year for the same membership that otherwise costs $47.

For information: Sierra Club Outings, 85 Second St., San Francisco, CA 94105; 415-977-5521; www.sierraclub .org/outings.

VOLUNTEER SENIOR RANGER CORPS

The Volunteer Senior Ranger Corps program, already operating in about a dozen national parks, is a new program established by the National Park Service and its partners. It gives grants to parks to help them recruit senior volunteers and enhance relationships with local communities. Those at least 50 years of age may apply by contacting the park where they'd like to work. Each participating park—such as Glacier National Park, Delaware Water Gap National Recreation Area, and Fire Island National Seashore—determines its own projects for the volunteers. To date, the projects include such activities as trail monitoring, investigating archaeological sites, restoring native plants in overused areas, and teaching groups of urban children how to fish.

For information: EASI, PO Box 250, Catlett, VA 20119; 540-788-3274; www.easi.org.

VOLUNTEERS FOR ISRAEL

In this volunteer work-and-cultural program in Israel for adults 18 and older, you'll put in eight-hour days for two to three weeks, working alongside members of the Israel Defense Forces. You'll sleep in a segregated dormitory and work in small groups at a reserve or supply military base, doing whatever needs doing most at that moment. You may serve in supply, warehousing, or maintenance of equipment

OPERATION ABLE

If you're over 40 and in the market for a job but don't know where to start looking for one, hook up with **Operation ABLE**, a nonprofit organization affiliated with a network of agencies that will help match you with a likely employer. You're in luck if you live in the Chicago area, where there are many regional offices and a job hotline (312-782-7700), a referral service for job seekers in the Chicago area. But there is also a network of independent ABLE-like organizations, modeled after the original, in several other cities, including Boston; Los Angeles; Lincoln, Nebraska; Rockville, Maryland; Southfield, Michigan; and St. Albans, Vermont.

Operation ABLE tries every which way to get you into the working world. It provides job counseling, group training activities, and individual career assessment and guidance; teaches job-hunting skills; matches older workers with employers; operates a pool of temporaries; and offers many other services.

For information: Operation ABLE, 180 N. Wabash Ave., Chicago, IL 60601; 312-782-3335; www.jobhotline.org.

or in social services in hospitals. You'll wear an army uniform with a "Civilian Volunteer" patch. Board, room, and other expenses are free, but you must pay for your own partially subsidized airfare.

For information: Volunteers for Israel, 330 West 42nd St., Stes. 16–18, New York, NY 10036; 212-643-4848; www.vfi-usa.org.

VOLUNTEERS IN TECHNICAL ASSISTANCE (VITA)

VITA provides another avenue for helping developing countries. A nonprofit international organization, VITA provides volunteer experts who respond—usually by direct correspondence—to technical inquiries from people in these nations who need assistance in such areas as small-business development, energy applications, agriculture, reforestation, water supply and sanitation, and low-cost housing. Its volunteers also perform other services such as project planning, translations, publications, marketing strategies, evaluations, and technical reports and often become on-site consultants.

There is no minimum age, but you must have enough time to serve.

For information: Volunteers in Technical Assistance, 1600 Wilson Blvd., Ste. 1030, Arlington, VA 22209; 703-276-1800; www.vita.org.

20

Over-50 Organizations

When you consider that there are more people in this country over the age of 55 than there are children in elementary and high schools, you can see why we have powerful potential to influence what goes on around here. As the demographic discovery of the times, a group that controls most of the nation's disposable income, we are a prime marketing target. And, just like any other large group of people, we've got plenty of needs.

A number of organizations in the U.S. and Canada have been formed in recent years to act as advocates for the 50-plus population and to provide us with special programs as well as opportunities to spend our money on their products or services. Here is a brief rundown on them and what they have to offer you. You may want to join more than one of them so you can get the best of each.

AARP

AARP offers so many benefits that you'd be mighty foolish not to join as soon as you turn 50 and become eligible for membership in this 35-million-member organization that serves as an advocate for the older population and has become one of the most effective lobbying groups in the country. Its newsletter, *AARP Bulletin*, and a bimonthly magazine, *AARP The Magazine*, go to more homes than any other publications in the U.S. The cost of membership is $12.50 for a year, $21 for two years, or $29.50 for three years (and that includes your spouse or companion who may be under 50). Overseas members pay $28 per year. Here are some of AARP's benefits:

- Group health insurance, life insurance, automobile insurance, homeowner insurance, mobile-home insurance, long-term-care insurance
- A broad assortment of money-saving discounts on airfares, cruises, hotels and motels, auto rentals, vacation packages, entertainment, legal services, online services, and more (to view them, see www.aarp.org/privileges)
- A mail-order pharmacy service that delivers prescription and nonprescription drugs
- A motoring plan that includes emergency road and towing services, trip planning, and other benefits
- A national advocacy and lobbying program at all levels of government to develop legislative priorities and represent the interests of older people
- About 4,000 local chapters with their own activities and volunteer projects

- Fully staffed offices in all 50 states plus Puerto Rico and the U.S. Virgin Islands
- Special programs in a wide range of areas such as consumer affairs, legal counseling, financial information, housing, health advocacy, voter education, employment planning, independent living, disability initiatives, grandparent information, and public benefits
- Tax-Aide, a program conducted in cooperation with the IRS that helps lower- and moderate-income members with their income tax returns
- 55 ALIVE Driver Safety Program, an eight-hour course offered nationwide to improve your driving skills and, in many states, help you qualify for a multiyear discount on auto insurance premiums
- Legal Services Network, which assists members in finding prescreened attorneys to help with legal problems
- Free publications on many subjects relevant to your life

For information: AARP, 601 E St. NW, Washington, DC 20049; 888-OUR-AARP (888-687-2277) or 202-434-2277; www.aarp.org.

ALLIANCE FOR RETIRED AMERICANS

This organization, created in 2001 by a coalition of the AFL-CIO, affiliated unions, and community-based organizations, is dedicated solely to "economic justice" for seniors and now has about 2.9 million members. Its purpose is to mobilize millions of older people to make their voices heard for public policies that will "protect and expand programs vital to the health and economic security of older Americans." Annual dues of most union retirees are paid by their unions; others pay a membership fee of $10 a year.

For information: Alliance for Retired Americans, 888 16th St. NW, Ste. 520, Washington, DC 20006; 888-373-6497; www.retiredamericans.org.

CANADA'S ASSOCIATION FOR THE FIFTY-PLUS (CARP)

Canadians over the age of 50 are invited to join CARP, a 50-plus lobbying group with over 400,000 members, retired and employed. For a membership fee of $19.95 (Canadian) a year for singles or couples, members get many benefits, including discounted rates on out-of-country health insurance, long-term care insurance, extended health and dental plans, and automobile and home insurance. They can also take advantage of an expanded travel program with an auto club and discounts on airfares, travel packages, hotels, and car rentals. Members may also participate in the activities of local chapters in their own communities.

CARP publishes a lively, informative magazine called *FiftyPlus*, with six regular issues per year, that offers articles on a wide range of subjects such as health care, travel, hobbies, politics, and people. CARP is a major advocate, national and provincial, on issues of great concern to mature Canadians. Free financial seminars are held frequently throughout the country.

For information: CARP, 27 Queen St. East, Ste. 1304, Toronto, ON M5C 2M6; 800-363-9736 (in Canada) or 416-363-8748; www.50plus.com.

CANADIAN SNOWBIRD ASSOCIATION (CSA)

CSA is an organization with about 80,000 members, mainly seniors and retirees, who travel outside Canada for up to six months of the year. As their advocate and lobbying group, CSA addresses issues of concern to Canadian seniors such as health care, absentee voting rights, cross-border problems, residency requirements, U.S. tax laws for Canadians wintering abroad, and estate tax rules on Canadian-owned vacation property in the U.S. And it endorses travel insurance as well as out-of-country health insurance.

Membership costs $20 (Canadian) per household a year, and benefits include a magazine, travel offerings, an automobile club, a currency-exchange program, home and automobile insurance, and social gatherings in popular snowbird locations such as Florida, Arizona, Texas, and California.

For information: Canadian Snowbird Association, 180 Lesmill Rd., Toronto, ON M3B 2T5; 800-265-3200 or 416-391-9000; www.snowbirds.org.

CATHOLIC GOLDEN AGE (CGA)

A Catholic nonprofit organization that is concerned with issues affecting older citizens, such as health care, housing, and Social Security benefits, CGA has well over a million members and more than 200 chapters throughout the country. It offers many good things to its members, who must be over 50. These include spiritual benefits, such as masses and prayers worldwide, and practical benefits, such as discounts on hotels, campgrounds, and car rentals.

Other offerings include group insurance plans, pilgrimage and group travel programs, and an automobile club. A new benefit program is Access to Care that offers discounts on the cost of long-term care facilities, assisted-living facilities, and home health care. Another is the Health Care Card that allows members to save money on the costs of prescriptions as well as on vision, dental, and hearing services. Membership costs $8 a year or $15 for three years.

For information: Catholic Golden Age, RD2, Box 249, Olyphant, PA 18447; 800-836-5699; www.catholicgolden age.org.

GRAY PANTHERS

A national organization of about 20,000 intergenerational activists, the Gray Panthers work on multiple issues that include peace, jobs for all, antidiscrimination (ageism, sexism, racism), family security, the environment, campaign reform, preservation of social security, health care, and housing. They are active in more than 50 local networks across the U.S. in their efforts to promote social justice. Annual membership is $20.

For information: Gray Panthers, 733 15th St. NW, Ste. 437, Washington, DC 20005; 800-280-5362 or 202-737-6637; www.graypanthers.org.

MATURE OUTLOOK

Canadians over 50 can join Sears' Mature Outlook program and get a multitude of benefits, including discount coupons for Sears products and services purchased in the stores, through the catalog, or with Sears HomeCentral; discounts on hotels and rental cars; 10 percent off at Sears Restaurants; travel offers; and a subscription to *New Outlook* magazine. Annual membership is $19.99 (Canadian) for Sears Cardholders, $24.99 for noncardholders.

For information: Mature Outlook, PO Box 4200, Sta. A, Toronto, ON M5W 3A8; 800-265-3675 (800-650-9950 for service in French); www.sears.ca.

MILITARY OFFICERS ASSOCIATION OF AMERICA (MOAA)

This independent nonprofit organization is open to anyone who is an active or retired commissioned or warrant officer in any of the seven U.S. uniformed services, including the National Guard and Reserve. Members receive lobbying representation on Capitol Hill and a bimonthly magazine, plus a number of other benefits including discounts on car rentals and motel lodgings, a travel program with "military fares," group health and life insurance plans, and a loan program that allows members to borrow funds for the education of their children and grandchildren.

Although national in scope, MOAA has over 420 local chapters with their own activities and membership fees. Annual dues to the national organization are $20. Auxiliary membership is offered to members' spouses, widows, or widowers, who pay $15 a year.

For information: MOAA, 201 N. Washington St., Alexandria, VA 22314; 800-234-6622 or 703-549-2311; www.moaa.org.

NATIONAL ASSOCIATION OF RETIRED FEDERAL EMPLOYEES (NARFE)

As you can probably gather, this is an association of more than 400,000 federal government retirees, current employees, and their spouses. The primary mission of NARFE is to protect the earned benefits of retired federal employees, and it has become an active lobby program in Washington and throughout the states. Annual membership costs $25, plus local chapter dues. Members will receive a monthly magazine and are entitled to discounts as well as special services.

For information: NARFE, 606 N. Washington St., Alexandria, VA 22314; 800-627-3394 or 703-838-7760; www .narfe.org.

NATIONAL COMMITTEE TO PRESERVE SOCIAL SECURITY AND MEDICARE (NCPSSM)

NCPSSM is a grassroots education and advocacy group "devoted to the retirement future" of Americans with the goal of protecting and enhancing the two major federal programs for seniors, Social Security and Medicare. Its current major concerns are the preservation of the Social Security system without privatization and the addition of an affordable, voluntary, and universal prescription drug benefit to Medicare as well as the expansion of Medicare to cover new preventive services.

Members, who pay $10 a year, receive consumer information, trimonthly newsletters, a Congressional scorecard guide, invitations to events and programs, and a chance to voice their concerns and opinions.

For information: NCPSSM, 10 G St. NE, Ste. 600, Washington, DC 20004; 800-966-1935; www.ncpssm.org.

NATIONAL EDUCATION ASSOCIATION (NEA–RETIRED)

With a membership of more than 220,000 retired education employees from teachers to school bus drivers, NEA-Retired acts as an advocate for their special interests such as pensions and health care and supports public education through legislative lobbying as well as reading programs, mentoring, and intergenerational activities. Among its benefits of membership are life, health, disability, and casualty insurance programs; savings and investment plans; credit and loan programs; discounts; educational guides; and a bimonthly magazine, *Active Life*. Join for $15 a year or $100 for life, plus local dues that vary depending on your state.
For information: NEA-Retired, 1201 16th St. NW, Washington, DC 20036; 202-822-7149; www.nea.org/retired.

OLDER WOMEN'S LEAGUE (OWL)

OWL is a national nonprofit organization that has local chapters dedicated to achieving economic, political, and social equality for older women. Anyone, of any age, is allowed to join. OWL provides educational materials, training for citizen advocates, and informative publications dealing with the important issues—such as Social Security, health care, retirement benefits, and employment discrimination—that women face as they grow older. Annual dues are $25.
For information: OWL, 1750 New York Ave. NW, Ste. 350, Washington, DC 20006; 800-825-3695 or 202-783-6686; www.owl-national.org.

Index